Misreading Law, Misreading Democracy

Misreading Law, Misreading Democracy

Victoria Nourse

Harvard University Press

Cambridge, Massachusetts
London, England *2016*

Second printing

Library of Congress Cataloging-in-Publication Data

Names: Nourse, Victoria F., author.
Title: Misreading law, misreading democracy / Victoria Nourse.
Description: Cambridge, Massachusetts : Harvard University Press, 2016. | Includes bibliographical references and index.
Identifiers: LCCN 2016009533 | ISBN 9780674971417
Subjects: LCSH: Law—United States—Interpretation and construction. | Legislation—United States. | United States. Congress. | Statutes—United States. | Legislative histories—United States.
Classification: LCC KF425 .N68 2016 | DDC 349.73--dc23
LC record available at https://lccn.loc.gov/2016009533

To my mother

Contents

Prologue:
The Paradox of American Civic Illiteracy 1

1. Congress Is Not a Court 14

2. Statutory Interpretation Theories Misunderstand Congress 34

3. A Legislative Decision Theory of Statutory Interpretation 64

4. Petty Textualism, Canons, and Cognitive Bias 103

5. What Is Legislative Intent? Evidence of Context 135

6. The Constitutional Argument for Legislative Evidence 161

Epilogue:
Courts and Congress as Faithful Agents of Democracy 182

Notes 191

Acknowledgments 247

Index 249

Misreading Law, Misreading Democracy

We think we know how Legislators argue, but do we?

JEREMY WALDRON

Every issue of law resolved by a federal judge involves interpretation of text—the text of a regulation, or of a statute, or of the Constitution.

JUSTICE ANTONIN SCALIA

You have to learn the rules of the game. And then you have to play better than anyone else.

ALBERT EINSTEIN

Prologue

THE PARADOX OF AMERICAN CIVIC ILLITERACY

THEN-SENATOR JOSEPH BIDEN: Who do you think gets Congress more wrong—the press or the law professors?

FORMER STAFFER: The law professors . . .[1]

One of the "dirty little secrets" of legal education today is that it teaches so little about so much—democracy. There is no more basic activity of a lawyer than reading a statute. As the most prominent judges in the nation have explained, this is the heart of what it is to be a lawyer. Constitutional cases are few. Statutory cases are many. Legislation should rank as the first of all law courses, but it is often merely optional and left to students' whim. First-semester curricula at the most prestigious schools, such as Harvard, Yale, Stanford, and Chicago, still steep their students in vast amounts of ancient, superseded common law, leaving the entirely false impression that statutes are secondary and odd. This curriculum should seem more troubling since academics spend so much time, in constitutional law and elsewhere, discussing democracy. Even in the Supreme Court, where the people think the Constitution reigns, the vast body of the work is statutory, not constitutional, law.

This civic illiteracy poses more danger than the average lawyer expects. Today, constitutionalists fret about what they call "the countermajoritarian difficulty"—that the unelected judge may strike down the will of millions of Americans in the name of the Constitution. Unnoticed is a parallel world in which judges do not purport to overturn but merely interpret laws, a world in which similar difficulties reign. In statutory cases, judges have the power to *read the law* counter to the will of the people. Today, this poses not only a countermajoritarian but a supermajoritarian difficulty because it has been at least 30 years now since major bills required a vote of a supermajority of 60 senators. If this book is correct, without greater understanding about how Congress works, judges of all political stripes and philosophies of legal interpretation, liberal and conservative, are capable of reading the law to serve the interests of those *who opposed the law in Congress*, creating a law of and by the few, rather than the many, much less the super-many required to pass any contemporary statute. Unlike more celebrated and seemingly robust exercises of constitutional power, the judicial power to read the law against the people is all the more worrying because it is articulated not as an exercise of power but the humble act of a judge who claims to be a "faithful agent" of Congress.

In a nation calling itself democratic, there should be something more troubling about the fact that elite lawyers learn so little in law school about our most representative institution, the Congress. Unfortunately, unless we embrace dictatorship or military rule, we are left with the need for a large, multi-member representative body. The American Congress is rarely popular; it cannot be, as it acts slowly, with 535 members, and engages in public, passionate disputes. Newspapers have always made fun of members and their petty foibles, paying little attention to what Congress actually does. Meanwhile, lobbyists reap the rewards of this ignorance, selling the most basic of information about Congress for high prices, information that should be public but seems to elude erudite commentators.

It is one of the great American paradoxes that lawyers love our democracy as much as they hate Congress. Most recently, the Supreme Court has fueled this paradox by showing overt disdain for Congress. In the 2015 health care case *King v. Burwell*, the chief justice likened Congress to a cartoon.[2] The next term, one justice announced from the bench that Congress received a "D" in legislative drafting.[3] Another justice regularly calls Congress's legislative materials "garbage."[4] During oral argument, the justices debate such congressional basics as "Is a conference report really different from a committee report?" (Answer: yes. One is proposed legislative text.)[5] Can one really know so much about democracy if one knows so little about Congress? As Justice Kagan, the former dean of Harvard Law School, recently remarked, she was never taught a darn thing in law school about how to interpret a statute.[6] This should not be surprising since the major Harvard book on the matter, the renowned classic Hart and Sacks's *The Legal Process*, taught to many of the justices currently on the Court, includes fewer than a dozen pages on legislative procedure in a 1,387-page volume.[7]

I do not blame the judges or lawyers. I blame legal education for this state of affairs. Law schools should have a strong self-interest in teaching statutory interpretation because it sits at the core of legal practice. Outside the academy, among judges, the call has been clear for some time. Precisely because it is so important in real lawyers' lives, statutory interpretation has begun to generate a lively and active debate among judges, spawned initially by Justice Scalia and energetically resisted by Justice Breyer on the Supreme Court. Justice Scalia touted his own view in a lengthy book, *Reading Law*,[8] in which he suggested that Congress get out of the way, and all doubts about statutes should be resolved by rules created by judges, known as *canons of construction*. In reply, Judge Posner, hardly a liberal, took to the popular press, expressing what can only be said as shock, declaring Justice Scalia's theories improvident and inconsistent with constitutional originalism.[9] As Justice Breyer says, overemphasizing text and canons "can lead courts astray, divorcing law from life."[10]

Truth be told, Justice Scalia deserves enormous credit for putting the question on the academic agenda in the 1980s, insisting, as I do, that law schools must reform their curricula and teach legislation. By the 1990s, the study of statutory interpretation had taken its first run down the academic runway. As Professor William Eskridge wrote, like Cinderella, "once scorned and neglected, confined to the kitchen, [statutory interpretation] now dances in the ballroom."[11] Eskridge's groundbreaking work has spawned lengthy and sustained theoretical treatments from extraordinary scholars Einer Elhauge, John Manning, Daniel Rodriguez, Jane Schacter, Scott Shapiro, Matthew

Stephenson, Adrian Vermeule, and Jeremy Waldron. More recently, theory has been supplemented by empirics by professors James Brudney and Aaron Bruhl, Lisa Bressman and Abbe Gluck, Anita Krishnakumar and David Law.

The real traction in statutory interpretation is not in academic theories—which may have little impact on actual legal practice—but in the great debates spawned by those who do the work: the lawyers and the judges. This book speaks to their concerns. It offers method as much as theory. It teaches lawyers to answer textualist claims with counter-claims and, more importantly, to discipline and simplify the search for legislative history. Unlike any existing approach toward statutory interpretation, and contrary to what is generally taught in law school, this method reflects the *basics of legislative procedure*—Congress 101. This is particularly important in an age of unparalleled legislative battle; without this understanding, judges and lawyers risk embracing the meanings not of the supermajority necessary to pass the legislation but of a merry band of filibusterers.

My suspicion is that lawyers and law professors think that they know the legislative process and find the rest overly complex or unorthodox. I tested this proposition at a legal education conference at Harvard a few years ago. I asked an extremely impressive body of professors and students if they knew the most important rule in democracy. No one said anything, so I gave them the rule number—number 22. There was a very, very long pause. Finally, from the back of the room came a wrong answer: "interpleader" (a rule of civil procedure). Rule 22 is the cloture rule in the Senate; it means that you need 60 votes to pass any bill, and it has single-handedly frustrated the Senate for decades. Ask any member of Congress; ask any president or White House counsel. They live and die based on Rule 22. There is nothing new or unorthodox about this; lobbyists have, for the past 30 years, sold themselves to clients on the theory that they can "get to 60."

Just as law professors hold to the "love democracy/hate Congress" paradox, they also hold to the "we know it/it's too hard" paradox. Many law professors and judges seem to think they know how Congress works and at the same time insist that it is much too hard to learn basic legislative procedure. Justice Scalia and his "textualist" followers argued that lawyers should blind themselves to Congress's records—legislative evidence—because it is just too complex. For all those judges and lawyers who somehow think it too difficult or confusing to learn about congressional procedure, I ask you to consider why it is so difficult if democracy is so important. No law professor proclaims with vigor that constitutional procedure or administrative procedure or civil procedure is too difficult to teach or learn. At some level, all subjects are complex and apparently unorthodox at first encounter. That there is complex litigation does not eliminate the possibility of simple litigation or Civil Procedure 101. Suspend disbelief: proceed to Chapter 3 for Congress 101. In a world of high-tech databases, and free ones, like Congress.gov, the complexity and expense argument against legislative evidence is over, although I do admit, as I suggest in the Epilogue, that Congress could make its processes far more transparent.

To defend my claims about the need for disciplined, intelligent understandings of Congress, I must answer some very basic questions about statutory interpretation. For those readers worried that they are about to find themselves immersed in legislative spinach, here is a quick summary. First, what is plain meaning? Plain meaning is a conclusion, not a method. Linguistics tells us that there are at least two plain meanings to any term (prototypes and logical or extensivist categories); any sophisticated lawyer should understand this distinction to resist or deploy textualist arguments. Second, do forays into the legislative record survive the critique that there are many purposes to a statute? Yes. Find bipartisan legislative agreement on a core example as the most restrained application of the statute and refuse to adopt as authoritative the meanings of those who opposed the bill. Third, can canons of construction operate as a substitute for legislative evidence? No. Judges must look outside their own institution to resist unconscious bias, lest they fall prey to picking and choosing canons, not to mention picking and choosing text, to achieve their preferred result—what Nobel Prize–winning cognitive scientists call the "focusing illusion." Fourth, is searching for legislative history a matter of "legislative intent"? No. It is a search for documentary evidence, not spirits. The entire notion of legislative intent is a diversion for the practicing lawyer; one can argue any statutory case without using the term *legislative intent*, which suggests that its cash value is minimal. Finally, is it unconstitutional to rely upon legislative evidence? No. The Constitution's text allows each house the power to control and record the evidence of proceedings under Article I, section 5. Just as Supreme Court opinions are evidence of the reasons for the Court's votes, Congress's public documents recount the reasons for Congress's votes.

Chapter 1

As a general rule, law schools teach Congress "through the rearview mirror," from the ways in which courts must address Congress—the interpretation of statutes. Chapter 1 provides a countervailing, but minimalist, understanding of why Congress is not a junior varsity court. Imagine a simple world in which we knew only two things about Congress: that legislators are individually driven by an electoral connection[12] to their constituencies and collectively hampered by the supermajoritarian difficulty—the real-world fact that all legislation which passes through the Congress today requires a supermajoritarian vote of 60 senators.[13] From these two facts, we can predict that ambiguity may be institutionally rational for legislators in ways it is decidedly irrational for judges. No politician worries that she will lose an election because her opponent cried: "Vote for me, I was precise." No majority leader, Republican or Democrat, who has to secure 60 votes on pension or health care reform would deny that she would gladly secure the last vote if the cost were a bit of ambiguity.

Statutory ambiguity may be as rational for legislators as it is irrational and deeply annoying for judges. It is not enough to blame Congress for failing to spend more time dotting *I*'s and crossing *T*'s when terrorists and debt ceilings loom. This is as silly as blaming courts for putting on green eyeshades and focusing on commas rather than large policy concerns. Ambiguity is structurally induced in Congress. It is not simply a matter of foreseeability or the malleability of language, as has been traditionally thought; it is demanded by a difficult process requiring the collective agreement of 535 members. This reality should make judges and lawyers more resistant to finding so-called plain meaning. It should also warn that interpretive discretion is inevitable: judges have to make choices about how to read law. More importantly, in making choices, judges must understand that the stakes of failure have increased exponentially. If a judge errs, her errors may remain fixed, without congressional redress, simply because a minority of senators blocks action.

Chapter 2

Academics' and judges' major theories of statutory interpretation—textualism, purposivism, and contract theory—misunderstand Congress. Taken to its extreme, each adopts an idea of Congress threatening to contradict its own theory of statutory interpretation. If Congress were as chaotic as textualists think or as rational as purposivists or game theorists believe, then text would never be plain for textualists, and it would always be rational for purposivists and game theorists. Applying a realist, minimalist view of Congress yields serious questions for each statutory interpretation theory. First, textualists have no consistent theory of text. Any single term may yield at least two plain meanings, prototypical and extensivist, and Congress has incentives to use both—to speak to the people with stereotypical popular meaning and to judges in legalist specialized forms. Unlike the hope of some textualists, there is no guarantee that picking the more "specialized" meaning will be more libertarian or insulate the textualist from siding with the bill's opponents. Second, purposivists have no consistent theory of purpose. This has allowed their opponents to cleverly suggest that interpreters must embrace any member's purposes, including the purposes of those who opposed the bill. If purposivists are to look at Congress from a realist view, they must seek a bipartisan agreement on core applications or paradigms, armed with a more disciplined approach toward legislative evidence, making clear to distinguish between statutory supporters and opponents. Finally, contract theories and their positive political theory cousins have much to tell us about how Congress really works but have few viable, simplified ways for judges and lawyers to apply metrics designed for the political science classroom.

Chapter 3

Without legislative context, statutory texts can become entirely arbitrary. Take the term "fifth." It might mean the Fifth Amendment to the Constitution, the fifth patient at a clinic, or a fifth of gin. Linguists and philosophers know that pulling text from context yields the potential for many meanings, giving the interpreter broad power to choose among those meanings. But it does not take an academic to explain that. Senator Orrin Hatch was right when he said that text without legislative context can turn into an exercise in "judicial adventurism."[14] So, too, was Senator Specter, who when still a Republican argued that the refusal to look at legislative evidence meant that judges were simply writing their own statutes.[15] As the current Republican chairman of the Senate Judiciary Committee said during confirmation hearings for the chief justice, despite his respect for Justice Scalia, he didn't agree with his position rejecting legislative history.[16]

Chapter 3 provides the basic principles and method for understanding legislative procedure—Congress 101. First, statutes are *elections*, not competitions among scriveners; there are winners and losers in the legislative battle, and if one does not take this into account, it is just as easy for a liberal or a conservative judge to make rather serious anti-democratic mistakes, in effect treating a dissenting opinion as a majority decision. Second, statutes follow a *sequence* over time, with the later text trumping earlier text: statutory reasoning should privilege the end of the process as we move to a whole text, not the beginning. (Stop writing legislative histories and start reverse engineering the statutory text; it is quite a bit simpler.) Third, Congress has its own rules of legislative interpretation that judges should understand and that can help when all other interpretive tools fail or when a judge is tempted to think Congress lost its mind (what judges call legislative "absurdity"). It turns out that what is unthinkable or "absurd" to a judge is quite thinkable—and sometimes required—by Congress's rules of proceeding. Fourth, the standard typologies of legislative history are bad proxies for reliability. Bipartisan evidence is the best legislative evidence; by contrast, the seeming gold standard under the current typology—committee reports—can be completely overtaken by changes in statutory text, or even issued after the statute is signed by the president (in which case it should be ignored). After bipartisan evidence, group-authorized evidence should take precedence to resolve statutory ambiguities. By contrast, when members do not act on behalf of the group, or when they flout the group's rules, their statements should be ignored.

Misunderstanding Congress can make legislative evidence a good deal more difficult to discover and more likely to invite the "picking and choosing" of one's friends, whether in text or history. In some of the most significant statutory interpretation cases in our history—cases about affirmative action, discrimination, health care, and judicial nominations[17]—the Supreme Court has made rather obvious mistakes in recounting the legislative evidence. In some cases, this has caused the Court to focus on the wrong text; in others, to misunderstand the priority of some texts to others; and in still others, to make the statute's bipartisan core harder, rather than easier, to find. This should seem strange: no lawyer would confuse a majority from a dissenting opinion, a pleading from a jury instruction, but these are precisely the kind of mistakes that lawyers make when they read the Congressional Record. Understanding simple rules governing legislative process may prevent such readings. These rules form what I call a *legislative decision theory* of statutory interpretation.

For decades, the theoretical split between major theories of statutory interpretation—purposivism and textualism—has hinged on time and generality. Textualists believe statutes' meanings are fixed and simple; purposivists believe that judges should update statutes over time to fit with complex policies. Textualists believe that granular detail matters; purposivists describe statutes in general terms. In fact, the most important question for lawyers and judges is whether to look to the legislative record. My answer is a resounding "yes." Both textualists and purposivists must look to the record, and if they do not, they are at risk of finding the wrong text, ignoring textual conflict, or adopting the opinions of those who opposed the bill. It is just as easy to pick out your favorite "friendly" text as it is to pick out your favorite "friendly" piece of legislative history, and this will be more true if one does not know how to read the statutory text in legislative context.

Chapter 4

Chapter 4 rejects the idea that canons of construction should replace legislative evidence. It critiques a particular form of textualism—"petty" textualism—which litigants relied upon in recent and important Supreme Court cases, like the health care case. Forty years of studies by economists, cognitive scientists, and linguists should warn us against a method that picks out one word from a statute, adds a canon of construction, and ends there. Such methods are "petty textualism" because they focus on small bits of text and blind themselves to legislative context, replacing that context with canons of construction. Courts should resist this project not only because all canons (even the ones with Latin names) have counter-canons and thus provide no restraint but also because a vast amount of research outside the law—in economics, cognitive science, game theory, and negotiation—tells us that canons cannot cure textualism of the "focusing illusion."[18] That illusion should warn judges that the choice of the key text is itself a choice. In the recent health care case, lawyers isolated four words from a 900-page law, and in the act of isolating those words, they created an argument that assumed what they were trying to prove—the very choice of text implying something contrary to other provisions in the law. As linguists and philosophers know, one risks fallacy by wrenching text from context. As cognitive theory shows, one must look outside the judiciary, beyond canons of construction, to resist lazy thinking and unconscious bias. De-biasing procedures require that judges know the "rules of the game" governing the other party to an exchange.[19] In the statutory context, that means looking to legislative evidence, as Congress understands it, rather than single words chosen because that choice, the very isolation of text, implies the lawyers' preferred result.

Chapter 5

The committed textualist, if she has read this far, will indignantly reply that all this talk about legislative evidence is mere "legislative intent," and "intent" cannot replace the law. Here, I address the age-old, and philosophically fraught, question: "what is legislative intent?" It turns out that the term is the subject of enormous jurisprudential interest but has been confusing lawyers for decades, if not centuries. Justices Scalia and others who refused to look to Congress's records insist that looking for public legislative evidence is like looking for a hidden, secret ghost, in legislators' minds. I reply that this is a kind of cheap "intent skepticism," in the sense that no one applies it to other large organizations, like Harvard or Apple or Time Warner, even though they are regularly personified. The term *intent* can be excised from arguments about statutory interpretation and debates about legislative evidence. Lest this seem radical, consider how constitutional originalists have shifted their discourse away from intent toward original public meaning.

This chapter punctures the canonical claim made originally in the 1930s by liberals like Professor Max Radin and asserted more recently by conservatives, like the late Justice Scalia, that Congress can have no "intent" or, that if one is looking for intent, one is necessarily looking for spirits or states of mind. To paraphrase the scientist Alan Turing, the question is not whether a computer has a mind, nor is the question whether Congress has a mind, but how the computer or Congress makes decisions. Congress acts as a group through its rules and procedures.[20] Those rules not only provide a key contextual guide—like the rules of chess—for interpreting text and legislative evidence, but they also provide ways to categorize and dismiss evidence that is not authorized by the joint group enterprise. If such rules are legitimate to explain how corporations act, one wonders why they are not good enough to explain Congress. Chapter 5's conclusion helps explain basic limiting factors on legitimate legislative evidence, such as why individual statements of legislators alone cause concern and why courts should reject evidence that has no ability to influence the group or lacks group authority.

Chapter 6

Opponents of legislative evidence have one last beachhead: the Constitution. Textualists have insisted that, for a judge to look at public legislative evidence is to act unconstitutionally. This chapter rejects that conclusion, providing a constitutional argument *for* legislative history, affirming the legitimacy of the approach taken by the vast majority of judges and lawyers over the course of the 20th century. I do battle using the very tools that textualists prefer: the constitutional text. Article I, section 5, the Rules of Proceedings Clause, supports the constitutionality of legislative evidence. This clause provides that each house may set its own rules for conducting business, just as the first Congress set up committees and conference committees to propose business and resolve controversy. The Journal Clause, in turn, provides for the publication of Congress's proceedings. Constitutional critics claim that the Bicameralism Clause, Article I, section 7, requires that a bill be passed by both houses. But the Proceedings Clause makes it clear that each house, not both, acts legitimately under the Constitution when it publishes documents of its proceedings. Any robust and realistic understanding of the separation of powers supports that textual claim.

Epilogue

If judges are to be faithful agents of Congress, they must imagine themselves democratic *fiduciaries*. Too much talk has been had about courts as the agents of Congress, suggesting the image of the passive proofreader, expecting Congress to produce perfect text. More attention should focus on the idea of "faithfulness" and what it means to be "faithful" to Congress. I argue that the judiciary must serve as democracy's fiduciaries, not its antagonists. This is true no matter how much the judge personally detests the majority party in Congress or desperately hated his or her own confirmation hearing. (I understand that completely.) Members of Congress owe a larger duty to democracy to try to come to greater inter-branch understanding, as Judge Katzmann has been suggesting for years. One cannot be faithful to an institution one likens to slimy meats, disliked vegetables, and refuse.

That said, Congress has work to do. Confirmation hearings must be regularized in ways that treat potential judges with respect; the current process is opaque and apparently arbitrary to many nominees, leaving judges with impressions about Congress from the very start of their career that are often less than favorable. The Congressional Record must be modernized by making its internal organization transparent in simple ways. Currently, bills are scattered across the Congressional Record; all relevant bill text and timelines should be consolidated. The record must be annotated to allow the average citizen to understand relevant procedures and reflect whether the speaking member voted for or against the bill or pending amendment. Finally, in an ideal world, if Republicans and Democrats agree that legislative evidence is relevant, as the current Republican chairman of the Senate Judiciary Committee Chuck Grassley has said, senators must insist that judicial nominees, particularly Supreme Court nominees, pledge to refuse to blind themselves to legislative evidence. Given the vast numbers of statutory cases, and given the supermajoritarian risks, it is not enough to talk about vague judicial philosophies. *Nominees must be asked about how they read the law.* The public needs to know whether a judge is willing to blindly claim as "plain" a practice of reading the law against the people.

Conclusion

Demagogues and dictators thrive in worlds contemptuous of the representative assembly. It may not be too much of an exaggeration to say that, in a world where filibustering obstructionism dominates, reading Congress with basic intelligence may be necessary to secure our republic for another century. Whether one seeks to reform the filibuster, repeal every modern law as an invasion of liberty, or simply read the laws we have, democratic competence requires no less from those who, like many lawyers, purport to be experts on democracy.

1

Congress Is Not a Court

It was a bad meeting.

The Senate Judiciary Committee's chief counsel asked when the majority leader planned to "bring up" the crime bill. Silence. Nothing. No response.

As we left, I asked, "What was that?"

"Moose."

"Moose?" I inquired, with some perplexity.

"Guns," the chief counsel grunted.

However politically naive I was at the time (and I was), even I knew that gun control meant a crime bill filibuster. It took longer to realize that "Moose" referred to hunters and, more specifically, hunters in Maine. The light clicked: the majority leader, George Mitchell, was up for reelection that year and did not want to bring up the bill lest it endanger his election. Of course, Senator Mitchell's staff evaded the issue. Why? Because the calculus was more complex: two years later, after he was reelected, George Mitchell would bring up the crime bill, and eventually he would vote for it.

To lawyers trained primarily in the art of the courtroom and the appellate case, congressional politics has the whiff of incomprehensibility that I experienced upon hearing the term "moose" issue from the lips of the otherwise articulate and accomplished Judiciary Committee's chief counsel. But it is precisely "moose" that explains the institutional rationality of the players' actions: guns made the bill subject to a filibuster in a year when the majority leader, who represented Maine, was up for election. Put more bluntly, the leader was driven to time the crime bill based on what I will call the "electoral connection" and the "supermajoritarian difficulty." Note, however, that this did not determine Leader Mitchell's ultimate vote or even his policy position. It did, however, have a decisive impact on the legislative process.[1]

When it comes to Congress, contemporary legal theories about statutes risk irony, if not contradiction. Consider textualism, personified by Justice Scalia, the theory that judges should stop at law's plain meaning, blinding themselves to how Congress writes statutes. One leading textualist describes Congress as "arbitrary" and "strategic" and its processes "tortuous" and "opaque."[2] If Congress is all that, why should plain meaning ever arise? Textualists' opponents, purposivists, personified by Justice Breyer, reverse the irony. They idealize Congress. As their professors, Hart and Sacks, famously put it, members of the legislature are "reasonable men pursuing reasonable purposes."[3] But if Congress reasons so well, every statute should be plainly reasonable, not ambiguous enough to send judges running to the statute's history as purposivists insist. Political scientists' theories, known as positive political theory,[4] fare no better,[5] imagining Congress as either a devil incapable of making rational decisions or as an angel yielding efficient bargains. If the irrationality thesis were true, why would there be any statutes at all? If the bargaining were so efficient, why is passing legislation so difficult, and why are the bargains so difficult to divine?

Taken to extremes, these theories of what lawyers call "statutory interpretation"—how to read laws—adopt ideas of Congress capable of contradicting the theories themselves. If we take the textualists' view of Congress-as-chaos to its extreme, then why should we look to text? A truly chaotic Congress could not create plain meaning. If we take Hart and Sacks's "reasonable men acting reasonably" view of Congress, then purposivist theory risks similar irrelevance; a truly reasonable Congress will always make statutes plain. Finally, if we take the political scientists' view of Congress to its logical extreme, then interpretation would be the least of our problems; government would be impossible or unnecessary. Put bluntly, leading theoretical opinions on how to read statutes—by judges, lawyers, and political scientists—have no coherent or realistic idea of Congress.[6] In this book, I offer a minimalist theory that is both realistic and of use to lawyers and judges in statutory interpretation cases.

This is not a pedestrian enterprise; it is a matter of fidelity to one of the basic principles of democratic government—the power of the people, meeting through their representatives, to determine their own fate. No one believes that judges should exercise legislative power. In a democracy, the people's representatives are responsible for legislation. Legislation deserves deference because of popular sovereignty. As Jeremy Waldron has so eloquently described it, legislation is the process by which citizens come to govern themselves in a world of wide and persistent disagreement.[7] Statutes are the product of the people's will, and even if that rosy picture seems too rosy, its opposite—rule by judges—is universally reviled.

Theories of statutory interpretation assume quite a bit about Congress, and it is time to focus on those assumptions. As Professor Jerry Mashaw has emphasized, "our positive beliefs about what is, powerfully constrain and shape our normative beliefs about what is good or desirable."[8] I begin with two meta-principles, which any theory of statutory interpretation should satisfy. First, as a descriptive matter, lawyers' theories of statutes must be based on what we uncontroversially know about Congress, including its rules and incentives.[9] Second, as a prescriptive matter, any proper theory must be consistent with basic democratic principles, such as majority rule.

Critics might wonder what is so new about the first principle. Realism in statutory interpretation traces to the 1930s. Its original claim was skeptical: Congress was incapable of forming a collective "intent."[10] My own view is that this objection—what I call "cheap intent skepticism"—is wrong. Groups like Congress act, and they make decisions; when we look for "intent," we are looking for the meaning of those decisions, and that meaning can only be understood by looking at evidence of legislative context—not imagined minds—as I explain in Chapter 5. At the same time, I think it practically impossible for people to use the term *intent* without evoking this silly objection; therefore, as a pragmatic matter, I think Hart and Sacks were wise to try to come up with a different term. They chose *purpose*, which unfortunately suffers from many of the same problems as *intent*. I have chosen *decision*, as we use this term to describe judicial rulings—even when the court is deeply divided, the decision is merely plural, or soon overridden.[11]

Unlike sophisticated fine-grained empirical theories of politics debated among political scientists, my aim is not to predict legislative strategies, policy outcomes, median voter results, or party influence. The model is realist, relying on uncontroversial, widely accepted facts about Congress and its members' institutional incentives. This minimalist approach is deliberately parsimonious. It must first translate Congress to courts as a descriptive matter and then provide a means for courts to translate that understanding to statutory interpretation. *Legislative decision theory*—the core of this book—argues that, in all cases, legislative context is crucial to understand legislative meaning. Interpreters cannot understand that context fully, however, unless they have a basic sense of Congress 101.

Just as we are capable of theorizing about courts in general without reducing them to individual judges, we can analyze Congress as an institution without reducing it to its individual members. An opening caution for political scientists and economists: I reject the "view from nowhere"[12] that politicians' or judges' "preferences can be specified independently of their institutional location."[13] One may readily concede, with many economists, that individuals are rational actors, but rationality may be influenced enormously by institutional context. The claim that individuals' preferences are separable from those of institutions is wrong; preferences are endogenously formed. As Professor Graham Allison long ago explained, decisions are typically based on where you sit.[14] As we will see, this view yields a theory of Congress starkly different from that held by either major school of statutory interpretation—textualism or purposivism. Congress is not a green-eye shaded scrivener nor a junior varsity court and, if it were, democracy would be in worse trouble than it is today.

My minimalist approach yields a strong lesson for lawyers and judges who embrace the concept of "plain meaning." Ambiguity, not plain meaning, is to be expected of Congress. Any realistic approach to Congress concedes that the business of legislating among 535 persons will yield ambiguity. One need not posit bad motives, strategic behavior, or stupidity (standard scholarly claims about legislative behavior). Imagine trying to write a Supreme Court brief with 535 coauthors. Textual ambiguity emerges from Congress's institutional structure, something no court can change. If this is true, then the search for plain meaning, which has driven much statutory interpretation theory for the past 20 years, is a diversion. Instead, we should focus on how to find the "proper" text (looking at evidence about how the text evolved), and in hard cases find the best evidence of legislative context to resolve ambiguity. Statutory interpretation must focus less on finding "plain meaning" and more on resolving statutory ambiguity.

It is sad, but true, that the search for "plain meaning" may be nothing other than an exercise of judicial fiat. As I explain in Chapter 2, it is fairly easy to find "two plain meanings" in every case; just contrast the best undisputed example (a prototypical meaning) with all logical examples of a text (an extensivist meaning). This does not imply that plain texts should not be honored; they must, and everyone agrees that they must. It does mean that we need to think harder about "plainness" and "ambiguity." It also means that we need to worry that our decisions about what is "plain" are cognitively biased, blinding decision makers to conflicting texts, and that the "choice" of particular texts as "plain" may be question-begging, as I explain in Chapter 4.

The most important question for courts is *how*, not *whether*, to resolve ambiguity. Courts have two choices: they may use their own self-constructed tools of meaning (canons, precedents, asserted plain meanings), or they can look to the evidence of how Congress acted (legislative evidence). This book argues that courts must look to legislative evidence, even where "plain meaning" seems apparent, if for no other reason than to counter judges' and lawyers' likely cognitive biases. Put in theoretical terms, both textualism and purposivism have work to do: as I will show, textualists who ignore legislative evidence can pick and choose the wrong texts, and purposivists who ignore how Congress works can pick and choose the wrong legislative evidence. Although it is likely to seem oxymoronic for some, textualists and purposivists alike must learn how to understand the legislative record (what I call "legislative evidence"), but in a new, simpler, and more disciplined way, as described in Chapter 3.

The "Electoral Connection"

Cognitive science tells us that we often do not think clearly, and this is nowhere more true than when lawyers begin to think about Congress, otherwise known as the "sausage factory." The "self-serving" bias tells us that we tend to think that success is our own, and failures are the fault of others. If a CEO is successful, this reflects his brilliant contributions; if he fails, it was the market's fault. This should warn judges about attributing all problems in legislation to Congress. Similarly, the "overconfidence effect" should warn judges not to be so sure about what they think they know about Congress. People systematically overrate their knowledge; consider the 68 percent of faculty members who rated themselves to be in the top 25 percent of teachers.[15] Institutions aggravate these biases in conditions of information scarcity. Because Congress is not taught as a subject in many law schools, individuals hear the same claims over and over again from their fellow judges and lawyers and professors: Supreme Court opinions "stunning," academic articles "intriguing," and legislation "sausage." Given these biases, I begin from the other end of the spectrum, from very basic, uncontroversial, facts about Congress that are often ignored in the statutory interpretation literature.

Start with the most basic fact about the legislature: "the electoral connection."[16] No political scientist, on the right or left, rejects the idea that the "electoral connection" is the most distinctive institutional feature of Congress. The first and foremost characteristic of a legislature is its intrinsic link to citizens of nation and state. The legislature "acts as the eyes, ears, and voice of the people."[17] A representative lives and breathes, to paraphrase the great constitutionalist Charles Black, based on "what [the voters] think" of her back home.[18] As the political scientist Richard Hall puts it: "the representative from South Dakota who concentrates legislative time on South Africa, and the senator from South Carolina who takes little interest in textile tariffs, whatever their positions and whatever *we* may think of their actions, are not being ideal [representatives]."[19]

That "members of Congress care intensely about reelection,"[20] is a view shared by the greats of political science, from Douglas Arnold to David Mayhew, from Donald Matthews to Morris Fiorina, from Richard Fenno to John Kingdon, from Barry Weingast to John Ferejohn.[21] Those who write within very different political science traditions—whether they were part of the great behaviorist revolution of the 1960s and 1970s, the rational choice revolution of the 1980s and 1990s, or some entirely different variant—share this assumption. Even those political scientists who find no correlation between people's views on particular issues and voting records,[22] or who insist that voters have the "haziest of awareness"[23] of specific policy issues, or that party or ideology or public interest matters, recognize that the electoral connection has a role to play.[24] As Douglas Arnold put it, members try to anticipate what their constituents want—or at least what their potential opponents at election time think that their constituents want.[25]

The Importance of Audience: An Intellectual Experiment

Open the Congressional Record. Imagine that you have never seen it. Notice that the record does not look much like an appellate argument or trial brief. Most legislative debate begins with a ritualistic invocation of groups supporting a bill and cosponsoring legislators. Why list these organizations or representatives? Because these groups are surrogates for those to whom the bill is directed: the people. Notice that there is often very little discussion of particular statutory texts and a good deal of discussion of general purposes and principles, in light of the political issues of the day. "We shall solve the health care crisis, we shall win the war, and we shall end violence against women." Why general purposes? Because the sponsor is talking to his or her constituents, and what they want is action: most average persons want to know what Congress is doing about the "budget crisis" or "health care," not whether Congress is amending 18 U.S.C. 924(c). Notice that, in these opening speeches, there are almost no references to dictionaries, the common law, Supreme Court cases, or even how the bill will be "interpreted."[26]

Most lawyers unfamiliar with politics see this behavior as strange, as something less than what law should be, as a silly refusal of otherwise capable men and women to sit down and write statutes clearly. It is almost as if legislative critics are stamping their feet like a frustrated parent, saying, "you, Congress, can't you please write more clearly!" Why don't we see you on C-SPAN sitting on the House floor drafting text? The frustrated member of Congress is likely to respond with passive aggression, ignoring the parental-sounding criticism because she has more important things to do. But if she were to answer, she would say, "With respect, your honor, no one votes for scriveners. I would not be doing my constitutional duty if I were to sit at my desk all day worrying over single words and canons of construction. No one at my rallies will be holding up a sign saying *Vote for X, she understands the latin canon ejusdem generis.*"

Of course, this exaggerates. Members of Congress are often lawyers who share a common language with judges, but it remains true that the legislature, as an institution, forces representatives to speak a different dialect to a different audience. Litigating lawyers talk to judges in courts and are generally taught in law school to talk to courts; politicians talk to the average Joe, the electorate. If this is a failure, it is a constitutionally prescribed failure. As Madison said in the *Federalist Papers*, the Constitution is structured to identify the "man" (and now "woman") with the constitutional mission of the place: in the case of Congress, the Constitution commands that members represent, and in the case of the court, the Constitution commands that judges stand above the political fray.[27] The popular branch, wrote Madison, "should have an immediate dependence on, and an intimate sympathy with, the people."[28]

The truth, as we will see, is that representatives have more than one audience—they must speak both to the people and to expert lawyers, judges, and administrators. One of the leading students of legislative behavior, Professor Nelson Polsby, once explained this constitutional principle by distinguishing between the American Congress, which is a "transformative" legislature, and the British Parliament, which is an "arena" legislature.[29] Arena legislatures are "forums for discussion of ideas and policies."[30] By contrast, the American legislature is a "transformative legislature," which must "actively translate ideas into laws."[31] "The act of transformation is crucial because it postulates a significance of the internal structure of legislatures, to the internal division of law, and to the policy preferences of various legislators."[32] Because of our separated powers system, which divides the legislative from the executive, the American Congress, relative to [parliamentary] legislatures, "is much more activist, and subject to 'conflict, compromise and individualism.' There is a constant give-and-take at work, as inputs from throughout the political system [the 'electoral connection'] are transformed into legislative output."[33] The American legislature is constantly struggling to translate politics into law.

Constituent-Talk

A brief intellectual experiment illustrates how the electoral connection makes judges and legislators act and speak in ways sure to produce regular misunderstandings. In what follows, I attempt to "light up" (to borrow Jeremy Waldron's felicitous phrase) the differences between judges and legislators in terms of "audience"—the better to understand the vertical dynamics of the legislature.[34] As we will see, the process is complex; statutes are directed to multiple audiences, including courts and agencies. But for parsimony's sake, let us see the point first—that, relative to judges, legislators speak openly to a different, more public audience—and then we can begin to complicate the story.

Imagine a citizen encountering the justices of the Supreme Court and asking them to please address important public problems: health care, crime, negative campaign advertising. Now imagine that in the weeks that follow, we hear the following from the Supreme Court. The chief justice stands up and refers to a failed health care law and bemoans "broken promises to the American people."[35] Now imagine the next justice rising and, after reading the text of a criminal law, saying, "Our wives, our mothers, and our colleagues are afraid to walk in grocery store parking lots, to jog in public parks, or to ride home from work late at night in city buses. They are losing a fundamental human right—the right to be free from fear."[36] And imagine the next justice rising, reading a lengthy campaign finance statute, and saying: "I think these issue advocacy ads are a nightmare. I think all of us should hate them . . . we [sh]ould get some of this poison politics off television."[37]

To anyone mildly conversant with the Supreme Court, there is something wrong with this picture. These do not sound like the statements of Supreme Court justices, for it is not the justices' job to respond to citizens' needs for legislation. The statements I have provided are in fact from members of Congress. The first, on health care, is from Senator Olympia Snowe; the second, introducing the Violence Against Women Act, is from then-Senator Joseph R. Biden; and the third, during the debate on the McCain–Feingold campaign finance bill, is from Senator Paul Wellstone.

Now shift your imaginative attention to the Congress. Imagine that a senator, unprompted by citizen demand or public uprising, were to rise and make the following statement on the floor:

> *Buckley* did not consider [section] 610's separate ban on corporate and union independent expenditures, the prohibition that had also been in the background in *CIO, Automobile Workers, and Pipefitters*. Had [section] 610 been challenged in the wake of *Buckley*, however, it could not have been squared with the reasoning and analysis of that precedent. The expenditure ban invalidated in *Buckley*, [section] 608(e), applied to corporations and unions, and some of the prevailing plaintiffs in *Buckley* were corporations. The *Buckley* Court did not invoke the First Amendment's overbreadth doctrine to suggest that [section] 608(e)'s expenditure ban would have been constitutional if it had applied only to corporations and not to individuals. *Buckley* cited with approval the *Automobile Workers* dissent, which argued that [section] 610 was unconstitutional.

If you guessed that this was not a senatorial statement, but a Supreme Court opinion, you would be correct. It is taken from Justice Kennedy's opinion in *Citizens United v. FEC*.[38] Notice how coherent and precise is the rhetoric and how unlikely it is that citizens or voters could make heads or tails of these statements. The justices value precision, detail, and expert meanings within a precedential system. Representatives speak primarily to their constituents; the justices speak primarily to their peers in the elite legal community and to the Supreme Court's own past precedents.

The skeptic should consider one final intellectual experiment: imagine if the individuals in these institutions switched places. Would lawyers really want members of Congress to spend their time at the Supreme Court or the American Bar Association? What if Supreme Court justices appeared on CNN or the Glenn Beck show or in the lobbies of Congress? Even the public would find this strange and inappropriate behavior for members of Congress and justices of the Supreme Court. Congress is not a court, and courts are not Congress. For many, however, it takes this kind of intellectual thought experiment to begin to treat Congress as something more than a junior varsity court.

For those who remain unconvinced, individual vice may yield collective virtue. To a lawyer looking for a right answer to a tough interpretive problem, it may all appear "vicious babble." That same "babble," however, may constitute virtuous representation writ large. As Jeremy Waldron has written, statutes are "essentially—not just accidentally—the product of large and polyphonous assemblies."[39] It is essential to the most minimal notions of democratic consent that the minority have the opportunity to voice its opposition. Democracy's legitimacy depends upon this idea. Relative to other forms of legislature, "the United States Congress is extraordinarily effective" at voicing "opinions held by significant numbers of voters back in the constituencies."[40]

There is nothing particularly new about this idea. The cynic Machiavelli warned that the legislative "tumults that many inconsiderately damn"[41] may yet yield good laws. John Locke believed that " 'tis in their Legislative, that the Members of a commonwealth are united, and combined together into one coherent living Body."[42] No one explained it better than John Stuart Mill:

> Representative assemblies are often taunted by their enemies with being places of mere talk and bavardage. There has seldom been more misplaced derision. I know not how a representative assembly can more usefully employ itself than in talk, when the subject of talk is the great public interest of the country. . . . A place where every interest and shade of opinion in the country can have its cause even passionately pleaded . . . is in itself, if it answered no other purpose, one of the most important political institutions that can exist anywhere, and one of the foremost benefits of free government.[43]

This intellectual experiment reveals the electoral connection as a powerful mediating force driving legislatures—a force largely absent from the incentives driving federal judges. To say that the electoral connection distinguishes legislatures from courts is not to say that representation works, is fair, or is undistorted.[44] Members may imagine an electorate speaking in a distinctly "upper or lower class accent" or excluding entire groups from electoral consideration. Representatives may be far more responsive to concentrated interest groups than large latent majorities. They may follow party dictates despite the call of their constituents or pass purely "symbolic" legislation.[45] They may even reject their constituents' specific demands in the name of the public good. But even if these things are all true, the relative institutional point remains the same: a representative is subject to institutional constraints involving collective action and links to voters in ways unthinkable for an unelected judge.[46]

The Multiple Audience Problem

If I am right about the electoral connection, then one of the most basic forces driving legislatures is different from—in fact antithetical to—forces driving courts.[47] This helps explain resilient institutional misunderstandings: these misunderstandings occur not because members of Congress and the judiciary attended different law schools or occupy different social strata but because the institutions provide strong incentives for particular forms of rationality and speech. For legislators, drafting ambiguity may be quite rational, indeed "normal," not because they prefer it but because the institution—and its need to act—produces conditions demanding it.

Consider the following example. During debates about the Violence Against Women Act, opponents claimed that its civil rights remedy would cover every act of violence between a man and a woman, leading to massive numbers of cases brought to federal court.[48] (Lest this seem odd, a similar "ubiquity" claim was made about a federal sexual harassment law when it was first debated). To assuage opponents, the drafters decided to accept the argument—quite literally. They added bill language saying that the law did not cover "random acts of violence."[49] From the majority's perspective, they gave away nothing because the bill was never drafted to cover such acts. The amendment attempted to defuse a political argument. There is no guarantee, however, that this language would not, in some future legal case, become the subject of interpretive controversy. (What is a "random" crime, for example?)

It would be comforting to think that we could insulate statutory text from the electoral connection: members of Congress would speak to voters in their grand speeches, but when it comes to statutory text, they would speak only to courts. But there is no "acoustic separation," as Professor Meir Dan-Cohen once put it, between the call of the voter, the citizen, and the court.[50] We cannot put legislators in a soundproof chamber when speaking to their constituents and then in another when marking up a bill. It is true that speaking to voters may involve arcane legalisms as easily as vernacular speech. But it cannot be true that statutes are only written for courts, lest we give up Madison's injunction that the "man" (and now "woman") must be identified with the constitutional place. As Justice Scalia once wrote, it would be horrifying if, like Nero, we posted statutes "high up on the pillars, so that they could not easily be read," so that the ordinary person could not know the laws to which she had consented to be governed.[51]

Because text cannot be separated from the electoral connection with any ease, statutes can be a crazy amalgam of the vernacular and the precise. This raises what I will call the "multiple-audience" problem. Statutes, like congressional debates, are exercises in communication along two conflicting dimensions—communication between representatives and citizens (the vertical dimension) and between between legislatures and courts and agencies (the horizontal dimension). There would be no purpose to a statute if it were not supposed to communicate a conduct rule to the average person: "do not discriminate," "do not harass," "do not kill."[52] Of course, statutes are also, to varying degrees, directions to those who would apply the statutes and thus are communications to legal experts (lawyers and agencies and courts). Precisely for both these reasons, statutory language is often an amalgam of legal and popular meaning.

One way of thinking about the statute-making process is that the legislature is trying to translate public and representative (vertical) concerns into a more precise (horizontal) lawyerly dialect. This complicates but does not negate my point: it is not that the vernacular is the only language of statutes (it is not), nor that public audiences always matter, but that if we are to understand Congress's internal incentives, we must consider the possibility that even *statutory text* reflects the demands of a popular electoral audience. Representatives may have powerful reasons to ignore precision and the lawyerly voice. To assume, then, as textualists often do, that the context of a statute is a community of elite lawyers runs against what we know about Congress's audiences and incentives. We must consider that legislatures may have an incentive to privilege prototypical, ordinary "joe" meanings rather than legalistic meaning, a point I explain in Chapter 2. It also helps to explain why representatives may well embrace ambiguity. In short, it helps to explain why Congress is not and cannot be a court.

The Supermajoritarian Difficulty

No one who studies Congress thinks it easy to pass legislation.[53] It is far easier to block than to enact legislation, given the many steps in the process at which the bill may be stopped. In the House, one moves from committee and subcommittee hearings and markups, to the House Rules Committee, to debate on a Rule approved by the Rules Committee, to substantive debate and amendment on the House floor.[54] In the Senate, one runs a similar gauntlet through subcommittee and committee, but one must face the unique requirements of a system that operates on unanimous consent, allowing individual senators to block the process, to "filibuster," unless there is a vote to "close" debate, known as a "cloture motion." If both houses pass bills, they must go to conference committee to work out the differences and then both bills must return to the Senate and the House to be approved. That still leaves the need for the president's signature and allows potential congressional override.

The difficulty of congressional action is not simply a practical consideration: it reflects our peculiar bicameral system. The Constitution undergirds this system by creating two chambers, allowing each chamber to set its own rules, and entrenching equal state representation in the Senate, empowering small populations to block legislation.[55] As political scientists like Robert Dahl and Keith Krehbiel and savvy constitutionalists like Sanford Levinson have argued, the structure of our government is far less majoritarian than most assume. Legislation on any popularly salient issue requires supermajorities.[56]

This is not simply because of the threat of filibuster but because state representation is entrenched in the Senate. Because of bicameralism, this means that minorities (small states) can always block legislation. In other words, legislative action requires massive consensus. We can call this the "supermajoritarian difficulty."

Structure-Induced Ambiguity

The supermajoritarian difficulty, when combined with the electoral connection, creates enormous pressure for statutory ambiguity. Although there are few electoral costs of ambiguity (no one lost an election because of imprecision), ambiguity may yield essential gains in supermajority consensus. These twin pressures also create enormous possibilities of misunderstanding between courts and legislatures. Courts prize interpretive virtues, "precision in drafting, consciousness of interpretive rules, discovery of meaning in past precedent, and detached reflection on the language of particular texts."[57] Legislatures, on the other hand, prize "action and agreement, reconciling political interests, and addressing the pragmatic needs of those affected by legislation."[58]

Empirical evidence of how legislation is drafted supports the pressures for ambiguity. When Professor Jane Schacter and I interviewed those staffers most likely to have a lawyerly view of the matter, those on the Senate Judiciary Committee, they told us that institutional incentives often prevailed over the need for clarity:

> Over and over again, staffers explained their choices in terms of constitutive virtues—that deliberate ambiguity was necessary to "get the bill passed," or that statutory language was drafted on the floor because a bill was "needed" by a particular senator, by the leadership, or by the public. Even staffers' reliance on lobbyists was an attempt to understand how the bill would "affect" people in the world. It was not that the staffers did not know the rules or recognize the interpretive virtues; it was that those virtues frequently were trumped by competing virtues demanded by the institutional context of the legislature. In an ideal world, the staffers seemed to say, they would aspire to both clarity and

agreement, but, if there were a choice to be made, the constitutive virtues would prevail.[59]

In such a world, ambiguity can become rational, even normal. Notice that this form of "rational ambiguity" supplements two important, but different, claims about the legislative process and ambiguity. Traditionally, theories of statutory interpretation have focused on time as the source of most interpretive problems: Congress cannot possibly foresee all statutory applications. In my view, this is an empirical claim that may or may not be true; one must look to the legislative evidence in any particular case. Later, dynamic theories of statutory interpretation suggested a different version of the temporal difficulty: norms change over time so that Congress's decisions may, at a later time, seem old-fashioned or out of date.[60] This "dead hand" problem is important but it is unclear how often it arises in the real world relative to the average statutory ambiguity case.[61] If my claim is correct, ambiguity is a more serious problem than either of these claims assert. Even without the passage of time, or a change in social norms, on Day Number One, structural incentives *within* the legislature create incentives to embrace statutory ambiguity.[62]

Structure-induced ambiguity is also different from game theorists' argument that members of Congress act strategically to influence how courts will interpret a statute.[63] In politically salient matters, members of Congress "anticipate" the actions of other elite institutions; for example, they must consider whether the president will veto a bill and, in some cases (particularly where judge-made law is the target of a piece of legislation), may try mightily to influence the way in which courts interpret statutes.[64] But it is also possible to exaggerate the degree to which strategic action, as opposed to the "electoral connection," coupled with the "supermajoritarian difficulty" produces ambiguity. Bargaining in legislatures is done horizontally—anticipating the consequences of actors next in line such as judges—and vertically—anticipating the consequences to citizens.[65] Legislators are always talking to third parties, their constituents, and unless those third parties are included in the model of "the game," it is just as likely—indeed, in my view far more likely—that the electoral connection will produce far more ambiguity than legislators' self-conscious attempts to manipulate courts.[66] Put bluntly: no one ever won an election by declaring that she manipulated more judges with the strategic use of legislative debate.

Theorizing Ambiguity

For some time now, theorists of contract interpretation have offered theories and taxonomies of ambiguity; not so legislative theorists who have largely been preoccupied with "plain" meaning. Theorizing ambiguity is important given the institutional incentives we have seen but also because it helps us to understand how ambiguity arises from institutional forces—not simply the passage of time, the vagaries of language, or cognitive biases. It tells us that no matter how clear Congress wanted to be, no matter if all members of the House and Senate studied and adopted a resolution to demand "clear texts," the institution would frustrate their aims.

Both sides in any bargain have the incentive to believe that they are gaining something. But in matters legislative, given that the parties are addressing a public audience, the existence of simultaneous horizontal and vertical relationships—to other institutions and to the voters—allows a variety of false compromises, in the sense that the gains from trade are, from the perspective of linguistic clarity, false. The gains from trade are political, not linguistic: they are gains in the electoral connection, not gains on an abstract clarity or rationality index.

Consider three different ambiguity scenarios: (1) the-ships-passing-in-the-night problem, where the relevant legislative negotiators think the statute is clear but the two parties think it has different meanings; (2) the keep-all-the-voters-happy problem, where the majority gives the opponents language allowing them to claim victory with their constituents but does not prevent the majority from claiming victory themselves; and (3) the unprovided-for-case problem, where the language of the statute is drafted with one prototype in mind, leaving other meanings unaddressed and therefore yielding the apparent "unprovided for" case.

Let us look at the ships-passing-in-the-night problem. Here is an example extrapolated from habeas corpus reform legislation in the late 1980s and early 1990s. At the time, there was a great debate concerning retroactivity and the meaning of the then-extant constitutional case *Teague v. Lane.*[67] I was on the floor of the Senate, at the direction of the manager of the bill, when the following occurred. During discussions on a compromise amendment, one senator was using the term *fundamental rights* to narrow habeas corpus claims. Other senators believed that the term *fundamental rights* would expand then-existing habeas claims. Had this amendment passed, it would have passed even though there was absolutely no consensus on the meaning of the term *fundamental right.* The authors were ships-passing-in-the-night agreeing to a single term for diametrically opposed reasons.[68]

Now, let us consider the "keep the voters happy" scenario or the "logrolling language" problem. Representatives, as we have seen, use textual language to assuage constituencies as much as to direct courts. The need for massive consensus leads to the incentive to defuse opposition with a form of linguistic logrolling, adding language that either repeats other language in the bill or otherwise may yield judicial ambiguity. Remember the example given earlier, in which drafters of the Violence Against Women Act added the words that would exclude "random" acts of violence, on the theory that this addition did not change the meaning of the law at all. Or consider the Tower amendment to the 1964 Civil Rights Act, addressing discrimination in employee testing.[69] Tower opposed the bill and wanted to narrow the testing language agreed upon prior to cloture. His post-cloture amendment failed because the parties had already negotiated the question of testing in the existing substitute bill language.[70] As Senator Humphrey put it, the testing question had been "discussed, discussed and cussed."[71] Tower's amendment lost. Nevertheless, Humphrey agreed to a modified compromise amendment. Having just emerged from the longest filibuster in history, there was an incentive to resolve the problem and move on. Keeping the other side "happy," civil rights supporters logrolled language onto the existing bill. Once that new language became the focus of litigation, however, that language raised questions, yielding a preeminent Supreme Court case on "disparate impact."[72]

If there are incentives that make redundancy rational, there are also incentives to switch between the language of the expert and the language of the voter. Consider the byzantine history of Federal Rule of Evidence 609, governing the impeachment of witnesses by prior felonies. The original bills applied to all witnesses, in civil or criminal cases, but in debating the bills, some legislators focused on a subset with a particular prototype—criminal defendants. The conference committee added language focused on the prototype, and the conference report's explanation toggled between these two meanings—the general and the prototype.[73] The resulting statute appeared to the Supreme Court as offering a "null set" because the prototype was not satisfied—the case before them involved a "witness" but a particular kind of witness different than the prototype—a civil plaintiff, not a defendant.[74] Members of the Court found the statute's language quite "unfathomable."[75] In fact, this kind of ambiguity may be a regular feature of statutory interpretation problems: some representatives are focusing on the best example (the prototypical meaning—criminal defendants) while others are focusing on all possible meanings (the conceptual or legalist meaning—all witnesses). The resulting statute may appear to yield what is known in conflict-of-laws as the "unprovided for" case.[76]

Conclusion

In a simple world in which we knew only two facts about Congress—the electoral connection and the supermajoritarian difficulty—we would know that there are basic institutional incentives leading to statutory ambiguity—whatever the fortuities of language, future events, member stupidity, or sausage-making deals (the causes most students of statutory interpretation embrace). Critics will reply that my account leaves out a good deal of important political theory. This is intentional: assumptions in a robust, powerful, theory must be simple. If they are too complex, they provide no testable claims or predict variation in outcomes. Perhaps more importantly, the aim here is different from much political theory but far more important for lawyers.[77] The aim is to provide a means of making familiar that which seems strange, of translating one institution—the Congress—to another—the courts—in terms that lawyers and judges can readily understand and use. Unlike attempts to study Congress in all of its dimensions, whether conducted by law professors or political scientists, *my aim is to simplify*. The key relative difference that judges and lawyers must keep in mind is the most basic one: compared to courts, Congress has an entirely different audience (voters) and an entirely different institutional and collective context (535 members). These two facts alone predict statutory ambiguity.

Legal academics have appropriated a good bit of political theory in the past 35 years, but very little of it satisfies my minimalist threshold—the uncontroversial. Interest group theory remains contested and yields highly indeterminate results.[78] Neither a party-driven model nor a median voter model[79] can explain something as basic as why most bills pass by large bipartisan majorities (something supermajoritarianism predicts).[80] Arrow's cycling theorem has been contested for decades: its predictions of legislative chaos fail to explain variation (why any bill passes) much less passes by large bipartisan majorities.[81] As the political scientist Keith Krehbiel has argued, none of these theoretical positions explains one of the most basic facts of a supermajoritarian system: persistent yet far from invariant gridlock, even in cases where there is no divided government, and even when a political party appears to have a filibuster-proof majority.[82] Twenty years of theorizing has been devoted to showing that, despite Arrow's cycling prediction, Congress does reach equilibrium, and generally it reaches equilibrium through institutional rules and procedures.[83]

To say that ambiguity may be rational for Congress in ways that it is not rational for courts should not lead to the hasty conclusion that statutory interpretation is, for that reason, an impossible enterprise. It is to invite judges and lawyers to resist the temptation to see Congress in their own image. It is to urge them to appreciate our most democratic institution for what it is, for good and ill. In the rest of this book, I argue that to understand Congress's most basic rules, and electoral incentives, should help judges and lawyers interpret statutes; at a minimum it should improve the use of legislative evidence and the tracing of statutory text. Judges aim to be faithful agents of Congress, but if they do not understand Congress 101, that mission is impossible. As in more sophisticated political theory, what is missing should be more important to lawyers, judges, and academics: *the rules of the legislative game.*

2

Statutory Interpretation Theories Misunderstand Congress

Never mind about these hair-splitting technicalities with reference to the bill; but remedy any defects that you believe to exist in it. If we all had to run as constitutional lawyers, few of us would get elected [laughter], and remember that what the workingmen ask you to do for them is simply that this Congress shall give, so far as it can, protection to them against this infamous contract system.

REPRESENTATIVE O'NEILL
(SUPPORTER OF THE 1885 ALIEN CONTRACT LABOR ACT)[1]

People who can instruct us in morals and religion and in every species of elevation by lectures . . . are not prohibited [under the Act].

SENATOR MORGAN
(OPPONENT OF THE 1885 ALIEN CONTRACT LABOR ACT)[2]

OUR MOST PROMINENT theories of statutory interpretation misunderstand our most representative body. Textualism, purposivism, and contract theory[3] each fail to account for two basic facts about Congress: the electoral connection and the supermajoritarian difficulty. Each has a tendency to treat Congress as a failed legal institution, whether as a junior varsity court or a failed contract regime. I argue that each of these theories needs a more "realist" approach toward Congress.

Textualism

In 1987, Justice Scalia gave an extremely influential set of lectures in which he set forth a doctrine of statutory interpretation known as the "new textualism."[4] The text of the statute has always been the starting place for theories of statutory interpretation, but Justice Scalia's "new textualism" placed text at center stage. As Professor Bill Eskridge explains: "Scalia's main point is that a statutory text's apparent plain meaning must be the alpha and the omega in a judge's interpretation of the statute."[5] Although traditional practice, reaching back to Blackstone, allowed judges to consider multiple factors, including the statute's purposes, textualists narrowed the range of permissible evidence to the text. "Legislative history should not even be consulted to confirm the apparent meaning of a statutory text."[6] If a law is within the text, "end of case," the judge should go no further.[7]

The Scalia Tanner lectures contain one of the most eloquent statements in print about the importance of legislation: "every issue of law resolved by a federal judge involves interpretation of text—the text of a regulation, or of a statute, or of the Constitution."[8] Scalia was concerned that, over the years, a culture had emerged in which "lawyers routinely . . . ma[d]e no distinction between words in the text of a statute and words in its legislative history."[9] Lawyers had corrupted statutory interpretation with a tendency to "have the meaning of a law determined by what the lawgiver meant, rather than by what the lawgiver promulgated."[10] In no uncertain terms Justice Scalia declared: "I object to the use of legislative history on principle, since I reject intent of the legislature as the proper criterion of the law."[11]

Scalia's theory influenced a generation of scholars and students equally eager to reject legislative evidence. Textualism has garnered sophisticated academic proponents, such as Harvard professors John Manning and Adrian Vermeule. Increasingly popular among judges and law students, it is easy to understand, particularly for lawyers fond of dubbing legislation "sausage." Lawyers love rules, and here is a simple rule: when "construing statutes, consider the text, the whole text, and nothing but the text. Period." [12] Because this approach is simple, it appears objective and likely to reach determinate results. As Professor Jonathan Molot has explained, some have declared complete victory: that "we have all become textualists."[13] Despite its many attractions, however, "new textualism" has not had the kind of radical effect its authors might have hoped: courts, including the Supreme Court, still look at legislative evidence of Congress's meaning. In my opinion, it would be close to malpractice for a litigator not to cite confirming legislative evidence, given open disagreement on the Court about this topic.[14]

Justice Scalia's Tanner lectures illustrate "new textualism" with a now famous 19th-century opinion, *Rector, Church of the Holy Trinity v. United States.*[15] The question in *Holy Trinity* was whether a minister who contracted to serve a New York church fell within a statute aimed to prevent large-scale importation of immigrant laborers. The case is a rather easy target. Justice Brewer's majority opinion openly declares Justice Scalia's point: "it must be conceded that the act of the [church] is within the letter of the section," the statute applying not only to "labor or service" but "'labor or service of any kind.'"[16] To top it off, the Court notes that the statute exempted singers, lecturers, and domestics and thus "strengthens the idea that every other kind of labor or service" came within the law.[17] Having noted these textual arguments for covering the good rector, the Supreme Court ignored them, reading the statute to exclude ministers, reasoning that "however broad the language of the statute may be, the act, although within the letter, is not within the intention of the legislature, and therefore cannot be within the statute."[18]

To Justice Scalia, *Holy Trinity* was grossly wrong: "well of course I think that the act was within the letter of the statute, and was therefore within the statute: end of case."[19] *Holy Trinity*, he argued, is "cited to us whenever counsel wants us to ignore the narrow, deadening text of the statute, and pay attention to the life-giving legislative intent. It is nothing but an invitation to judicial lawmaking."[20] As this suggests, one of Justice Scalia's greatest claims for "new textualism" was constraint for activist judges: "textualism constrains judges' decisions more than other methods do, and it gives judges a principled method for interpreting statutes separate from their own 'policy preferences.'"[21]

Justice Scalia's wonderfully written critique has spawned a vast scholarship and erudite exchanges, many of which stand as the great jurisprudential battles of our day. There are grounds on which I stand firmly with Justice Scalia. As Justice Frankfurter properly insisted: "read the text, read the text, read the text."[22] Justice Scalia and his academic followers are also correct that ghostly "intent" should not supplant text. In the rest of this book, I part company. Legislative evidence is neither ghostly nor something in members' minds; it is publicly available documentation; the intent question is a red herring (Chapter 5). The Constitution does not reject legislative evidence; it requires courts to respect the rules of Congress's proceedings in Article I, section 5, proceedings which create that evidence (Chapter 6). New textualists pick and choose texts, wrenching words from context, in ways that make hash of the claim that the method is neutral or restrained (Chapter 4). These claims are made in later chapters. I set the foundation for them by considering the ideas of Congress embedded within new textualism and competing theories of statutory interpretation. In each case, textualists, purposivists, and even political theorists, have imposed ideas on Congress that are more ideas about courts and law than they are about Congress.

Textualism's Devil/Angel View of Congress

Emerging from textualism's scholarly elaboration is what I will call a devil/angel view of Congress, with heavy emphasis on the devil. Justice Scalia's most ardent interpreters are resolutely pessimistic about the legislative process. Here are just some of the adjectives his former clerk and Harvard Professor John Manning used in a single, rather short article in describing the legislative process: "intricate," "opaque," "awkward," "complex," "cumbersome," "highly intricate," "strategic," "arbitrary," "nonsubstantive," and "tortuous."[23] At the same time, textualists hold out hope, as Professor Jane Schacter has written, that the theory will somehow *discipline* Congress to write better statutes.[24] Overtly or perhaps secretly, textualists dream of Congress as the honorable wordsmith, the veritable green-eye-shaded scrivener, but see only a crass unprincipled dealmaker.

If the devil view were correct—if congressional action were truly chaotic—then it is doubtful that what came out of the legislative chamber (the statute's words) would be any less "tortuous" than Professor Manning describes. The devil view simply goes too far, and it should go too far even for honest textualists. Given their view of Congress, textualists must take one of two positions. They must either concede that Congress is plain on some occasions (in which case they will have to explain the variation between the "chaotic" Congress and the "plain meaning" Congress), or they have to take the position, which the cynic might take, that the plain meaning is never Congress's plain meaning but judges' plain meaning conferred upon the statute by jurists with the power to determine what is plain or not.[25] The latter view, though, takes us full circle. Justice Scalia's fear was that, by looking at legislative evidence, courts exerted their own will.[26] Honest textualists must answer the critic who says that "judicial activism" is in finding meaning plain when it may not be plain at all.[27]

The devil view was originally grounded in sophisticated, but controversial, political science. New textualists claimed that legislative intent is impossible because there can be no stable majoritarian set of preferences.[28] At least in part, this view reflects the influence of Arrow's cycling theorem on political science and, through political science and economics, on law.[29] As Manning explains: "Invoking the economics and game-theoretic insights of public choice theory, textualists emphasize that laws frequently reflect whatever bargain competing interest groups could strike rather than the fully principled policy judgment of a single-minded majority."[30] Since then, public choice theory, and its extremely pessimistic conclusions, have come under much greater scrutiny by political scientists and lawyers.[31] The theory simply proves too much: if democracy is never possible, how can one explain the Civil Rights Act of 1964 or the Violence Against Women Act ? Without being able to prove variation—an impossibility if democracy "never" happens—such theories do not meet the most basic standards of predictive social science. Even if these theories were correct, however, they would still pose a problem: where does statutory plain meaning come from if it must emerge from such a process? And if statutory plain meaning does not reflect democracy, then why should it deserve deference?

The textualist will respond that the text is a better alternative than legislative history. Legislative evidence is too hard to find, to decipher, and to understand. Let us bracket for the moment this practical claim, one called into serious question given new technology and easy to use databases, not to mention Google. Text is also better, they argue, because more constitutionally legitimate. Individual legislators' statements have not been approved by two houses and the president, and thus they violate bicameralism.[32] Put bluntly, both text and legislative history may be chaotic, but text has greater constitutional legitimacy. Again, this argument goes too far: legitimate chaos may be legitimate, but it is still chaos. Taken to its extreme, this argument would give legitimacy to a list of random zeros and ones, as long as the list was passed by the Senate and House and signed by the president. Later, in Chapter 6, I treat the constitutional arguments against legislative history in depth, countering them with a response grounded in the Constitution's own text, but here it is sufficient to recognize that the bicameralism argument could confer legitimacy on gibberish.

Now let us turn to the angel ideal: textualists criticize Congress in the hope that doing so will induce legislators to write clearer statutes. Visions of expert scriveners dance in textualists' heads. But remember the electoral connection. Can one really see people protesting on the steps of the Capitol with signs reading, "Vote no on lack of precision!" or "He forgot the dictionary!"? We can with little worry of exaggeration assert that no member of Congress ever lost a single vote because of semantic inexactitude. Textualists admire precise language, consult dictionaries, and look to the ancient common law. But this is not what one sees in floor speeches on C-SPAN or reads in the Congressional Record. Senators do not sit quietly at their desks with dictionaries in hand either in committee or on the floor. House members do not have the latest Supreme Court case on their desks, much less Blackstone or the *Federalist Papers*.

Congress as scrivener-in-chief does not accord well with congressional reality. More importantly, it is suspiciously self-referential. Although the "scrivener" model is almost completely foreign to political scientists and policy analysts (not to mention those who work in Congress),[33] it haunts lawyerly discourse about statutory interpretation. In part, this is to be expected: legal education privileges courts mightily. Recently, the academy has come to emphasize administrative law as an antidote to judiciocentrism, but legislation courses remain heavily outnumbered, and few experts on statutory interpretation have any experience in congressional lawmaking.[34] Whether intentionally or not, the textualists' dreamed scrivener image looks a lot more like the judiciary—a kind of junior varsity court—than Congress.

Two Kinds of Plain Meaning

Textualism cares little for the one institutional feature that universally distinguishes Congress from courts: the "electoral connection."[35] As I explained in Chapter 1, in both text and history, the Congress is speaking to multiple audiences, the people as well as courts. What, however, are we to take from this view? What if we were to look at statutes as laws that should be interpreted in terms of "prototypical," or popular, meaning?

Consider, for example, *Holy Trinity*. What was the meaning of "labor or service of any kind" to the average person on the street in 1885? I wager that the prototypical meaning would be manual labor.[36] As linguist and law professor Larry Solan has argued, ordinary meaning is prototypical meaning, which is to say that it is meaning which picks the best example, rather than all logical extensions, of the term.[37] The best example is typically the best undisputed application of the law based on bipartisan legislative evidence. Supporters of the bill believed that manual labor was covered, as did bill opponents. The common prototypical example was manual labor. Lest one think differently, consider how the statute would have been written if its prototypical "mischief" were a ship full of clerics shackled in the hold. As the *Holy Trinity* court explained: the "whole history and life of the country"[38] rebelled at the idea that an upper class minister on a voluntary journey that Senators likened to "importing laborers as we import horses and cattle."[39]

Justice Scalia insisted on a different plain meaning: he found the meaning prescribed by the "letter of the law," what I call "legalist" meaning. Justice Scalia's analysis emphasized that the statute provided for "service or labor *of any kind*," implicitly suggesting that the law itself rejected a narrow meaning. Where prototypical meaning looks for the "best undisputed application" of the statute, legalist meaning looks for all potential logical applications of particular isolated categories. Notice that the latter approach will, by definition, push the law toward fringe or peripheral meanings, expanding the law beyond its uncontested core.[40] One can conceive of this in the following diagram:

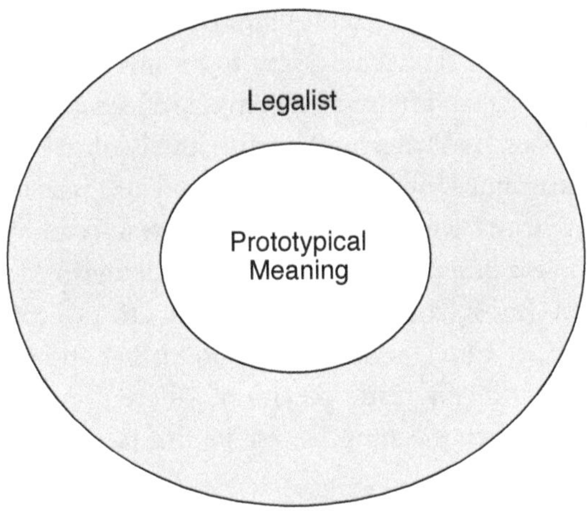

There is nothing terribly modern about this idea. It can be traced to the 16th century, expressed in the shell-and-kernel metaphor: "the letter of the law represents the shell, and the sense of it the kernel." Interpreters argued that, just as you would prefer to be nourished by the nut rather than the shell, interpreters would "receive no benefit by the law," if they "rely only upon the letter."[41] Here, the kernel represents prototypical "sense," while the shell represents the legalist "letter of the law." A similar distinction can even be found in Blackstone's affection for the "sense" and "spirit" of the law, or Locke's lament, that the ordinary citizen may "very well understands a Text or a Law, that he reads," until he consults an interpreter . . . "who by that time he hath done explaining them, makes the Words signify either nothing at all, or what he pleases."[42] Moderns will recognize that the debate persists: in the mid-20th century, Professors Hart and Fuller engaged in a famous jurisprudential debate about distinguishing core from peripheral meaning.[43]

Many textualists are quite open that they are looking for expert, legalist meaning. Professor John Manning writes that textualists seek out "technical meaning, including the specialized connotations and practices common to the specialized sub-community of lawyers."[44] Such a concession leads critics to argue that new textualists tend to see "words written on a piece of paper, rather than a collective effort by elected representatives to govern on behalf of their constituents."[45] Detaching text from any larger conversation between the public and its representatives reflects the lawyerly love of logical puzzles. As Professor Merrill astutely observes, "the textualist judge treats questions of interpretation like a puzzle to which it is assumed there is one right answer. The task is to assemble the various pieces of linguistic data, dictionary definitions, and canons into the best (most coherent, most explanatory) account of the meaning of the statute."[46] Other critics go further and urge that textualists aim to find "linguistic precision" where it does not exist by relying on "abstract meaning," even in the face of contrary evidence.[47]

This tendency to prefer legalist, peripheral meaning, raises serious questions about the consistency of textual theory. Generally, textualism is advertised as a more "restrained" view of statutory interpretation, relative to "intentionalism" or "purposivism." First, as we will see in Chapter 4, the very choice of text, the cutting of a chain of words into smaller pieces, and holding only these chosen words in high relief, has a tendency to privilege and enrich the meaning of the words chosen, relative to the whole text, with the result that the choice of text may assume, by implication, precisely what the interpreter is trying to prove. Second, it is ironic, but true, that legalist meaning will expand the domain of the statute relative to an uncontested application, whereby I mean an "uncontested" application that neither the bill's opponents nor proponents would reject. Textualists claim that they are more restrained in their interpretations, but one must wonder why it was wrong for the Supreme Court in *Holy*

Trinity to limit the statute to its prototypical example—manual labor. Surely any libertarian will see that applying the statute to ministers expands the reach of the statute beyond its uncontested domain—the importation of slave labor for railroads and factories.

More importantly, although textualists reject legislative evidence, they are perfectly willing to add their preferred forms of evidence to resolve ambiguities—lawyerly meanings, canons of construction, and the common law. The preference for specialized meanings speaks loudest in textualists' affection for the "common law" baseline. The "common law" for lawyers is the set of rules existing in a prior age, before legislation, and typically associated with the ancient private law of tort and contract. As one prominent textualist writes: "Textualists assign common-law terms their full array of common-law connotations; they supplement otherwise unqualified tests with settled common law practices."[48] The common law is the province of courts, not the public, and generally not the legislature. I doubt that even a committed textualist, if asked, would suggest that legislators are, as a matter of empirical fact, expert in matters of common law meaning. To be sure, legislators are lawyers, but the common law tends to be the province of academics and judges, not the average practicing lawyer who has neither the time nor the inclination to peruse Blackstone. After all, as Justice Scalia himself so eloquently insisted, we live in an age of statutes. In such an age, it is perfectly reasonable to believe that persons who are in the business of making statutes know more about statutes than they do about the common law.

Some textualists will reply that it is not fair to tar textualism with affection for arcane lawyerly meanings; textualists seek "ordinary meanings." Justice Scalia maintained that the appropriate procedure for determining meaning was to find "the *ordinary meaning* of the language in its textual context."[49] There is reason to wonder, however, whether Justice Scalia and others unconsciously equate "ordinary" meaning with expert or specialized meaning. In one recent study of Scalia's dissents, the author found that "when Justice Scalia says plain meaning, he refers to something different than 'ordinary meaning.' 'Plain meaning' usually refers to a *specialized* but accepted meaning of a term."[50] In another empirical study, the political scientist

Frank Cross found that "overall, the plain meaning standard seems ideologically manipulable and incapable of constraining preferences to provide greater consensus."[51] Yet another more recent empirical study by Professors Ward Farnsworth, Dustin Guzior, and Anup Mulani, based on more than 1,000 subject responses, found that "plain meaning" (or the finding of no ambiguity) correlated to ideological bias, whereas "ordinary meaning" did not.[52]

Here lies a deep and important problem within new textualist theory. For all its affection for "plainness," new textualism is ambiguous on precisely what type of meanings it will apply.[53] While some textualists, like Professor Manning and Judge Easterbrook, tend to emphasize "expert" meaning, others, like Justice Scalia, emphasize "ordinary" meaning. Indeed, some textualists are quick, even within a single article, to refer to ordinary meaning and specialized meaning as if there were no difference between the two.[54] Perhaps new textualists are assuming that the average citizen is a lawyer—something I am quite sure the voting public would find odd if not offensive. But perhaps that helps to explain empirical work showing that Congress has a greater tendency to "override" plain meaning decisions, suggesting that the meaning was not plain or ordinary to those in the legislature who are far more inclined to the vernacular. [55]

Congress's "multiple audience" problem requires a theory about when courts should apply expert meaning and when they should apply public, or prototypical, meaning. Textualism has no such theory; it either assumes that prototypical and legalist/peripheral meanings are the same or prefers legalist meaning, without defending that choice. Sophisticated textualists like Professor Manning bow to audience by referring to relevant "interpretive communities."[56] Shifting the inquiry to a "relevant community" has the important virtue of noticing that there is an audience for statutes and that context is crucial to meaning, but it raises its own ambiguities: how are we to determine the relevant community? Why is the relevant community one of expert litigators rather than expert legislators? Why are expert lawyers who refuse to look to the legislative record, beyond the text, better interpreters of legislative meaning?

Finally, and perhaps most importantly, textualism fails to consider the possibility of "structure-induced ambiguity." Textualists have a tendency to view ambiguity as a deliberate failure of Congress: members could have been clear but preferred to be vague. Indeed, textualists are fond of talking about how legislatures spend time trying to manipulate courts into particular interpretations.[57] Does this make any sense, given the "electoral connection"? Just imagine our putative representative going home to claim, "I manipulated more courts than any other representative in Congress" (rather than "I voted for war" or "I voted for health care"), and one begins to see that this claim is likely to be exaggerated. For our purposes here, it is only important to recognize that new textualism is ambiguous on the issue of ambiguity: new textualists' theory of Congress's chaotic nature should make ambiguity the norm, but textualists insist that there are plain meanings.

New textualists' not-so-disguised contempt for Congress raises the most serious worries when it comes to the supermajoritarian difficulty. New textualists are insistent that their theory reflects democratic formalism—that the words of the text best reflect the democratic process. If one cares about the democratic process, however, one must recognize that there are real life consequences to people's lives at stake when a court interprets a statute, and these stakes are more than linguistic precision. As we have recently seen in the context of the health care law, a court's construction of a law may mean the end of that law if a new Congress is unable to reenact it. For all those who worry about the countermajoritarian difficulty of constitutional law (the most insistent worry of 20th-century constitutionalism), they should be at least as worried, if not more, about the supermajoritarian difficulty in statutory interpretation. In constitutional law, it is at least transparent that a court is claiming its power to supersede the legislature. In statutory law, the court may destroy semantically imprecise legislation even as it claims to act as a faithful agent of Congress.

Purposivism

If the "new textualism" has captured the imagination of a scholarly generation, this was not always the case. For much of the 20th century, there was a rough consensus that courts should interpret statutes by looking for congressional "intent." The approach tended to be eclectic, but generally courts would look at the text of the statute as well as legislative history. In the post-war era, a new consensus called "purposivism" developed to clarify the notion of intent. Harvard's "legal process" school urged lawyers to look for the "purposes" of a statute: "decide what purpose ought to be attributed to the statute and to any subordinate provision of it which may be involved and then, interpret the words of the statute immediately in question so as to carry out the purpose as best it can."[58]

Let us return to *Holy Trinity*. The purposivist looks for a reasonable purpose to attribute to Congress. According to Justice Brewer in *Holy Trinity*, Congress's prime purpose was to cover large-scale operations in which corporations imported cheap immigrant labor for mining, railroad, and other industries. Quoting from a district court opinion, he explained that "the motive" of the act was a matter of "common knowledge." "Law capitalists in this country" had contracted "with their agents abroad for the shipment of great numbers of an ignorant and servile class of foreign laborers." The employer agreed "to prepay the passage," and the "laborers agreed to work after their arrival for a certain time at a low rate of wages."[59] A modern purposivist would find support for this position in the legislative history. The text is then read in light of that purpose. Although there are two possible meanings of laborer—all workers and manual labor—the ambiguity is resolved in favor of the law's purpose—to apply to manual labor. The rest of the text is read to support this purpose. Section 4 covers laborers, artisans, and mechanics, again supporting the manual labor interpretation. Repeating the theme, section 5 exempts non-manual labor, such as professional artists and lecturers. Indeed, the good minister might be likened to a lecturer on religious topics (as we see from the quotation at the beginning of this chapter from the Congressional Record).[60]

Critics have suggested that this analysis is too simplistic.[61] Statutes may have many purposes; perhaps the law's point was to limit all foreign immigration, except for those specifically exempted, like artists and singers. Professor Vermeule cites legislative history suggesting that some members believed the term "labor" could be interpreted to mean any kind of labor.[62] The committee report cited by Justice

Brewer, moreover, did not result in any amendment to the text of the law to limit it to "manual labor." Why did the statute list exemptions, if the authors did not assume the bill covered all labor? Could the purpose of the law be to limit its exemptions to performers? The "professionals" exempted do not include "ministers." There are replies to these claims, but the typical purposivist response has been to ignore such questions and emphasize a dominant general theme, or the judge's authority, under legal process analysis, to find a "reasonable purpose." In her detailed account of the legislative evidence, Professor Chomsky emphasizes that the dominant theme of the debate was to prevent large-scale slave labor importation, what was called "cooly labor" at the time.[63]

From this, we may unearth purposivists' assumptions about Congress. Purposivists tend to have a rather rosy and vague view of Congress. The legal process masters, Professors Hart and Sacks, wrote that courts should "assume, unless the contrary unmistakably appears, that the legislature was made up of reasonable persons pursuing reasonable purposes reasonably."[64] Few students of Congress, and certainly no political scientist, would venture to embrace such a view. Like purposivists' critics, I believe that this view is far too rosy—even if taken as a normative ideal rather than a descriptive matter (what Congress "should be" as opposed to what it "is"). Congress can only be that which its institutional incentives—principally the electoral connection—allow it to be. Congress is a place of conflict, where unreasonable people are often battling with other unreasonable people. To idealize Congress simply opens up purposivism to attack as a theory of statutory interpretation more romance than law.

This is not to say that purposivism, as a theory of statutory interpretation, is wrong; the truth, as Judge Katzmann has made clear, is that most judges are both textualists and purposivists.[65] Scholars agree. As Professor Schauer has eloquently put it: "Although it would be a mistake to ignore the extent to which . . . the statutory text is the dominant factor in statutory interpretation, it would be a mistake as well to neglect the important fact that the text, even if it is a starting point, is often not the ending point."[66] Statutes are passed to achieve ends in the world. Those ends are often the subject of popular debate in and outside Congress. Even textualists concede that purpose is relevant, although they argue that purpose can be gleaned solely from text.

This does not relieve purposivists from scrutiny for their ideas of Congress. Their attachment to a rosy view seems as unrealistic and self-referential as the textualists' "junior varsity" court approach. The truth is that "reasonable persons acting reasonably" seems to describe *judicial, not legislative, virtue*: "precision in drafting, consciousness of interpretive rules, discovery of meaning in past precedent, and detached reflection on the language of particular texts."[67] Courts prize reasonableness; they look at law as if it were serving a rational policy (as opposed to "position-taking" or symbolic action, as a political scientist might). Perhaps this is not surprising given what the great anthropologist Mary Douglas has shown: institutions tend to "think" themselves, indulging "self-serving" explanations—in this case, purposivists, like textualists, appear to deploy assumptions about courts and impose them on Congress's proceedings.[68]

There is reason to believe that purposivists' attachment to the rosy view may well be something other than it first appears. Purposivists claim they honor the Congress's law-making or policy-making capacities. One way of looking at the "rosy legislature" claim then is not as a description of Congress so much as a description of a principle of *deference to Congress*—a principle that few, even textualists, are prepared to reject. To the extent purposivism's view of Congress is a theory of deference to Congress, it declares a principle with which no theory of statutory interpretation quarrels. In fact, it is quite consistent with one of the few truisms of constitutional law, that judicial deference to the political branches is not only wise but, on statutory matters, constitutionally commanded.[69] Unfortunately, this does not answer textualists' claim that their theory better defers to Congress by looking solely at text because there are too many purposes reflected in the legislative evidence.

Another, related, way to look at the rosy view is that it is not so much a theory of Congress as a theory of courts as the "faithful agents" of Congress. This is obviously related to deference, but focuses less on Congress *simpliciter* than the *relationship* between the Court and Congress. As Professor Eskridge puts it, a good agent serves the principal's ends by filling in gaps and responding to real and sometimes changing circumstances. If told to collect all the ashtrays in the building, the faithful agent does not pull the ashtray off the wall next to the elevator.[70] In fact, in any reasonable "agency" relationship, we affirmatively do not want the agent to pull the ashtray off the wall. There is nothing inconsistent with this view, however, and a more realist view of Congress. Presumably, if the agent has orders, or evidence of his orders, he will look to them to resolve his mission. Even if he has conflicting orders, he will look for the orders upon which his superiors agreed to guide him.

Let us return again to *Holy Trinity*. What if purposivists were to acknowledge that Congress is a place of conflict and that "purpose" is really a metaphor for moving beyond that conflict and finding a "best application," one upon which opponents and proponents agreed; in short, the "core" or "prototypical" problem Congress was trying to solve. The overwhelming majority of the legislative evidence assumes mass importation of manual labor as the prototype. To be sure, opponents argued that the bill was poorly drafted and covered all sorts of labor.[71] As one of the law's major supporters pointedly claimed, in a quotation at the beginning of this chapter, the opponents' textual position was the product of pointy-headed lawyers who would never get elected because they would care more about words than their constituents![72] We will never know whether opponents deliberately courted ambiguity by sponsoring an exemption for "professionals" but, even if true, that would do nothing to undermine the claim that, if asked, even opponents would accept that the core case, the best undisputed application, was manual labor.[73]

A purposivist can readily accept this account without claiming that Congress does in fact or should act as reasonable persons acting with reason reasonably all of the time. In fact, purposivists who cling to this vision are taking the more radical position of Professor Cass Sunstein, who argues for a republican theory of statutory interpretation, based on a vision of Congress as grand deliberator.[74] Any realist view suggests that there are strong institutional incentives against some forms of deliberation. For example, is the "no compromise compromise" discussed in Chapter 1 really a form of deliberation? It seems far more like no deliberation. To be sure, the idea that Congress never deliberates is grossly overdrawn. I personally can think of many cases in which Congress truly did debate questions, when members were on the floor, on questions of the exclusionary rule, or habeas corpus reform; indeed, as legislative scholars know, there are inspiring examples such as debate over authorizing the first Gulf War.[75] The question of debate, however, veils the dominant structural incentive at play: the electoral connection. In some cases, the electoral connection will drive serious debate, but sometimes it will drive precisely the opposite: no debate.[76]

In my view, purposivism does not fare well as a realist, evidence-based theory of Congress. Like other theories of interpretation, purposivism has little regard for who won or lost the legislative debate. Purposivists have never really answered the question about "which" purpose counts, and this is one of the principal objections to the approach. They have been skewered upon the clever notion that all sorts of purposes can be found in the legislative record as long as you cite those who opposed or sought to moderate the bill. Given this problem, one way of reconciling purposivism with the realities of a conflict-ridden legislature is that it is not really about all purposes or even reasonable purposes but about something more concrete, the best undisputed application. As traditional purposivist theory assumes, one must look to the legislative record to find the best undisputed application, one agreed upon by proponents and opponents of the law. This recognizes that there are structural ambiguities and conflict in the legislative process, but the aim of legislative inquiry, in cases of ambiguity, is to find concrete points of bipartisan agreement in the legislative record.

This approach—a "realist purposivism"—shifts the focus from purpose to prototype, from a purpose imputed to Congress by the judiciary to a core application found in the record. As a first pass at a statute, the most restrained view is the one that limits the statute to prototypical meaning. I define that here as the best undisputed application revealed by the legislative evidence, not supposition about reasonable legislators or imposition by reasonable judges. The inquiry does not end there, although it makes sense of many of the cases we will see later in the book.[77] There may be excellent reasons to depart from this basic undisputed meaning. In hard cases, there may be no evidence of an undisputed application or conflicts about undisputed applications. This view will not resolve conflicts between statutes or within a statute. On the other hand, the purposivist who takes this approach is capable of acknowledging that there may be many purposes to a statute, and that the analysis must start with what Congress agreed upon—the undisputed "mischief" prompting the need for the law, and perhaps most importantly, that one should not embrace the purposes of those who opposed the legislation.

To purposivists, who tend to be liberals with an affection for the regulatory state, this approach might seem disturbing, since prototypical meaning is associated with narrowing statutory scope.[78] To new textualists it will seem strange for similar reasons, as they associate themselves with narrowing meanings and think of purposivism as expanding statutes' domains.[79] Despite widely-held assumptions to the contrary, there is no logical entailment of either textualism or purposivism with narrowing or expanding statutes. *Holy Trinity* is a perfect example. The textual meaning, according to Justice Scalia, was clear: laborer includes the minister because ministers labor. His "plain meaning" (the legalist, extensive meaning) *expanded* the reach of the undisputed prototypical meaning of the statute, manual labor. In short, a realist purposivism would *narrow* the reach of the statute, excluding the minister, relative to the new textualist interpretation that includes him. Translation: the realist purposivist, in this case, is libertarian, or at least liberates ministers to emigrate to the United States. There is no guarantee that this realist version of purposivism will always yield such outcomes. The undisputed application is a beginning, not an end, to inquiry.

Purposivism-as-search-for-the best undisputed meaning has affinities with modern and ancient approaches. It has modern analogues in Professor Jed Rubenfeld's theory of judicial review and his emphasis on "paradigm cases."[80] It has ancient analogues in the common law "mischief" rule, urging courts to determine the core problem the statute sought to solve. Professors Hart and Sacks sought to modernize the language of statutory interpretation by using the term *purpose* and then qualifying that term with the ubiquitous and normative term "*reasonable*." There is nothing wrong with this; indeed, it strikes me as entirely contemptuous of Congress to think that they do not *try to act reasonably*, even if reasonableness is viewed from their own particular institutional situation, reflecting legislative, rather than judicial, rationality. But the term *purpose* is broad, has affinities with "intent," and suffers from vagueness. Just as there are at least two kinds of plain meaning, there are at least two kinds of purposes for any bill. Those who opposed the legislation will have their purposes contrary to those who supported the bill, and even those who supported the bill may have many purposes.

Purposivists could adopt a more realistic view of Congress—one that accepts its essentially conflictual nature. The term *purpose* does have the virtue of reflecting one "reality" of Congress, because it operates at a general level, speaking to a generalist lay audience, rather than at the granular level of legalist scrivener-in-chief. At the very least, distinguishing between undisputed applications and peripheral cases provides an answer to the conventional objection that there are many purposes to any law. First, it is grounded in actual evidence rather than supposition, one that asks: what would supporters and opponents agree upon as the best example of the problem prompting the law? Such a move from purpose to prototypical "best example," is not a panacea.[81] It has downsides: it may entrench bias in the case of old statutes, a problem that has engaged statutory interpreters since the 1990s, when Professor Bill Eskridge put it front and center in his dynamic theory of statutory interpretation.

In theory, there is nothing preventing purposivists from jettisoning the rosy view put forth by Hart and Sacks and acknowledging a more realist idea of Congress. It would only strengthen some aspects of the theory. If one begins with the idea that statutes are likely to be ambiguous (the principle of legislative-structure-induced ambiguity), then one must go somewhere to resolve that ambiguity. Purposivists, unlike textualists, urge that ambiguities should be resolved by looking at evidence produced by a popular body (legislative evidence). It may appear ironic, but that aspect of purposivism would only be strengthened by a less-than-rosy view of Congress, one that did not insist upon the kind of deliberation more characteristic of the faculty lounge than the halls of Congress. The aim would not be to write a "history" of debate but to find the "common prototype," a bipartisan view of the statute's core.

As I emphasized in Chapter 1, there are two features of the realist Congress. The first is the electoral connection; purposivists can easily accommodate that aspect by emphasizing the need to look to legislative evidence and the power of popular, prototypical, best examples—two features the new textualism rejects. The second is the supermajoritarian difficulty. The difficulty with looking for a "core" example in legislative evidence is that legislative processes are adversarial; the Congressional Record documents a battle in which there are winners and losers. As we will see in Chapter 3, in *Holy Trinity*, bill *opponents* took Justice Scalia's and Professor Vermuele's position—that the bill covered all labor including professionals. Like textualism, purposivism has no theory of legislation in which some policies win and others lose. As we will see in Chapter 3, in a supermajoritarian world, purposivism, like new textualism, can be manipulated to favor the purposes of tiny minorities, if it is incapable of distinguishing between those who won and those who lost the electoral battle. A realist view would focus on the best undisputed example, agreed upon by proponents and opponents, based on the legislative record.

Contract Theories

In recent years, a number of scholars have brought sophisticated positive political theory, including game theory, to statutory interpretation, a view partial to the idea that statutes are like contracts. Professors John Ferejohn and Bill Eskridge led the theoretical charge with a masterful analysis of the court–Congress–president game.[82] Let me say at the outset that I am deeply sympathetic to these claims, and the theory I offer in Chapter 3 is quite consistent with a realist version of positive political theory, as long as the analysis considers what great theorists of positive theory, like Ken Shepsle, acknowledge: the power of Congress's rules to understand its behavior. But when it comes to analyzing legislative history, positive political theory has too often hypothesized imaginary bargains without recognizing the power of those rules to shape the basic deal.[83]

Although textualists often cite positive political theorists as allies, the theories are quite distinct—and in some cases opposed to each other.[84] Second-generation textualism has now eschewed reliance on some versions of positive political theory. More importantly for my purposes, whereas textualists reject intentionalism and legislative history, many positive political theorists, such as Dean Daniel Rodriguez and Professor Barry Weingast, embrace both.[85] They are quite ready to delve into the legislative history; indeed, their aim is to create a more "scientific" intentionalism. These scholars aim to create a scientific theory of "legislative rhetoric," weeding out unreliable from reliable legislative history. I have no real quarrel with that aim: I agree with these theorists that it is irrational not to look at legislative evidence, since this provides more and better information about Congress than judicially made canons of construction (judges' major alternative source of information). But in *some* forms at least, I believe the idealization of Congress as grand bargainer misunderstands Congress and (somewhat ironically, given positive political theory's own focus on agenda setting and pivots), fails to pay enough attention to Congress's own rules about bargaining.

Although there is a sophisticated political science literature supporting this view of legislative history, it is easier to describe this approach as a "contract" theory, as it aims to use bargaining theory to "recast" the deal struck by Congress.[86] In one sense, this is not new: judges and statutory theorists have suggested "imaginative reconstruction" for years, the notion that a judge should reconstruct how Congress would have debated a new issue.[87] But game theory provides a richer analytic veneer to the contract idea, adding a new vocabulary of "cheap talk," "costly concessions," and "signaling." As the trio of political scientists known as McNollgast put it over a decade ago, "ascertaining legislative intent requires separating the meaningless actions (or signals) of participants in the legislative process from the consequential signals likely to reveal information about the coalition's intentions."[88] *Cheap talk* is defined as "communication that is costless for the speaker to make and that is unverifiable and therefore untrustworthy," and *costly signaling* is "communication where the speaker pays a price for inaccuracies."[89] Costly signals can be trusted; cheap talk cannot. For example, in *Holy Trinity*, the original committee report supporting a "manual labor" interpretation would be rejected as "cheap talk" since the authors anticipated that the bill would not pass; there was no actual legislative "cost" to making such a statement in a committee document.

Curiously, although political scientists assert these theories, they rely in significant part on a *legal*, as opposed to a *political*, theory of legislation. Statutes are contracts: "both formalize bargains among actors with diverse and partially conflicting interests."[90] As in contract law, "the role of the courts is to fill in the gaps in legislation by interpreting the intentions of the law's enacting coalition."[91] Just as a court finds the "actual agreement" of contractual parties, these analysts aspire to find the "original intent" of legislation.[92] The contractual analogy explains why McNollgast rejects Justice Scalia's distaste for legislative history: "one cannot argue that a contract between two parties does not embody their mutual agreement because both parties delegated the negotiation to their lawyers and then signed it after only superficial perusal of its contents."[93] McNollgast rejects textualism's willingness to blind itself to relevant information: "theoretically well-grounded interpretations of legislative signals will produce better information than poorly grounded readings of the history or than a decision to ignore all of the history because some of it is uninformative."[94]

Given its emphasis on contract, game theorists' idea of Congress is neither devil nor angel but the efficient marketplace. In an early paper, McNollgast explained that their analogy to contract was based on the "economic approach to the law of contracts," which evaluates legal regimes "according to their efficiency."[95] Legal rules increasing the cost of negotiation were disfavored; common law rules were viewed as efficient to the extent that they furthered the purposes of the contracting parties. McNollgast argued that rules of statutory construction should increase efficiency: "viewed in the light of contract law, the purpose of canons of statutory interpretation is to facilitate legislative agreements and thereby advance the efficiency of the legislative process."[96] This, McNollgast contended, could be accomplished by scouring the legislative history to find the moderate coalition necessary for bill passage: "Consequently, if statutory interpretation is guided by the principle of honoring the spirit of the legislative bargain, it must not focus only on the preferences of the ardent supporters but also *on the accommodations that were necessary to gain the support of the moderates.*"[97]

Consider contract theorists' claim that the 1964 Civil Rights Act was the product of a compromise between the Humphrey majority and the Dirksen moderates.[98] Contract theorists argue that relying only on Senator Humphrey's "winner's" legislative history "devalues the pivotal role of moderate legislators whose assent is essential to reaching a bargain that can achieve majority (and, because of the filibuster, supermajority) support."[99] They explain:

> For example, speeches made at the introduction of legislation are ordinarily cheap talk. This stage occurs before any of the legislative compromises necessary to pass the act and, therefore, cannot reflect the critical compromise provisions in the final act. . . . *In contrast, discussions on the floor of the legislative chamber that focus on the meaning of critical compromises offered in amendments are costly signals. Because they risk losing the votes of the moderates, ardent supporters pay a large price for attempts to downplay or inaccurately describe the compromise during floor debates preceding acceptance of the compromise.*[100]

Bravo, Dean Rodriguez and Professor Weingast, I say. Finally, someone has actually paid attention to the legislative process. Bill supporters do wax lofty: they will end "child poverty in America," "rid the airwaves of poisonous political advertisements," or "end violence in our time." So, too, these authors recognize what courts often do not: the dangers of "loser's" history. Just as ardent supporters are likely to engage in grand rhetoric exaggerating the bill's wonderous effects, ardent opponents are likely to engage in grand rhetoric extolling the bill's grave weaknesses. Major political theorists are clear on this point: "members who voted against the legislation in key votes, who filed minority reports against the legislation in committee, and who offered rejected amendments to kill or gut the legislation should be regarded as outside the enacting coalition, even if they voted in favor of the bill on final passage."[101] In short, they recognize that, just as one does not cite the dissent of a Supreme Court opinion for the decision's meaning, one should not cite those who filibustered a bill for its meaning, lest the Court operate as an engine of anti-democracy.

It is unclear, however, whether this particular form of positive political theory does in fact get at key compromises if it fails to attend to the way the rules of the legislative process shape actual bargains. The 1964 Civil Rights Act does include moderate concessions; without accepting compromises, Democrats could never have obtained the votes to surmount the then-filibuster threshold of 67 senators. The problem comes in assuming that *every text* accepted or proposed by a moderate—if those senators can in fact be identified—amounts to a compromise, without looking at the actual debate. New textualists, for example, seem to assume that every text is a compromise so that each piece of text deserves special isolated consideration, a claim that may be entirely false as an empirical matter. To find a real compromise, the interpreter needs to look at the legislative evidence.

Legislative rules create moments of central compromise. As the political scientist Keith Krehbiel explains and firsthand accounts of the legislature corroborate, getting to 60 votes is central to any bargain in the Senate.[102] Contract analysts are correct that the majority will seek moderate votes clustered around a pivot; the crucial pivot is cloture. Senators willing to resist cloture may demand changes to the bill as a price for their vote.[103] So, in the 1964 Civil Rights Act, H. R. 7152, the original bill before the Senate *was not the bill* considered after cloture. Instead, there was a "substitute" bill (styled as an amendment but striking out the entire original bill). A substitute representing the basic negotiations—the Mansfield–Dirksen substitute—was Dirksen's price for cloture.[104] There is nothing unusual about this procedure: it is almost sure to happen with any bill of controversy, both then and now.

Not every textual amendment occurs at this pivotal point in the process. Consider, for example, Senator Tower's post-cloture amendment on employee testing. Congress debated employee testing issues during the negotiations leading to the Mansfield–Dirksen pre-cloture compromise "substitute" text. Negotiators agreed upon a text permitting an employer to administer tests under section 703(h) if the tests related to bona fide merit systems. After cloture—emphasis on *after* cloture—Senator Tower tried to "re-litigate" the testing battle by offering an amendment that would undo the earlier compromise, permitting businesses wider testing latitude. Civil rights supporters rejected the amendment as unnecessary, the bill manager claiming that the issue had been "discussed, discussed, and cussed."[105] The parties compromised on a new text. The bill's proponents claimed the compromise text did not change the original bill in any significant way; they wanted to keep the bill moving, as opponents were still stalling—filibustering-by-amendment.

Without looking at the rules of proceeding and the particular parties involved—without looking hard at the actual legislative evidence (here, roughly under 15 pages)—assuming "moderate" compromise may be unwarranted. Because of the rules of legislative sequence, not all text is alike when it comes to legislative compromise. We can say with some confidence that text added in a bipartisan substitute bill yielding cloture should be respected with special care, as the reflection of a supermajority, the agreement of opponents and proponents. This does not necessarily follow for all textual amendments. A post-cloture amendment is not, by definition, made at the key procedural moment for moderates; post-cloture amendments are often attempts by zealous opponents to "undo" the moderate compromise.

In this particular case, Senator Tower was a serious filibustering opponent who fought and voted against the bill.[106] After cloture, he continued filibustering by returning to the testing issue, trying to make the bill more friendly than the substitute bill to business on the testing issue. There is nothing unusual in this. Post-cloture amendments are often attempts to test whether substitute's negotiators have accurately captured the preferences of the whole Senate. Tower's original amendment to permit virtually all testing as long as it was "professionally developed" failed (emphasis on *failed*). Instead, Tower agreed to new language inserted in the proper place near the original "bona fide merit" system language and closer to the substitute language.[107] In the language that passed, Tower gave up an expansive pro-business testing provision for one that modified the bill's existing language on bona fide occupational qualifications. This hardly seems much of a concession; in fact; the new amendment barred testing "used" to discriminate, language absent from the original Tower amendment.[108]

Most importantly, the Tower amendment raises a general question going to the very assumptions of contract theories. Contract theory assumes that there was a deal made when we have seen that rational ambiguity may yield false compromises. It is one thing to read the record and find where the parties generally agree, or to assume that key procedural hurdles are pivotal points of compromise. It is far more complex and difficult, perhaps impossible, to know whether in any individual case, outside key pivotal procedural moments like cloture, whether the compromise is important to bill passage. Indeed, it may be impossible in some cases to distinguish the moderates from the true opponents of the bill. Political scientists use voting scores to define the "moderate" member, metrics foreign to the judicial arena.

For example, it is just as easy to interpret the Tower amendment as an example of what I called in Chapter 1, "legislative-ships-passing-in-the-night" as a true or significant compromise. To see this, however, one must return to the basic principle of the "electoral connection." Remember Professor Mayhew's cacophonous Congress: senators are speaking to their constituents in these matters as much as to their congressional opponents. It is entirely possible that the "dealmakers" are not talking to each other at all. Instead, they are talking to their constituents, and the "cost to constituents" drives the bargain. Contract theories pay little attention to constituency-talk, or what some game theorists call "audience costs." As the game theorist Professor Nolan McCarty explained in a very sophisticated model of presidential–congressional relations, "almost all models of bargaining ignore the possibility that the two primary negotiators want to send signals to a third party."[109] Political scientists studying international affairs, such as Professor James Fearon, have known for some time that games must take into account what are termed "audience costs," by which they mean costs to the domestic audience of particular position-taking in international conflicts.

Consider the following "constituency" scenario as applied to the Tower amendment. Senator Dirksen was very concerned about a problematic court case in his state of Illinois, which seemed to imply that businesses could impose no tests at all. He reached a compromise in the Dirksen–Mansfield substitute. But he did not like the compromise. After cloture, not wanting to appear inconsistent, he sent the senator from Texas, Senator Tower, to try to undo the cloture agreement and obtain a more favorable compromise for business. Senators Tower and Dirksen wanted to let business interests know that, even after cloture was obtained, they were trying to gain more for business on testing than had been gained in the substitute bill. Meanwhile, Senator Humphrey and his civil rights proponents wanted to tell their supporters that nothing had changed, that the amendment that ultimately passed simply clarified the existing compromise on "bona fide" merit systems. Tower could claim to his constituents that he had obtained specific testing language. Humphrey could claim to his constituents that testing could not be "used" to discriminate. There was no agreement on how to prove what would later be called "disparate impact."

Contract theory's failure to incorporate audience costs is not a technical objection but a theoretical one about the difficulty of finding "moderate" compromises. There is every reason to believe, for example, that the false compromise story I have told is more plausible than a "key compromise" account. The vertical, electoral connection debate I have sketched may produce far more benefit to the legislator than any costs that legislator might suffer from ambiguity in a court down the line. To be sure, legislators have an interest in writing a bill clearly enough to make the bill effective. Timing, however, makes it likely that, for the legislator, the vertical electoral incentives are likely to trump the horizontal effectiveness incentives. A representative's electoral fate depends upon the claim that she has done something; a court may undo that, but the judicial intervention is most likely to happen long after the election. For example, the Violence Against Women Act's civil rights remedy was passed in 1994 but was not adjudicated unconstitutional until 6 years, and thus 3 House electoral cycles, later. Moreover, even if the court rules against the representative, that might not yield electoral costs: it might simply add to the salience and importance of the position-taking of the representative. More people might vote for her precisely because the court rejected her position.

The theoretical problem lies in assuming *that contracts exist when they may not.* Game theory assumes that a contract is a contract; a deal is a deal, whether it exists in business, the international arena, or a legislature. In other words, contract theory fails to appreciate that the peculiar nature of Congress—its electoral connection—and its rules may shape the bargain, just as the rules of chess shape the game of chess. As John Ferejohn, a very savvy political theorist, has explained, the idea of what he calls "separability"—the notion that preferences are exogenous to institutions—is radical and "likely to be wrong."[110] Without understanding how institutional rules and procedures can change the game, game theory becomes a self-fulfilling prophecy. Assumptions in, assumptions out. If you accept that there is a contract, then it follows that the contract should be honored, but there is every reason to believe, from an evidence-based perspective, that this is too simple—that compromises cannot be assumed, but must be proved by recourse to the record and tracing of texts.

Given this, one may fairly ask whether game theorists are creating, rather than finding, "costly concessions," based on the assumption that statutes are like contracts. In fact, statutes are more like elections. They are winner-take-all. When a court applies a statute, it does not consider the voting strength underlying the bill. A law is given the same interpretation whether the vote was close or not, 99 to 1 or 61 to 39. If contract theory assumes that there is a deal when there is not, reconstructing that deal in favor of the "moderating coalition," may turn out to be a way of giving *the opponents of the bill like Tower* more power than they had in Congress. This is particularly important in light of the supermajoritarian difficulty. We know that bills are difficult to pass because the Senate rules allow a minority to block passage. If that is right, a contract theory adopting the assumption that every text supported or authored by a moderate (if moderates can be identified outside the cloture context) risks exacerbating the supermajoritarian difficulty. If in a true majoritarian (51-vote) system, the text would pass without the moderate coalition, then giving strength to views of alleged moderates injects the equivalent of the filibuster rule into judicial statutory interpretation. Worse, if one misdescribes a senator like Tower as a moderate, when in fact he was a bill opponent, giving his statements (here statements on a *failed* amendment text) judicial credit as the authoritative meaning of a subsequent and different text may allow those who lost the fight in Congress to win in court.

Conclusion

Three principal theories of statutory interpretation risk basic misunderstandings of Congress. Textualism, purposivism, and contract theories all impose legalistic visions of how courts and judges operate onto a very different institution central to our democracy. Understanding Congress more realistically, in the parsimonious sense I explained in Chapter 1, gives us new ways of looking at some very old problems. It turns out that, contrary to conventional wisdom, textualist plain meaning approaches have the power to expand the reach of statutes beyond bipartisan prototypical meanings, challenging the notion that textualism is inherently libertarian or more conservative than purposivism. If prototypical meaning is narrower than legalist meaning, a plain meaning approach will extend text to the legal periphery expanding statutes' domains. Second, and also somewhat paradoxically, if purposivism is reconstructed as looking for evidence of undisputed application, based on real evidence of bipartisan agreement, it may help to answer a persistent question about how to find one purpose among many in the legislative record. A realist purposivism serves to ground the search for purpose in real life (a concrete "best" example agreed to by bill supporters and opponents) and narrow the scope of statutes to undisputed bipartisan legislative meanings. Third, despite far more sophisticated understandings of Congress, contract interpretations of statutory history may exacerbate the supermajoritarian difficulty if they assume hypothetical moderates or hypothetical bargains without real legislative evidence, or if they fail to consider that the rules of the legislative game provide the most reliable means of finding pivotal compromises. Finally, and most importantly, all these theories can yield results that are highly undemocratic: without paying attention to the actual evidence—the legislative record—textualists, purposivists, and contract theorists can each embrace results favored by a filibustering minority, unwittingly enlisting judges into a counter-majoritarian effort more serious precisely because the effort may be entirely unconscious.

3

A Legislative Decision Theory of Statutory Interpretation

"The creation and interpretation of statutes are now paramount concerns of the legal profession. . . . But about the nature of the legislative process . . . the typical law school curriculum is practically silent."

JUDGE RICHARD POSNER[1]

"There has been scant consideration given to what I think is critical for courts discharging their interpretive task—an appreciation of how Congress actually functions, how Congress signals its meaning . . ."

JUDGE ROBERT A. KATZMANN[2]

FOR TWO DECADES, academics and judges have debated *whether* to refer to materials outside the text of a statute. Textualists say no;[3] purposivists say yes.[4] For most lawyers and judges, this question is largely irrelevant. Lawyers feel compelled to turn to legislative history, as do judges. And as long as they do, the question should not be *whether*—but *how*—to use legislative history. Neither textualism nor purposivism has a method for using legislative history, or at least a method that I believe comports with basic uncontested principles about how Congress works; as a result, each can unwittingly invent a plain meaning to a statute directly opposed to Congress's decision.

My antidote for this illiteracy is a legislative decision theory of statutory interpretation.[5] That theory requires basic knowledge of

Congress 101. Just as any lawyer leaves law school understanding the basics of Courts 101—that there is a difference between dissenting opinions and majority opinions, that higher courts trump lower courts, that pleadings arrive before jury instructions—lawyers should leave law school with a similar understanding of Congress 101. This does not require mastery of arcane parliamentary rules or deep cultural knowledge of congressional norms.[6] Unfortunately, Congress 101 is not taught in law schools. This should be more worrisome for, as political scientists generally believe, legislative procedures help Congress achieve stability and equilibrium in an otherwise chaotic atmosphere.[7] As even those skeptical of legislative history have explained, these rules are Congress's "constitution."[8] "Without a positive theory," any normative theory of statutory interpretation may be misguided and even futile.[9] Judges agree, as we see from the quotations at the beginning of this chapter, from Judge Posner and Judge Katzmann, that understanding "how Congress actually functions" is essential in an age where statutes dominate the job of judging.

For many lawyers and academics, love of democracy fights with fears of spinach. Lawyers who are otherwise happy to learn the complexities of high theory—law and economics, critical legal studies, jurisprudence—are resistant to learning the basics about Congress. The Constitution, if nothing else, should be more influential on this topic. It commands that Congress set its own "rules of proceedings." Since judges and lawyers are enjoined to follow the Constitution, presumably those basic "proceedings" should be part of legal education. I find it very odd that judges and lawyers are willing to understand the arcana of tax law, habeas corpus, administrative procedure, and even evidentiary rules but are fearful of learning even the most basic of rules—let us say the cloture rule—that govern our democracy.

Just as it is possible to teach Civil Procedure 101 so that students know the difference between a pleading and a summary judgment motion, it is possible to understand the basics of Congress 101. Some recent scholarship has suggested that legislative procedure is too complex and unorthodox for easy consumption.[10] The first time you go into a courtroom, it seems complex, too. If you knew nothing about civil procedure and evidence, trials would seem very, very complex. Developments like e-discovery or multi-district litigation or managerial judging could all be described as unorthodox. The truth about today's new "obstructionism" in legislation is not that it is unorthodox; the basic procedures have been in place for some time. The "new normal" in legislative procedure is simply a hyper-partisan use of old processes. Since the 1990s, omnibus legislation and filibusters have reigned, and they have reigned based on rules and procedures that have been in place since the 1970s.

Here are the basics: (1) some texts win and others lose; (2) creating legislative text is a sequential process in which later text trumps earlier text; (3) key compromises are often made in the Senate at cloture, which is the political pivot on almost every important bill; (4) a few key internal rules, I call "legislative canons," lead members to make assumptions about text that are not well known to judges or scholars. That is the gist of what I am asking lawyers and judges to understand.[11] Basic knowledge of these principles can be extremely helpful in simplifying the search for, and, more importantly, understanding relevant legislative evidence. The problem is that law school does not teach lawyers much about these processes, and as a result, lawyers find themselves capable of confusing the decisions Congress rejected with those they accepted, even if they would never confuse a dissenting, with a majority, judicial opinion.

Most importantly, we need to stop talking about legislative history and start talking about *evidence* of legislative *decisions*. Legislative decision theory posits the basic principle of "reverse-engineering" legislative decisions. *The aim should not be to imagine that one is actually writing a history, a story about legislation, but looking for the last textual decision relevant to the interpretive question.* Now made easy by computerized databases, this approach is far more efficient than an attempt to construct a coherent story about a conversation between warring parties. The legislative evidence may not resolve the matter, but it can provide greater insights into the decisions that were or were not made. My aim is that lawyers learn to read the Congressional Record intelligently, as an intelligent member of Congress would read the record, not as a lawyer who sees it as the record of a strange, backward, foreign country.

Statutory interpreters who identify themselves as "purposivists" should find this a refreshing endorsement of their recourse to legislative materials and a long overdue response to those who contend that looking at legislative materials is too complex or biased. This approach should also be good news for positive political theorists, who have claimed, for over a decade, that existing theories of statutory interpretation—including textualism—fail to appreciate "how legislation is actually created and how elected officials" operate.[12] Legislative evidence has fallen into some disrepute, and it is time to resurrect it as a democratic necessity. Purposivists' critics have been correct to urge that purposivism needs a method, and legislative decision theory is that method—one that disciplines the search for legislative evidence based on a minimalist positive political theory of Congress.

Textualists will be perplexed to discover that I believe they must look to legislative evidence to avoid the risk of "picking and choosing" texts.[13] Textualists are used to lambasting their foes with this kind of selectivity, charging that purposivists pick and choose legislative history or purpose. Textualists do the same thing; they simply pick and choose texts. Without looking at legislative evidence—by creating "orphan texts," stripped from context—textualists are capable of creating entirely arbitrary meanings. As I show in Chapter 4, "petty textualism" tends to fixate on a particular word, and by doing so, it rejects statutory context relevant to the case in ways that assumes what the interpreter is trying to prove. We know from behavioral economics and cognitive science that this kind of "focus" amounts to an "illusion," a cognitive failure of basic rationality. There is no text without context, and that includes the whole text and meaning from legislative evidence, not a "petty textualism," that focuses with blinders on a word or two, ripped from any larger text, with a dollop of ancient canons that only intensifies the illusion of precision.

Purposivists rightly recognize the importance of legislative evidence. But they also appear to hold out hope that if they phrase the problem at ever higher levels of generality—law as norms, law as integrity—the result will be more democratic. In fact, there is no guarantee of such a result. Imagine if one claimed to understand a trial court's evidentiary rulings by looking to the "purpose" of a trial.

Of course, statutes are purposeful, but whose purpose counts? It is sad but true, as we will see, that there are cases in which purposivist judges have embraced the purposes of a bill's inveterate *opponents.*

Textualists may cry foul by urging that purposivists improperly look for legislative "intent." The intent issue is a diversion. One can easily discuss legislative evidence without ever using the term *intent.* In Chapter 5, I analyze the question of "legislative intent" in much greater analytic detail, reckoning with the academic greats on the subject, arguing that *intent* is simply a metaphor for *evidence of legislative context.* Every lawyer and judge would be better off leaving such issues to the philosophers and avoiding the term *legislative intent.* When one looks for meaning, one searches for public legislative evidence of public legislative context, not the ghostly "spirit" of the law.

This chapter begins with the basics. It offers five Congress 101 principles, illustrating each with recent prominent cases, like the Supreme Court's 2015 health care decision, *King v. Burwell,*[14] as well as famous cases taught in statutory interpretation classrooms across America—*Rector v. the Church of the Holy Trinity, United Steelworkers v. Weber; Green v. Bock Laundry, TVA v. Hill, Public Citizen v. American Bar Association*[15]—and those struggled over by courts of appeal, such as *Amalgamated Transit Union Local 1309 v. Laidlaw Transit Servs., Inc.*[16] My focus, unlike the positive theory I first articulated in the *Yale Law Journal,* is less on the "rules of Congress" than on the *normative* aspects of legislative decision theory. My fear is that ignorance of legislative process has allowed both purposivists and textualists to achieve anti-democratic outcomes, turning legislative losers into judicial winners. After setting forth the basics of Congress 101, I consider objections, arguing that legislative decision theory reduces complexity, respects democratic decisions, and encourages both Congress and courts to discipline themselves.

Principle #1: Statutes Are Elections

Legislating is about conflict. Laws typically pass by large bipartisan supermajorities, but statutes do have determined opponents. Courts and lawyers would never cite a dissenting opinion as authoritative without explanation; so, too, they should not cite congressional opponents for the authoritative meaning of a law. The gold standard for legislative evidence is a core bipartisan agreement.

Principle #2: Statutes Follow a Sequence

Laws develop over time. Textual decisions are made sequentially. Courts and lawyers know appeals trump earlier trial decisions; so, too, they should know that later text and legislative evidence may trump earlier legislative evidence.

Principle #3: Congress's Rules Can Help Interpret Statutes

Legislative conflict is mediated by legislative rules and procedures. Courts and lawyers adopt their own rules—known as canons—to solve difficult interpretive cases; so, too, Congress has a few discrete rules that can provide interpretive guidance, if used as a legislative canon.

Principle #4: Typologies of Legislative History May Mislead

Conflict, sequence, and rules make it unlikely that one "type" of legislative history will always be the most reliable. Courts and lawyers know that types of cases (i.e., labor, civil rights) do not determine outcomes; so, too, even the best "type" of legislative history can be misleading without an understanding of legislative context, to wit, Congress 101.

Principle #5: What Is Unthinkable to a Judge May Be Quite Thinkable to a Member of Congress

Courts and lawyers know that foreign countries' institutions may appear "unthinkable." So, too, they should understand that congressional procedure may lead to outcomes that appear as if they came from a foreign country. What seems "unthinkable" for a judge, and therefore "absurd," may be demanded by Congress's rules of proceeding.

Congress 101: Five Basic Principles

Since the 1990s, courts and scholars have made sweeping critiques about legislative history: it is far too complex and heterogeneous to be understood; always manipulated or produced by non-legislators; reflective of a "chaotic" or "tortuous" institution.[17] As Professor Adrian Vermeule has rightly insisted, these are empirical claims.[18] We cannot know that legislative evidence is impossibly complex unless we look at the hard case for the critics—when legislative history is easy and at its best. Moreover, many of these claims—particularly about the difficulty of finding legislative evidence—were issued before high-tech databases made the job as easy as typing Control-F. Just put the number of a recent committee report into Google and it will pop up. Even with these new high-tech tools, however, legislative evidence is at its best when understood within a framework of the rules of Congress's proceedings.

Just as no one would try to understand the meaning of a trial transcript without understanding the basics of a trial, no one should try to understand legislative evidence without understanding Congress 101. Of course, some will charge that my examples are anecdotal or particularly friendly to the argument but, if so, they are no worse than the standard fare, as claims both for and against legislative evidence rely upon precisely the same "friends" I invoke.[19] At its most minimal, my claim is for one simple, but powerful, interpretive canon: just as Congress is presumed to know and follow the "surrounding body of law,"[20] there should be an even stronger presumption that Congress knows and follows its *own* procedure and rules.

Principle #1: Statutes Are Elections

Legislation, like politics in general, is the product of conflict, yet this simple principle seems to elude lawyers' analysis of legislative evidence. Lawyers have no problem recognizing such conflict in the Supreme Court, easily distinguishing between majority and minority judicial opinions. But when it comes to legislative history, they have the odd habit of citing materials without regard to whether the source "won" or "lost" the debate. The easiest way to see what I mean by Congress 101 is the rule that majorities win—or, more accurately in Congress, supermajorities win. This is a basic principle of legislative procedure that no student of the legislative process would deny. Unfortunately, despite declarations to the contrary, losers' history is fairly easy to find in judicial opinions. In fact, opinions by the Supreme Court, both great and small, have relied upon losers' history, not simply to provide context but to prove the authoritative meaning of the act or the process by which the statute was created.

Take the recent health care case, *King v. Burwell:* although legislative history played no real role in the case, the majority opinion sought to explain Congress's "inartful drafting" by claiming that the statute had been passed in a strange tricky way, which avoided the "traditional legislative process."[21] The chief justice began by stating that "The Affordable Care Act contains more than a few examples of inartful drafting. (To cite just one, the Act creates three separate Section 1563s. See 124 Stat. 270, 911, 912.)" In a 900-page law, there is nothing remarkable about mistakes. However, opinion went on to state that there was something about "the Act's passage" that made it a particularly "unfortunate" process. The justice explained that "Congress wrote key parts of the Act behind closed doors," and cited a law review article written by a law librarian, stating that the act did not follow "the traditional legislative process."[22] The majority explained that this nontraditional process by which "much of the Act" was passed was a "complicated budgetary procedure known as 'reconciliation.'" As a result, there were "limited opportunities for debate and amendment," and the act "bypassed the Senate's normal 60-vote filibuster requirement." The conclusion: "the Act does not reflect the type of care and deliberation that one might expect of such significant legislation." The paragraph was polished off with a citation to a cartoon "in which a senator tells his colleagues 'I admit this new bill is too complicated to understand. We'll just have to pass it to find out what it means.'"[23]

To be fair, this account was similar in some respects to accounts offered by news journalists and even to ones appearing in the *Harvard Law Review*.[24] It also happens to be *wrong*, a point called to my attention by the Senate's former parliamentarian, who asked me why all the "law professors" could get it so wrong. First, the Affordable Care Act (ACA) was passed after an extreme Senate filibuster and entirely full deliberation; there were 2 years of debate. (Hein's legislative history is in nine volumes, and it is, in the author's opinion, incomplete.) Second, the ACA did not bypass filibuster or amendment; there were multiple filibusters, hundreds of amendments in committee, days of markup, and debates on amendments on the floor in a dramatic, and intense, Senate standoff that no senator, Republican or Democrat, could truthfully deny. Third, it is not true that "much" of the bill was passed by reconciliation; the reconciliation bill, which was a short separate bill, affected a minority of provisions, almost all of which were irrelevant to *King*. Even the short (14 pages in the Congressional Record) after-ACA reconciliation bill was hardly unorthodox lawmaking: every president since Ronald Reagan has used reconciliation to pass major tax cuts, health care laws, and other legislation.[25] The bottom line: the Court confused two different statutes. The ACA itself, Public Law 111–148, became law on March 23, 2010, after a lengthy debate and a month of extreme Senate filibuster. Seven days later, the president signed a different, much smaller law,[26] the Health Care and Education Reconciliation Act, Public Law 111–152, which was passed under the Budget Act and reconciled the first bill to existing budget targets.

Elsewhere, I have explained the rather dramatic debate that led to the ACA.[27] I am saddened, however, that the Court's account reflects such confusion about the legislative process. All one had to do was to search online for "reconciliation" to get the Congressional Research Service's explanation of the many bills passed by this method. It does not take a legislative expert to realize that once the president signed the ACA, there was no guarantee that Senators would approve the reconciliation bill. The House has no way to require the Senate to pass its bills. For purposes of this book, however, this is not only a question of descriptive accuracy; it is also a normative question. The Court's account leads to an entirely unnecessary appearance of political bias. Since the case could easily have been decided on textual grounds, as I explain in the next chapter, reference to the legislative process was entirely unnecessary.

What the Court did say makes matters worse because it appears contemptuous. In fact, the account's details appear (emphasis on appear) to be lifted from the *amicus brief of senators who filibustered the bill*. For example, the Court cites "3 section 1563s" as a sign of inartful drafting—a very precise example, which appears among the many,

many amicus briefs—that of filibustering Senators Cornyn et al.[28] Similarly, the Court states that the law was drafted "behind closed doors," a claim repeatedly made (at least 150 times in roughly a month period, by my count) by filibustering senators, including Senators Cornyn et al.[29] The Congressional Record gives this "closed door" claim a good run for its money since the bill and its amendments must by rule be printed. Whether true or not, the comment was gratuitous at best and, at worst, leads skeptics to conclude that, far from being deferential, the Supreme Court looks down on the Congress or believes democracy a cartoon.

Congress 101 tells us that "normal lawmaking" depends upon the filibuster; bills don't pass by 51 votes; they pass by overwhelming supermajorities precisely because of the filibuster. This basic fact, which has been true for decades, makes it far more important not to confuse statutory winners and losers. The system already prefers supermajorities by virtue of the structure of the Senate: small states have enormous power. For courts to turn legislative losers into winners risks magnifying the supermajoritarian difficulty, intensifying the malapportionment of the Senate.[30] In other words, it risks courts adopting views that the people's representatives have rejected in overwhelming numbers. Positive political theorists are correct that losers are likely to exaggerate the limits of a bill, just as winners are likely to exaggerate the benefits of the bill.[31] But embracing views of those who lost the debate should generate far more caution: surely the job of judges is not to aid legislative obstructionists. Courts cannot simply feign deference to popular sovereignty; they must practice deference, and they can practice deference only if they understand the institution to which they are deferring.

United Steelworkers of America v. Weber

There is nothing particularly new, nor particularly partisan, about roaming around the legislative record, citing anything that may help one's case, without considering whether one is citing those who won or lost the statutory fight. It happens among liberals and conservatives, textualists and purposivists. I begin with an opinion in *United Steelworkers of America v. Weber*, by Justice Rehnquist, because it is a prominent opinion admired by liberals for its use of legislative history, rather than a textualist approach. The question was whether a private company and its union could use a voluntary affirmative action plan to rectify "conspicuous racial imbalances" in the workforce.[32] Until 1974, the company had only hired white persons for skilled craft positions. As a result, less than 2 percent of the skilled craft workers in the plant were African American. A labor-management agreement reserved 50 percent of the openings in newly created craft training programs for African Americans. Brian Weber, who was white, brought suit, claiming racial discrimination under Title VII of the Civil Rights Act of 1964.[33]

In dissent, Justice Rehnquist engaged in an extraordinarily lengthy legislative history of the 1964 Civil Rights Act[34] in an opinion that has been praised by liberal scholars who nevertheless disagree with Justice Rehnquist's result.[35] In fact, I believe that the Rehnquist opinion reflects a flawed understanding of legislative process and risks normative bias against majorities—in this case large majorities who sustained an anti-segregation statute against the longest filibuster in history.[36] Justice Rehnquist's legislative history frames the debate in the House with a discussion of a minority committee report and, in the Senate, with a motion to kill the bill by filibustering opponents.[37] Committee reports are generally considered excellent sources of information, but in this case, the report appeared long before the text central to the case was ever created. The central text on affirmative action and quotas appeared in section 703(j)—in the substitute bill debated in the Senate months later.[38]

More importantly, from a normative point of view, the House report was a *minority* report, and the senators cited to frame the debate opposed the bill.[39] Legislation is full of conflict; in the case of highly charged legislation, legislating is the equivalent of war. In such circumstances, courts must be highly conscious of who won and who lost the war. At its best, the Rehnquist opinion might be defended as an attempt to show the agreement of those who supported and those who opposed the bill, but without making a distinction between the filibusterers and the supporters, there is the risk that the reader will take the statements or reports of those who opposed a bill as "authoritative," turning a filibustering minority's will into law.[40]

Griggs v. Duke Power Co.

Lest my account of *Weber* suggest a liberal bias, let me take a decidedly more conservative stance on a different and well-known discrimination case, *Griggs v. Duke Power Co.*[41] The precise issue turned on the validity of an EEOC rule requiring that job testing be related to the job. Companies wanted to give basic intelligence tests, and racial minorities resisted, claiming that the tests were biased and unnecessary for many jobs. The Fourth Circuit ruled, in part, against the discrimination claim and for employers, allowing them to use tests without having to satisfy the EEOC's rule requiring that the test be job-related. Any intelligence test would do. Judge Boreman reached his conclusion by relying upon the legislative history of the statute, in particular an amendment that had in fact failed—emphasis on *failed*—in the Senate, an amendment offered by a filibustering *opponent* of the bill, Senator Tower.[42] The Fourth Circuit's theory was that Senator Tower had justified his amendment as a definitive rejection of an Illinois case, *Myart v. Motorola*, that had struck down general intelligence testing as unfair to "disadvantaged groups."[43]

Relying upon legislative history to a *failed* amendment is problematic in itself. It is also problematic because the statute (before the amendment) required that tests be "bona fide merit" systems, suggesting that the EEOC's job-relatedness rule was consistent with the statute. But it is even more problematic because Senator Tower was a determined filibustering opponent of the bill. As a positive political theorist would say, he had every incentive to engage in "cheap talk" about the extent or breadth of his amendment, to make it sound as if it were a crucial legislative limitation and rejection of the *Motorola* case. Cheap talk is not an academic matter. Judge Mikva once explained that, when he was a member of Congress, he made statements in *opposition* to an important anti-racketeering law (RICO) that later became the *meaning of the law* when interpreted by the Supreme Court.[44] That can happen only because interpreters have failed to recognize one of the most basic facts about statutes: that legislation results from battle and that there are winners and losers in that battle.

No appellate judge in the *Griggs* case questioned whether it was appropriate to rely upon a filibustering senator's views.[45] The legislative history is not hard to find—it amounts to about a page or two on the failed amendment and then a substitute amendment (new text) added by consent with no discussion. In fact, the text of the substitute amendment is much different from the text of the original Tower amendment, a matter largely ignored by all courts. Senator Tower's original amendment would have allowed business greater room to use tests to discriminate relative to the underlying bill. Senator Tower's legislative statements interpreted the bill as potentially barring all testing because of racial disadvantage. Unlike the Fourth Circuit, the Supreme Court noticed that the amendment *failed*, and from that, it reached precisely the opposite conclusion. Although the entire concept of "disparate impact" did not exist in 1964, when the Civil Rights Act was debated, the Supreme Court concluded that Congress intended to embrace it—a leap that was not, in my view, required to decide the case based on the text of the statute (much less its legislative history).[46] For our purposes, however, just as Representative Mikva's statements against RICO were adopted as the meaning of RICO, Senator Tower's statements against the Civil Rights Act became the appellate court's authoritative interpretation of the act, and framed the Supreme Court's reversal of that interpretation. How an avowed segregationist became the inadvertent catalyst for disparate impact should at the very least be seen as passing strange.

Rector v. Holy Trinity Church

Academics fall prey to the same failures as judges. Take, for example, the scholarly debate about the canonical 19th-century *Holy Trinity* case, one of the central cases in the textualists' canon. The law reviews have offered two widely different interpretations of the legislative history, one by Professor Adrian Vermeule,[47] and the other by Professor Carol Chomsky,[48] neither of whom make much of a distinction between supporters and opponents of the law. Professor Vermeule has argued that the legislative history of the Alien Contract Labor Act supports Justice Scalia's plain meaning interpretation:[49] the labor act says "labor or service of any kind" and obviously covered a British rector brought to preach in New York.[50] Professor Chomsky disagrees, arguing that the legislative history is far more complex, focusing on the importation of slave labor or what was called at the time "cooly practices."[51] Chomsky emphasizes the parallel interpretation of the Chinese Exclusion Act as meaning "manual labor" when that act used the term *labor*: Since the Supreme Court had already interpreted similar legislation in a way that would exclude the rector, Congress did not intend to cover the rector, according to Professor Chomsky.[52]

Both professors cite those who opposed and those who supported the bill. In a very fine article, for example, Professor Vermeule sought to support the textualist view with legislative history, citing this exchange:

> Senator Morgan: "If [the alien] happens to be a lawyer, an artist, a painter, an engraver, a sculptor, a great author, or what not, and he comes under employment to write for a newspaper, or to write books, or to paint pictures . . . he comes under the general provisions of the bill. . . . I shall propose when we get to it to put an amendment in there. I want to associate with the lecturers and singers and actors, painters, sculptors, engravers, or other artists, farmers, farm laborers, gardeners, orchardists, herders, farriers, druggists and druggists' clerks, shopkeepers, clerks, book-keepers, or any person having special skill in any business, art, trade, or profession."
>
> Senator Blair responded: "The Senator will observe that it is only the importation of such people under contract to labor that is prohibited. . . . If that class of people are liable to become the subject-matter of such importation, then the bill applies to them. Perhaps the bill ought to be further amended."[53]

Professor Vermeule pauses to note that Senator Morgan, a Democrat from Alabama, opposed the bill, but his argument nevertheless relies upon Morgan's statements.[54] In fact, had he wanted to, Professor Vermeule could have cited a great deal more evidence that proponents knew their *opponents* were reading "labor" in its extensive, legalist sense (all work) rather than in its contextual, prototypical sense.[55] If we stick to the notion offered by a vast array of proponents (even the reluctant ones),[56] the rector in *Holy Trinity* was not covered because he did not fit the prototypical "contract labor" situation. No one was worried about a rash of clerics lured to America with deceptive offers of employment huddled in the hold of a ship.

If Professor Vermeule does not distinguish statements opposed to the act from those supporting it, neither does Professor Chomsky, who is far more reliant on the legislative history for her argument. Chomsky concludes that:

> It is difficult to read page after page of this House debate without concluding that the bill was meant to address the "contract labor system," the practice by industrialists of importing large numbers of workers from abroad to take the place of American laborers at reduced wages, and that this was understood by all legislators considering the bill.[57]

In reaching this conclusion, however, Chomsky treats us to statements by Senators Morgan and Hawley (who voted against the bill) just as readily as by Senators Blair and Platt (who voted for the bill).[58] Chomsky's argument would have been substantially strengthened had she emphasized that the proponents and opponents agreed that manual labor was covered under the bill. She would also have had a stronger argument if she noted that those who persistently complained about the breadth of the act were in fact *opponents* of the bill.[59] She might have even dented the armor of those naturally hostile to legislation by noting that her favored interpretation *narrows the statute's domain.*

Professor Chomsky and Professor Vermeule appear to give equal weight to congressional statements of losers and winners. Certainly, we should not read the legislative history to adopt the view of one of the bill's most urgent opponents, Senator Morgan, who states that the law was "vicious" and "class legislation."[60] Then why should his views on the bill's coverage be authoritative? Just because he insisted the law was poorly drafted and could include all labor does not mean his view should prevail. It is not a court's job to search out and enforce the position of determined congressional minorities. After all, Senator Morgan's views did not carry the day: the Senate vote was a rather lopsided 50 to 9.[61] If one digs deep enough, moreover, one learns that this same argument was made in the newspapers of the day when the case was first filed, precisely by those openly opposed to the bill.[62]

To say that losers' history should not determine meaning is not to say that it is entirely irrelevant. As Lisa Bressman and Abbe Gluck note, when opponents and proponents agree on meaning, that is very strong legislative evidence.[63] Moreover, minorities' views may be essential to understanding changes in textual meaning to provide context.[64] Costly concessions, as the political scientists say, are important: after all, it was the great opponent of the bill, Senator Morgan, who argued that "lecturers" on *religious* topics were in fact excluded from the act. Indeed, in my opinion, Senator Morgan makes a "costly concession" when he acknowledges that "lecturers" (exempted in the text) include lecturers on religious topics; this is an admission against interest, contrary to his general claim that the bill covered all workers, even high-class ones.[65] In short, there is a good deal of evidence that reading the record without attention to the great legislative battle, without regard to winners or losers, obscures important arguments even for erudite scholars of statutory interpretation.

Principle #2: Statutes Follow a Sequence

Sequence is the second, and equally crucial, principle of Congress 101. Trials and appeals do not happen instantaneously; neither do statutes. Trials and appeals involve sequential processes. Later events in the trial typically trump earlier events. Lest this seem confusing, think about how an appellate ruling trumps a trial ruling, and you will see that a later-in-time Senate substitute bill typically trumps an earlier House bill, or a conference committee report (which comes at the end of the process) typically trumps an earlier committee report on the same matter. This is particularly important in legislating since major bills, unlike trials, often take years to come to final debate.

Historians worry about using the present to interpret the past. Precisely the opposite presumption should apply in reading legislative debates. *The very notion of legislative "history" should be treated as a misnomer.* Later textual decisions trump earlier ones. Put in the simplest terms, legislative history should be *read in reverse.* The last act may occur in a debate on a post-cloture amendment or in a conference report or in committee, but one should always start by looking for the last decision-making point concerning the text at issue in the case. Texts change as new problems are envisioned, and this is why the changes most relevant in time to the final text are the most important; it is also why writing a legislative history from the beginning can be unncessary. If the bill changes in central ways, as we saw in *Weber;* when new text is added in a substitute before cloture, the old bill may become textually irrelevant to the issue. Moreover, this approach is more efficient: indeed, as we saw in the *Griggs* case, it whittled down the history to a page or so.

The principle of "reverse engineering" proceeds as follows. Because much text may change long after bill introduction, begin with the final text enacted as law. From there, look to the debate on the conference report. A conference report is proposed joint text because the House and the Senate have disagreed upon the proper text. If the matter is not debated on the House or Senate floor on the conference report, then one should go to the conference report; there may be material in the joint explanation to the conference report which explains the resolution of a dispute between the House and the Senate on any particular text. If there is nothing in the conference report's joint explanation, then one moves to the debate on the original bills on the floors of the Senate and the House. In the Senate, the post-cloture debate is most important because the bill will have been rewritten, in many cases, to obtain cloture, and thus differ substantially from the original. From there, one would move to the various committee reports on the bill. As we will see, committee reports may or may not be relevant depending upon whether they are bipartisan, have any relationship to the bill text that was actually passed, or were available at the time the bill was debated.

Although seemingly unconventional, this approach has some basis in longstanding practice. It explains the value of conference committee reports, for example. It is the conventional and correct wisdom that, of all legislative evidence "apart from the statute itself, [conference committee reports are] the most reliable evidence of congressional" decisions.[66] This is not because of deliberative quality: at the end of a bill, particularly a long-debated bill, much may be assumed and rushed.[67] Nor is it because of comprehensiveness: conference reports are not summaries or descriptions of bills, but reports of the textual resolution of issues in conflict between House and Senate, which in most cases affect a small subset of a bill. Precisely because the conference report's explanation will not explain texts that both houses agreed upon, these reports should not be read to imply much of anything about agreed-upon text, as we will see below.

At the same time, this approach is unconventional to the extent it recognizes the post-1970s reality that key decision-making moments in the legislative process are provoked by the Senate's need to invoke cloture. Today, the conventional sequence of events in modern lawmaking often centers around the filibuster. Since the 1990s, every major bill in the Senate has been subject to filibuster. The process is quite predictable but left out of the *Schoolhouse Rock* views of the legislative process. To obtain cloture (60 votes),[68] leaders and managers of the bill often change the bill after committee consideration. So, before debate, there will be a "substitute" bill introduced; in the case of the Civil Rights Act, it was the Mansfield–Dirksen substitute; in the health care case, it was the Reid substitute. As we saw in the *Griggs* case, the pre-filibuster "substitute" text was a very important baseline from which to judge the effect of the post-cloture Tower amendment to the substitute.

To illustrate this principle, return to Justice Rehnquist's opinion in *United Steelworkers of America v. Weber*[69] and Justice Stevens's opinion in *Green v. Bock Laundry Machine Co.*,[70] which provoked an important textualist concurrence by Justice Scalia. My claim here is not about results but methods: both Justice Stevens and Justice Rehnquist made the legislative history question much too difficult; both opinions invite the criticism that judges "pick and choose" legislative history. In each case, the relevant legislative history was a small fraction of that which the Court considered. More importantly, once we focus on the proper legislative evidence, we can hone in on the key textual questions in the case.[71] If this is correct, then legislative decision theory has something important to say to both textualists and purposivists.

United Steelworkers of America v. Weber

Reconsider Justice Rehnquist's dissenting opinion in *United Steelworkers of America v. Weber*.[72] In the writer's humble opinion, Justice Rehnquist's opinion demonstrates how *not* to read legislative history. Justice Rehnquist cites legislative evidence that is the equivalent of confusing pleadings for jury instructions. For example, the opinion begins its analysis of the legislative history by emphasizing that the statute's sections 703(a) and (d) were included in the early House bills, at the beginning of legislative action.[73] As a matter of congressional procedure, this is entirely irrelevant if later amendments limited or clarified these provisions. That is the core problem in the case: section 703(j),[74] the most relevant provision, was added in the Senate prior to cloture[75] and was specifically aimed at the quotas objection. Section 703(j) says that nothing in the bill was to "require" preferential hiring.[76]

From this rather inauspicious beginning, Justice Rehnquist's treatment of the legislative history meanders. The opinion includes long discussions of the House debate, but if section 703(j) is the central textual provision, how can these debates be relevant?[77] Section 703(j) only appears much later in the process, long after the House debate—long after, in fact, the longest filibuster in history, at a key moment of compromise in the Senate "substitute." This error is compounded by lengthy discussions of House floor statements. Even the House sponsors of the bill knew it would be significantly changed in the Senate.[78] Because of the *sequence* of the bill, the Senate debate trumps the House on matters of text added in the Senate. Put bluntly, House members could not possibly have debated section 703(j) *because it had not yet entered the bill.*

Justice Rehnquist's treatment of the Senate debate is better than that of the House, but it suffers again from lack of attention to sequence. He begins by explaining: "The Senate debate was broken into three phases: the debate on sending the bill to committee, the general debate on the bill prior to invocation of cloture, and the debate following cloture."[79] This is true but unhelpful. The debate on recommital is irrelevant: motions to recommit controversial bills are always efforts to kill the bill by those opposed to it; in this case, the motion was rejected.[80] The general debate prior to cloture, including various memos written by the supporters of the act and the Justice Department, is better than the motion to recommit but precedes the central piece of any Senate drama: cloture. In this case, the pre-cloture debate did not include the central text, section 703(j), which speaks directly to the question of quotas and was added in the pre-cloture substitute, qualifying prior text.

Justice Rehnquist's account of the legislative history is at its most persuasive when he cites statements occurring at the proper moment in the sequence: *post-cloture*[81] *statements* against quotas, made by supporters and opponents of the bill.[82] If one wanted to look to legislative evidence against the majority's position, the best evidence would be post-cloture statements like that of Senator Muskie, which addressed section 703(j). The point of such a history would be to show a bipartisan agreement against quotas. This may not resolve the matter in the case since the key text in section 703(j) depends upon whether the government had "required" the company or the union to impose a quota—a point I believe the majority should have emphasized to support its decision. But Justice Rehnquist's opinion would have been much stronger had it been a good deal shorter and had it reverse-engineered the key text. Focusing only on the most relevant legislative evidence may well have reduced his account to a few pages.

Green v. Bock Laundry Machine Co.

Bock Laundry involved Rule 609 of the Federal Rules of Evidence.[83] The civil plaintiff brought a products liability action against the maker of a machine used in a car wash. The defendant company sought to impeach the civil plaintiff based on the plaintiff's prior felony conviction. The question was whether Rule 609 covered civil plaintiffs: the Rule's opening clauses covered all witnesses, but its balancing test covered only "defendants."[84] All of the judges found the term *defendant* something of a puzzle: did it cover civil defendants but not plaintiffs? That would surely be strange, not to mention unconstitutional.

Justice Stevens sought to solve this puzzle by approaching the legislative history from the beginning. Conventional wisdom no doubt holds that the majority opinion appears, particularly to scholars, as erudite and comprehensive. The opinion begins with the common law, Wigmore, and other legal treatises, referencing "seminal articles" by Dean Ladd and the 1942 American Law Institute proposal, the ABA proposal, the D.C. Code, and important case law principles, such as the "*Luck* doctrine."[85] Congress is nowhere to be found in this putative treatise.[86] It seems quite unlikely, as Justice Scalia noted, that the average member of Congress had a clue about this history, better suited to an academic than an elected official.[87] If one thinks it dangerous and potentially self-interested to "look out for one's friends" in legislative history, how much more dangerous is it to search for one's friends among law reviews and treatises?[88] Ultimately, Justice Stevens, like the rest of the justices, including Justice Scalia, performs judicial surgery by inserting words into the text, namely the word *criminal* to modify the term *defendant*, rewriting the text to exclude Mr. Green's civil case.

The puzzle here, in my opinion, cannot and should not have been resolved by resorting to the 13-year history of efforts to reform federal evidentiary rules but by recognizing that all the trouble in the statute was caused at the end of the legislative sequence, in the conference committee. The House bill reversed the common law rule allowing impeachment of any witness in a civil or criminal trial by prior crimes; the Senate bill imposed the common law rule allowing impeachment of any prior felony in any civil or criminal trial. In other words, the conference had to reconcile the old common law view (passed by the Senate) with the total rejection of the common law view (passed by the House). The conference report split the baby, keeping general language both houses agreed upon and adding a compromise clause with the puzzling term *defendant* and a balancing test borrowed in part from a Senate committee bill.[89] However the Court resolved the case, which was quite difficult, it did not need to consider the 13-year history of the Federal Rules of Evidence to find the source of the problem and the one page of conference report materials on Rule 609. Reverse engineering shows that the troubling text "defendant," appeared at the end of the process, leaving the relevant legislative evidence to one or two pages in the conference report's joint explanation.

As I have explained at length elsewhere,[90] in *Bock Laundry*, there are many ways to read the conference report's joint statement—its legislative history (conference reports are "text," the joint statement the new "text's" legislative history). We know that the House and Senate both voted for rules with identical language at the start, covering all "witnesses," thus covering civil cases. We also know that since both houses passed that text, the conferees had no power to change it. That text must be reconciled with the balancing test, which applies only to defendants. It is charitable to say that the joint statement is less than precise about the meaning of the term *defendant*—referring to Rule 609 as covering witnesses, sometimes parties, sometimes the accused, sometimes the defendant, and even "someone else."[91] However one wants to resolve that problem, reverse engineering provides us with a much more disciplined method than roaming around in years of history, reforming the rules of evidence. Surely, one can hardly say that the most relevant legislative evidence is too voluminous: after we cull the 14-page conference report and joint explanation, the sections on Rule 609 amount to about a page and a half.[92] And, as we will see later, members in such a case are likely to follow the interpretive rule that added language (the odd balancing test) does not substantially change the agreed-upon scope of the rule (all civil and criminal cases).

Principle #3: Congress's Rules Can Help Interpret Statutes

If the first two principles are correct and easy to see, it is not so easy to see that, contrary to judicial expectation, Congress has its own rules that may help courts resolve knotty interpretive problems.

Consider an easy example based on an apparently difficult case. *Public Citizen v. United States Department of Justice* involved the American Bar Association's recommendations to the president on judicial nominations.[93] The question raised was whether the ABA had to satisfy the Federal Advisory Committee Act (FACA), which requires certain governmental entities "established or utilized"[94] by the president to open their meetings, balance their membership, and release public reports.[95]

Today, *Public Citizen* is taught as a controversial case. For textualists, the majority opinion commits judicial surgery, cutting the word *utilized* from the statute. As Justice Kennedy wrote in his concurrence, it is hard not to believe that the ABA was in fact being "used" by the president.[96] Any conclusion to the contrary depended on how the absurdity canon was applied. The majority argued that if *utilize* meant "use," in the ordinary sense, then it would yield absurd results, covering a meeting of the president with the NAACP or his own political party.[97] Ultimately, the majority decided to read the relevant statutory term *utilize* in a technical, rather than "ordinary meaning" sense—as something of a repetition of the statutory term *establish*, a result that seems odd as a linguistic matter but avoided apparent absurdity.[98] Among textualists, the majority opinion raises eyebrows not only for its apparent judicial surgery but also for its reliance on the much-debated canons of absurdity and constitutional avoidance.[99]

There was an easier way to resolve *Public Citizen*, although this road was taken neither by the majority (which performed the apparent surgery) nor by the concurrence (which held the statute could not be constitutionally applied to the president). This easier path rests on understanding when Congress added the term *utilize* to the statute. No lengthy legislative history is necessary to find the answer. The term *utilize* first appears in the conference committee report resolving House and Senate differences on FACA. The Senate bill going to conference covered committees "established or organized" by the president;[100] the House bill used the term *establish*.[101] In other words, the votes in both the House and the Senate prior to the conference were for "establish" or "established or organized." The term *utilize* is nowhere in sight. Indeed, "utilize" is added in the conference committee, contrary to the bills passed in both the House and Senate.

That "utilize" first appears in the conference report should raise a red flag for anyone knowledgeable about Congress's own *rules*. *Conference committees cannot—repeat, cannot—change the text of a bill where both houses have agreed to the same language*.[102] Both House and Senate rules bar such changes.[103] These rules limit opportunism by conference committee members and ex post control by drafting committees, since drafters are typically appointed as conferees and thus get another shot at legislation they themselves drafted. Even if these rules are flouted at times, members have an incentive to follow them lest the bill be stalled by a point of order[104]—a formal objection to proceeding with the bill as violating the rules—precisely at the point where the maximum effort has been expended toward passage.[105]

In *Public Citizen*, the conference report was simple, strong, proximate legislative history. It was the last act on the precise statutory term at issue—"utilize." Viewed within the principles outlined above, a court should defer to the meaning demanded by Congress's own rules. According to congressional rules, the conferees had no power to change the agreed-upon text in any significant way, and therefore a judge should interpret "utilize" precisely as a member of Congress would interpret it—as making no significant change to "established or organized." Ironically, this is precisely the result the Court reached, albeit in ways that seem highly strained and controversial.

One might argue that, since no senator or House member objected to the term *utilize*, it should be given a full, independent, meaning; in fact, members are likely to presume precisely the opposite. A faithful member of Congress would assume that, when both houses pass the same language, any added conference language must be read as making no substantial change in the agreed-upon bill. A court applying this "legislative" canon is not ignoring the text, but trying to avoid the conclusion that Congress has written an absurd statute, or the constitutional question raised by applying the statute to every committee with whom the President meets. Surely a court is more faithful to Congress by recognizing that the faithful member of Congress is likely to have assumed that the term "utilize" was irrelevant, rather than absurd, given the rules governing conference committees. A faithful textualist should apply this interpretation as well, because the Constitution's text requires deference to Congress's rules.[106]

This is particularly important in cases of demonstrable ambiguity or potential absurdity, such as *Public Citizen*. When a statute is capable of two meanings, a court may look to legislative evidence to resolve the ambiguity. If the ambiguity is created in conference committee, as it was here, then the court may resolve the ambiguity by conforming to Congress's own rules.[107] Those rules tell the congressperson to assume that the conference has not changed the core meaning of any text passed by both houses. Under the conference committee rules, a member looking at the term *utilize* would either object or assume that *utilize* did not, per the rules, change the statute in any significant way.[108] That is how a judge should interpret the meaning of *utilize* as well. If courts must respect Congress, as all statutory interpreters agree, then judges should interpret the meaning of *utilize* in the same way that Congress would, as making no significant change in the language "establish" passed by both houses.

This analysis requires no lengthy exegesis of the law's full legislative history but focuses instead on statutory history (which has always had a better pedigree than legislative history, being the history of text).[109] All this analysis requires is looking at the bills passed by the House and the Senate and finding that the *key statutory term* was added at conference. Even if one were to invoke the entire conference report, it is a mere 13 pages long, 8 pages of which are statutory text.[110] This is hardly the excessive "volume" or "heterogeneity" that has been asserted by legislative history's critics.[111] More importantly, if this analysis is correct, it avoids all sorts of rather controversial questions: it turns a case that is quite difficult on questions of absurdity, constitutional avoidance, and the president's power to nominate into a far more straightforward case.[112] Relying on "the rules" of the conference allows a judge to defer to Congress's decisions and, at the same time, restrains judges from picking out a judge's friends or enemies in the text or legislative history.[113]

Principle #4: Typologies of Legislative History May Mislead

If principles 1–3 are correct, they lead to the conclusion that conventional typologies of legislative history are misleading, if not wrong. It is often asserted that some kinds of legislative history are inherently better than others: committee reports are better than author statements, and author statements are better than the statements of random representatives.[114] Some scholars have asserted a de facto hierarchy of reliability when it comes to legislative history.[115] In fact, as Professor Vermeule has written, this hierarchy is "poorly theorized."[116] The standard hierarchy is not only under-theorized, it is wrong in terms of its judgments about reliability.[117] The best legislative history should not be defined by essentialist category, such as the category of all committee reports or all floor statements, but by sequence, relation to text, and bipartisanship.[118]

Committee reports have for some time been considered a reliable "type" of legislative history. Following the ancient but largely outdated Wilsonian wisdom that Congress in committee is Congress at work, the conventional wisdom urges that legislative history should focus on committee reports. This in turn has led to the belief that there is a hierarchy of legislative history, and committee reports sit at the top. In fact, there is no reason to believe that, even if there is a hierarchy, committee reports should sit on top. The decisional process is less vertical than horizontal, a debate between supporters and critics that, if represented, would appear a sideways funnel constructed by oscillating but diminishing wavelengths. The wavelength—or distance between proponents and opponents—would become progressively smaller until the text would be at rest.

Those suspicious of legislative evidence are likely to find it obvious that committee reports are not always the "gold standard." In the *Holy Trinity* case, for example, Professor Vermeule found that one of the committee reports on which the Supreme Court relied was in fact a committee report issued in a Congress prior to the Congress that passed the bill.[119] Professor Vermeule is clearly right in concluding that it cannot be "authoritative" history because the committee report on which Justice Brewer relied was simply too far in advance of the ultimate debate.[120] Bills change dramatically over time, and in fact the Alien Contract Labor Act was significantly changed after that report was issued.[121] One should always be cautious in asserting that committee reports are necessarily better than author statements or amendment debate. Of course, if the committee report refers to a decision on the particular matter and is roughly contemporaneous in time, then that may be the best legislative evidence.[122] This cannot be assumed, however, unless one traces the statutory text.

There remain two problems with typological analysis. The first refers to substantial but regrettable confusion about the very nature of committee reports. The second refers to timing; on occasion, even committee reports can follow the signing of a bill, in which case they risk post hoc manipulation. As to the first, a few quick reminders of what to some is well known but is still confused by some judicial interpreters. *Conference reports are not committee reports.* Conference reports come at the end of the process; committee reports typically occur at the beginning. *Conference reports are proposed text,* agreed upon by the conferees just prior to final passage; committee reports typically summarize the committee bill, text that may change dramatically over time.

To illustrate just how variable the practice may be with respect to committee reports, let us turn to what has become an iconic case for textualists, an issue considered by several courts of appeal, including the Ninth Circuit in *Amalgamated Transit Union Local 1309 v. Laidlaw Transit Servs., Inc.*[123] The case involved the Class Action Fairness Act, a law aiming to reduce delay in class action cases. The specific provision at issue involved the amount of time to appeal a decision to remand a case to state court (permitting an unusual interlocutory appeal). The statute provided that the appeal could be filed in "not less than 7 days."[124] Of course, "not less than 7 days" may mean 8 days or 8 weeks or 8 years. The common sense reader will say that "less" was simply a mistake; "less" really meant "within 7 days"—a scriveners' error. Many state legislatures allow courts to fix such an error, but there is no comparable federal canon.[125] In fact, the meaning of "less" occupied the sustained attention of appellate courts in the Ninth, Tenth, Eleventh, and Seventh Circuits.[126] Judge Easterbrook, for the Seventh Circuit, rejected any reference to the committee report and read the provision literally, explaining "that Congress has written a deadline imprecisely, or even perversely, is not a sufficient reason to disregard the enacted language."[127]

It turns out that this case involves one of the rules that senators know but the *Schoolhouse Rock* version of Congress omits: there is no requirement to file *any* Senate committee report. When a Senate committee "reports" a bill, the term *report* is a verb, not a noun. The committee sends the bill—the text—to the floor for consideration. A "report" of the bill need not, however, be accompanied by a "committee report" in the sense of a bill summary. As courts of appeals addressing the Class Action Fairness Act discovered, the committee report was released *after* the bill was signed by the president, and it included contested dissenting views.[128] So much for the idea that committee reports are always the "gold standard."

In fact, despite some significant debate about the committee report in the appellate cases, the contents of the report do not resolve the mystery of how Congress could have written "less" when it meant "no more than." For that, one has to look to the floor debate. The Class Action Fairness Act aimed to reduce delay in class actions; no one disputed that aim. On the floor, senators spoke at length about the precise number of days, noting that class action jurisdiction should be determined within 77 days, 7 of which was for the time to appeal a remand order. Proponents and opponents agreed on the importance of the 77-day limitation. In short, the debate reveals 7 days as a *ceiling, not a floor*.[129] As for the committee report, the curious thing is that there was nothing nearly as helpful in the report as the floor debate, and yet it occasioned all sorts of discussion within the courts of appeals about when the report was filed.[130] As this and the other examples I have given illustrate, it is sequence that matters more than typology when looking for legislative evidence. And, yes, even committee reports can disappoint, or constitute "post-enactment" history, which is generally viewed with suspicion by most experts in statutory interpretation.

Principle #5: What Is Unthinkable to a Judge May Be Quite Thinkable to a Member of Congress

We have come to a far more nuanced appreciation of the ways in which Congress's processes may defy lawyerly expectations. Let me call these "structure-induced misunderstandings": cases in which faithful legislators following the rules may operate under process-based expectations precisely the opposite of what a court might expect if the court looked solely to the textual language and not the procedural context of Congress's decision.

Let us return to the *Public Citizen* example. The justices thought the text "unthinkable," but given the nature of conference negotiations, last-minute additions are in fact quite "thinkable." Time is often short, and so conference reports tend to include minimal explanations.[131] For example, on matters for which both bills have the same text, the conferees will have an incentive, given time constraints, to say *nothing* about this agreement. Even though *members* will realize silence means textual agreement, judges and lawyers who focus only on the joint explanation (the legislative history of the conference substitute) may read meanings into that silence precisely the opposite of what a member might conclude. If both bills are the same (as they were in *Public Citizen*, on the term "established"), the joint explanation will say nothing about the meaning of "established." A judge, however, might read this silence as enormously significant when in fact it is foreordained.[132]

Conferees have every incentive to be silent on that which is agreed upon and to focus on that which is in dispute. It is not surprising, then, that the joint explanation in *Bock Laundry* focused on issues involving criminal defendants, where the statute has a dramatic impact—forcing plea bargains. Going into the conference, the bills were directly at odds; the Senate bill allowed impeachment in every case for all civil and criminal witnesses; the House bill provided no impeachment for all civil and criminal cases. In theory, the members could not change the coverage of the bill (civil and criminal cases), but in their compromise, they created a balancing test that seemed to leave out plaintiffs. The joint statement did not emphasize the agreed upon language between Senate and House (witnesses), but focused on the disagreements. This can create a reverse "salience" effect for judges if they believe the joint explanation is summarizing the bill (it is not). In such cases, that which is most disputed, about which there is the most discord (criminal defendants), is elevated above that which is not in dispute—the text agreed upon by both houses (coverage of civil and criminal cases).

"Structure-induced" misunderstandings do not arise only around conference reports. For example, reconsider our *Griggs* example, the case interpreting a single amendment by Senator Tower concerning job testing. The cloture rules give an incentive for bill opponents to revisit issues agreed to in the substitute. (Remember that, before the cloture vote, the parties will have generally agreed to a substitute bill compromising the major issues necessary to obtain 60 votes). Today, Senate Rule XXII encourages this by requiring that post-cloture amendments be introduced prior to cloture.[133] Given rule-produced incentives, proponents of the underlying bill will always suspect that post-cloture amendments amount to "redos"—efforts to gain benefits lost in the major substitute negotiations. Nevertheless, proponents will want to see the already-filibustered bill move forward, which will give them an incentive to agree to redundant language. Redundant language raises no immediate electoral costs to the proponents or opponents (who ever lost an election because she voted for redundant language?) but may cause substantial ambiguity. In other words, Senate rules create incentives to create surplusage at the amendment stage likely to offend judges' canonically induced preference for parsimony.

Consider, finally, another type of rule likely to create "structure-induced misunderstandings"—rules governing appropriations bills. The canonical case is *Tennessee Valley Authority v. Hill.*[134] The question was whether the Tellico Dam construction could be halted because it would endanger the snail darter, an endangered species. The Burger Court held for the tiny fish against the huge dam on the theory that the Endangered Species Act (ESA) was broadly worded and that there could be no "repeal by implication" based on Congress's repeated general appropriations for the Tellico Dam.[135] As a methodological matter, *TVA* is a mess. As one of my students found, the Supreme Court missed a relevant *statute* that should have resolved the matter.[136] Even in the absence of this statute, however, the Court's analysis shows deep misunderstandings about the legislative process by denigrating appropriations bills relative to authorizing legislation.

The appropriations committee had no power to amend the Endangered Species Act. Senate rules prohibit legislating on appropriations. Members operate under "rules that prohibit the inclusion of legislative language in appropriations measures."[137] Their only way to resolve the matter was to try to pass an appropriations bill limiting the use of TVA funds. (As it turns out they did, but no one seemed to notice.)[138] Let us assume, however, that the Court was left only with general statements in the appropriations bills' legislative history (a common way that appropriators signal agencies), plus the appropriations bills themselves. From the judicial standpoint, you have text of the ESA up against the text of the appropriations bills. Since appropriations bills are typically lists of numbers, the court decided the authorization bill should trump the appropriations bill.

This is entirely contrary to congressional intuitions. No authorizing chairperson believes that his or her program will be funded if the appropriators disagree. If, for example, an authorizing committee wanted to spend money on a war in Afghanistan, Congress could pass a bill to that effect, and the appropriating committee could completely undo the effect of that bill by introducing an appropriations measure with no money for such a war. At that point, the authorizing committee could *not* seek to amend the appropriations bill with contravening language, for that would violate the rules against legislating on appropriations. The sequence of these procedures from authorization to appropriations means that, as a general rule, appropriations supersede authorizations. The only exception to the rule against legislating on appropriations is that legislators may limit the use of funding for specific legislative purposes.

For members of Congress, then, appropriations trump authorizations. The Supreme Court's opinion in *TVA v. Hill* treats this in precisely the opposite way: authorization trumps appropriation.[139] The Court applied a judicial canon against "repeal by implication," which effectively reversed members' presumption that appropriations trump legislation.[140] Elsewhere, the canon against repeal by implication may be both wise and important,[141] but as Dean Daniel Rodriguez and political scientist Mathew McCubbins have argued, the Supreme Court's assumptions about Congress in *TVA* were more than "strange"; they defy positive political theorists' well-honed understandings of the appropriations process.[142] What judges see as ambiguity and lack of deliberation in appropriations matters[143] (since the bills have little text) is quite the opposite for those in Congress, where appropriations are the most important and actively debated bills in Congress.[144]

All of these misunderstandings might be dismissed as isolated and innocuous failures, but there is a consistent normative implication. In *TVA*, the Court missed the relevant statute, and in *Griggs*, the appellate court relied upon a failed amendment. In *Public Citizen*, there was an easy, legislatively supported "fix" to a statute branded "absurd." In *King v. Burwell*, the Court dismissed Congress as a cartoon.[145] These are not the statements and actions of courts deferring to Congress; these are statements and actions of courts contemptuous and ignorant of Congress 101. For years, the academy and lawyers have struggled with the so-called counter majoritarian difficulty of constitutional law, worrying about courts' ability to reverse the people's choices. These examples show the possibility of a far more persistent and pervasive difficulty—of supermajoritarian proportions—in the more common arena of statutory interpretation.

Responding to the Critics

Congress 101 should change how we read statutory text and history. Procedural context matters to courts when it is a matter of courts' own actions. So why should it be irrelevant to understanding congressional debate or text? If we force students to imbibe evidence, civil procedure, and administrative law, why not the rules that amount to democracy's internal "constitution"? Here, I respond to some major objections to the search for legislative evidence—complexity, cost, and lack of discipline. Aided by the power of technology and big data to resist the claims of excessive complexity and cost, I argue that a theory "internal" to Congress is far more likely to be disciplined and efficient than any "external" theory. Congress has *independent incentives* to know and follow its own sequential processes, apart from anything a court might do in a particular statutory interpretation case or a theorist might devise as a method to "discipline" Congress.

The "It's Too Complex" Argument

Some legal scholars or judges are quick to say that legislative procedures are too complex for lawyers or judges. Charitably interpreted, this claim assumes that lawyers do not, and cannot, know anything about legislative procedures. My quarrel is with that assumption. Are House and Senate rules any more complex than the Federal Rules of Civil Procedure or the Federal Rules of Evidence? Lawyers have no problem tackling the massive Code of Federal Regulations or the General Agreement on Trade and Tariffs but pale when faced with a document like the Senate rules that is substantially shorter. I have invoked fewer than a dozen congressional rules in this chapter and procedures with obvious analogues to judicial proceedings. Is it really "too complex" or difficult for judges and academics to learn basic facts about congressional process?

Others might argue that there really are no rules because Congress's rules are not entrenched.[146] Congress's rules may be evaded by unanimous consent in the Senate or a "special rule" in the House. But these are the exceptions that prove the existence of the rules. No one claims that the Rules of Civil Procedure or the Federal Rules of Evidence are not really rules because Congress does in fact amend them and courts are granted authority to make exceptions—in some cases exceptions entirely at the judge's discretion. Standing rules of the House and Senate do in fact regularize the processes affecting members' run-of-the-mill behavior.[147] Just because we have all heard stories about conference committees including extraneous material[148] does not mean that members do not go to extreme lengths to enforce the rules of conference committees. For example, on a weekend shortly before Christmas 2005, Senators Levin and Warner revoked their signatures on a conference report because House members sought to add extraneous material to an important habeas corpus bill.[149] This anecdote demonstrates what positive political theorists embrace: "legislators value the stability in legislative outcomes that flows from the legislature's internal structure and procedures."[150]

In fact, Congress's procedures stem from a simple premise: plurality. How can 535 people write a brief together without a division of labor (committees devoted to particular issues), rules for resolving disputes (sequential referral), and ultimate decisions finalized? For example, consider the unwritten rule that "legislative precedent" matters. In voting on bills or drafting bills, members often look to prior bills so that their policy positions are consistent over time and, in the case of drafting, so that it is easier to pass the bill; the author can argue that the bill presents no great change in law, and it has already passed the relevant legislative body. Just as no written constitutional rule binds the judiciary to precedent, no written rule binds the Congress to its prior textual precedents. And, yet, textual precedent has a powerful effect in Congress. Relying on precedent reduces information costs; it makes decisions easier. This is true of individual judges and individual representatives as well. Let us say that Representative *X* has voted for bill *Y* for three sessions of Congress; the likelihood is very high that he will vote for it again; the likelihood is also very high that his staff will want precisely the same language voted on earlier to avoid the costs of considering new and unexpected outcomes. Relative to the current uncoordinated system, one based on legislative decision-making processes is likely to decrease complexity and increase simplicity.

The Legislative History "Costs Too Much" Argument

One of the most significant arguments against using legislative evidence, akin to the complexity argument, is that even if legislative evidence is no more complex than other areas of law, relative to a focus on the text itself, it increases litigation costs. Some have even suggested that the costs of investigating legislative history "may . . . tend to skew judicial evaluation in favor of claims . . . advanced by affluent parties," with greater resources to mine the legislative record.[151] With the advent of new technology, including databases free to the public, arguments against the difficulty of finding legislative evidence must change. Databases like ProQuest, Westlaw, and Congress.gov now make searching for legislative sequence quite easy, and particular terms in lengthy reports can be found with Control-F. Just "google" a recent committee report's number and it will pop up, Google transferring you to the printing office's website.

Even if technology did not reduce the costs of search substantially, it would still be the case that an exclusionary rule (no legislative evidence) would not necessarily reduce interpretive costs below those that might be saved by legislative decision theory. As Professor Vermeule has made clear, there is no unified judicial agreement on any particular statutory interpretation approach, including a legislative history exclusionary rule.[152] The vast majority of courts still use legislative evidence. Relative to the present practice in which there is no central agreement on what counts as reliable legislative history, legislative decision theory's attention to sequence and tracing text may render the legislative history quite manageable. It may well be impossible, as Professor Vermeule has noted, to assess whether courts make more errors with legislative history than not.[153] However, relative to a rule of uncoordinated picking and choosing of legislative history, one that simplifies and objectifies legislative evidence reduces costs. It reduces costs by reducing the amount of relevant legislative evidence and increasing coordination among courts.

In theory, legislative decision theory could even reduce the total interpretive costs below the level imposed by a strong exclusionary rule, meaning a rule allowing the interpreter to consider text only. Just as legislative history is subject to "picking and choosing," so too is text. As we have seen above, reverse engineering helps target texts central to Congress's decision. Perhaps more importantly, the costs of an exclusionary rule cannot simply be calculated by what is left out. If a court does not use legislative history, it uses something else to resolve ambiguity, whether canons of interpretation, prior precedent, or other statutes, all of which impose interpretive costs. Such costs can be quite large as, for example, when a court canvasses the whole code, looking to vast numbers of other statutes.[154]

The exclusionary view also risks a different, but ultimately a more important, cost: entrenching the views of superminorities. Only by looking to the legislative evidence can a judge be certain that she is not embracing a result sought by a filibustering minority.[155] Once a court has embraced the view of the opponents of the bill, it may be extremely difficult to reverse. Given congressional inertia and the need for a supermajority to overcome the inevitable Senate filibuster, losing parties are likely to find it quite difficult to elicit congressional reversals of erroneous textualist interpretations in cases of low political salience or where minorities' interests are at stake. If a legislative decision approach reduces that risk, it may well be less costly than the exclusionary view, where cost is defined not purely in terms of information costs or judicial resources but in the larger normative sense of legitimacy in a democratic order. As we have seen, although textualism claims to be a majoritarian approach, there is nothing preventing such an approach from entrenching the will of the few at the expense of the many. The same is unfortunately true of purposivism, but here the risk is less because the advocates are at least willing to look at legislative evidence.

The "Let's Discipline Congress" Argument

A number of scholars have suggested that the problems of ambiguity would be solved if Congress were simply "punished" when it creates ambiguity. Textualists believe that focusing on text will "discipline" Congress. Textualists are not alone in the hope that judicial rules will force congressional action: Professor Einer Elhauge has written, in one of the most sophisticated forms of this approach, that courts should force Congress to reveal Congress's preferences more accurately.[156] In fact, such judicially imposed default rules are unlikely to succeed. As Professor Vermeule has argued, for such rules to be effective, judges must agree upon them, and there is no evidence that judges can or will reach a consistent agreement.[157] More importantly, even if judges were to agree, they would have to communicate their rulings consistently to Congress, and Congress would consistently have to "hear" those rules.[158] Outside decisions of wide public notice or importance to a powerful interest group, the empirical evidence suggests that Congress pays little attention to the internal minutiae of appellate decisions.[159] This reflects the obvious fact that no one ever lost an election by failing to pay attention to appellate case law. As Judge Robert Katzmann of the Second Circuit has recently written, it is an "illusion" that even a uniform judicial practice, such as one decrying ambiguity, "will change legislative behavior."[160]

Others have proposed that Congress pass its own federal rules of statutory interpretation.[161] If we have rules of evidence, why don't we have rules of statutory interpretation? This is an excellent question, but it is unlikely to incite legislative action by Congress, *particularly given that Congress may view itself as already having such rules.* Congress simply has no incentive to pass new rules in a world otherwise crowded with immediate political needs. Congress is a very busy place,[162] and statutory interpretation, however important in the abstract, is likely to garner little attention by representatives busy waging war, balancing budgets, and reforming entitlements. Moreover, even if such a proposal did capture the imagination of a member of the House or Senate, it would not be easily passed because theoretical disputes would soon be associated with larger, politically salient issues, making it difficult to reach consensus. For example, rules about textualism and purposivism would be debated in public, as rules of judicial restraint or activism, and this would tend to yield predictable and large political divisions, akin to those we see in Supreme Court nomination battles. Finally, even if a bill were passed, Congress would soon begin the process of undoing any compromise, just as it has felt free to "contract around" other grand projects aimed at congressional self-restraint.[163] Congress would be better off, as I suggest in the epilogue, by making its decisions far more transparent, by making changes to the Congressional Record and providing easier ways to trace statutory text and sequence.

Legislative decision theory offers significant advantages because it is a *self-enforcing* rule of statutory interpretation. Using Congress's own processes allows judges to apply the interpretive presumptions of a faithful congressional decision maker, hurdling the barriers of coordination and communication associated with competing proposals. It might also have the salutary side benefit, if it were to communicate anything to Congress,[164] of reducing incentives for legislative manipulation. If, for example, members know that losers' history does not count, then losers have no incentive to try to manipulate the record; and if Congress's rules do matter, then members will have an even greater incentive than they already do to conform to the rules.[165] Mirroring Congress's own incentives does not require one to embrace the unrealistic view that particular methods of statutory interpretation—what courts do—has an effect on Congress's drafting practices. It harnesses Congress's own internal incentives—with the possible salutary side effect that Congress will have an even greater incentive to follow its own rules.

The Democracy Deficit Argument

Some suggest that any recourse to legislative evidence suffers from a democratic legitimacy deficit because it involves reliance on statements of a *part* of Congress rather than the whole Congress. Curiously, no one makes similar arguments in other venues. No one argues that because corporate committees, the board of directors, or a corporate subsidiary, issues a report that the report is not legitimate because drafted by a *part* of the corporation. Similarly, no one argues that because only a small number of judges on a Circuit Court of Appeals—a three judge panel—decides a case that their decision is not legitimate because they are a *part* of, and may ultimately be overruled by, the entire Circuit en banc. Nor do lawyers argue that because only a narrow majority of 5 justices on the Supreme Court come to a united opinion, that the decision is somehow illegitimate because 5 justices are only *part* of the whole Court.

In Chapter 5, I address this "group agency" objection in greater detail, but even if we were to take this "partial democracy" argument at face value, legislative decision theory can accept and correct for it. Even when a court is relying upon a smaller body than the whole of Congress—the drafters of a committee report or an individual sponsor—it is not relying on them because of their individual character but because it believes that these documents or statements are representative of a majority's—typically a supermajority's—views. If the legislative evidence does not meet the criteria of the group authority under the rules (explained more fully in Chapter 5), then it should be rejected. Finally, in cases where there is an irreducible gap, one cannot say that there is in fact a truly democratic alternative—in the case of unforeseen events, for example, no majority formed on the interpretive issue in question. In such cases, the job of a court is to give legal effect to the statute in a way that is the most respectful of democracy—and that cannot simply be to impose the personal views of the least democratic body in our government, the judiciary.

Conclusion

If nothing else, legislative decision theory is more normatively appealing than any available theory because it respects what we know about Congress as a democratic body. If Article I of our Constitution means anything, it signals legislative primacy of place, which no student of the Constitution or statutory interpretation, textualist or purposivist, disavows. "Congress is the Constitution's first branch, with enumerated, sweeping powers."[166] It is not only the most "potentially powerful" legal institution in the country but also the institution theoretically "most accountable to the people."[167] "Federal judges—who have no constituency—have a duty to respect legitimate policy choices made by those who do."[168] Unfortunately, almost universal disdain for Congress has deprived lawyers and judges of the knowledge that would make them more effective citizens and better disciplined consumers of Congress's statutes. Legislative supremacy is not a principle of enforced judicial humility or haughty legislative overreach; it is a principle that aims for the judiciary to act as a fiduciary for the people. If we can agree upon nothing else about democracy, we should agree upon principles that count as anti-democratic. There should be little doubt that any theory whose methods allow for embracing the meanings of those who filibustered a bill or who lost the legislative fight should count as anti-democratic.

4

Petty Textualism, Canons, and Cognitive Bias

"In my mind, legislative history, properly applied, can have great value in the interpretive process. Text without context often invites confusion and judicial adventurism."

SENATOR ORRIN HATCH (R–UTAH)[1]

"I think when justices disregard that kind of material [legislative history], it is just another way to write their own law . . ."

SENATOR ARLEN SPECTER (THEN R–PENN.)[2]

LEGISLATIVE CRITICS FIND Congress 101 so strange they hope to cut Congress out of the process and resolve difficult statutory interpretation cases with an entirely different set of materials made by themselves—judicially created "canons of construction." The canon movement supplants congressional materials with ancient judge-made rules that most lawyers and judges of my generation were never taught and members of Congress do not know or follow.[3] Justice Scalia and Bryan Garner's book *Reading Law* admits this ignorance and offers a simple, straightforward 567 pages on 57 such canons (13 others are rejected as anti-canons), some of them known by their Latin names, such as *ejusdem generis* or *noscitur a sociis.*[4]

For its advocates, this canon lore is easy, rule-like, and transparent, even if it stands in some tension with textualism itself (why do you need canons, after all, if text is most often plain). If recent Supreme Court cases are any indication, the canon movement has had influence at the highest legal levels. Once thought dead, canons are experiencing a resurgence, as justices in recent terms have openly displayed their grammatical and Latin erudition in opinionated canon fire.[5] Since its publication just a few years ago, Justice Scalia and Professor Garner's book has been cited in more than 200 cases.[6] Not everyone agrees; Judge Posner, hardly a self-described liberal, has taken his not-so-disguised contempt for canon enthusiasm to the pages of the popular press.[7] Law professors, once largely derisive of the phenomenon, have developed a new range of fans.[8]

Ancient canons may seem innocuous to the uninitiated, but no lawyer should be confused about the canon war: *it is about power—judicial power.* In *Reading Law*, Justice Scalia and Professor Garner reveal an enthusiasm for canons directly contrary to Justice Scalia's view of legislative materials as "garbage."[9] By contrast, the 57 canons (with their historical grounding in Judaic and Christian biblical interpretation) are rule-like, virtuous, and objective.[10] One need not, as a logical matter, reject the canons as one of many sources of relevant interpretive materials. Many, perhaps most judges, such as Justices Breyer or Ginsburg, use them as part of a more pluralistic interpretive enterprise, in which the text, purpose, and legislative context are all consulted to find "convergent meaning." However, *canons cannot and should not replace legislative evidence;* indeed, in my opinion, faithful agents of Congress—fiduciaries of the democratic process—must consult legislative evidence, prior to applying canons, both as a matter of proper deference to the people's will, and the court's proper role in statutory interpretation, as Congress's agent, not master. Only by looking to a source outside of the courts, namely legislative evidence, can a judge properly exercise judicial restraint in resolving ambiguities.

The canon question is made all the more important because those judges and academics most insistent on text, like Justice Scalia and Professor Garner, are also canon enthusiasts: they seek to supplant legislative evidence with canons. Indeed, one of the prime "anti-canons" rejects Congress's evidence as a fallacy of statutory interpretation.[11] In the war between those who rely upon legislative evidence and the canon enthusiasts, someone is winning, and someone losing. In fact, Justice Scalia once warned that some canons are a "sheer judicial power grab."[12] When legislative evidence is ignored and, worse, replaced with judicially created canons that no one voted on and no average person (much less members of Congress) knows, the people's power to direct their government is not only diminished but supplanted. Consulting only canons in the face of relevant public legislative evidence is anti-democratic and contrary to judges' constitutional duty to defer to the political branches.

Federal judges cannot purport to be faithful agents of Congress if they consult only the rules they themselves make. Even those who study the canons, like Professor Barrett, recognize that there is a deep tension between democracy and canon fire.[13] Professor Gluck goes further and urges that the canons raise questions about why and whether the courts should be able to make such a vast amount of federal common law.[14] And then there is the simple practical objection that the complexity of the process will lead to politicized usage and judicial activism. The canons are complex. Justice Scalia approved 57 of them in *Reading Law*—and this complexity is why even some conservative judges reject them as an "invention" that has made law less "accurate, predictable, or sensible."[15] As Judge Posner has written, the 57 canons Justice Scalia approved provide judges "all the running room needed to generate whatever case outcome conforms" to their political views about some of the nation's most divisive issues, from "abortion, homosexuality, illegal immigration, states' rights, to the death penalty."[16] As retired Justice John Paul Stevens writes, "I have always been reluctant to place primary reliance on any canon of statutory construction when confronted with a question about the correct interpretation of an ambiguity," because like the charge of the light brigade, such "commands can have disastrous consequences."[17]

In theory, Congress could, like many states,[18] reject or modify all judicial canons through legislation. The canons are entirely judge-made law. In practice, however, Congress has little incentive to enact such legislation because the canons are largely irrelevant to legislative practice. Empirical work shows that legislative members and their staffers know little about the canons and do not use them to draft statutes,[19] or, in my view, may use entirely different—legislative—canons[20] based on the nature of legislative, as opposed to, judicial proceedings. Congress is entirely free to legislate against judicial canons; many states, for example, have legislated against the use of ancient Latin canons, including such classic, and classically unreliable, canons as *expresso unius exclusio alterius*, meaning that the inclusion of particular items of a class means that all other items of that class are excluded. Some states have asked that judges fix grammatical mistakes, and few have codified the Latin canons.[21]

This chapter critiques "canon textualism," a form of textualism seeking to supplant legislative evidence with canons of construction. My fear is that this form of textualism encourages judicial activism: judges writing their own statutes with their own materials, as the quotations at the beginning of this chapter, from Republican senators, warn against. Judges and lawyers exacerbate this risk when canon-textualism joins with a form of textualist method I call "petty textualism." The problem of "petty textualism" is bigger than any particular theory of statutory interpretation; it is a highly problematic *method of dissecting text* that has never been theorized. I introduce "petty textualism" here, because it tends to be associated with those who insist most rigidly on "textual" analysis, although, as we will see, petty textualism may infect more pluralistic analyses. Canon enthusiasts and petty textualists, as I have defined them here, *both exclude legislative evidence and enthusiastically embrace canons, which tends to aggravate the anti-democratic implications of their combined method.* At the very least these methods share a set of prominent adherents, and a moment in history in which Supreme Court interpretive practice has come to view legislative history with derision and embraced canons of construction with enthusiasm.[22]

Petty Textualism

Textualism as a methodology, as opposed to a theory, deserves greater analysis. We need to look deeply at textualism "as applied"—as a practice in actual cases—rather than an abstract theory. But there is a particular method of textualism I aim to isolate and analyze, a method I dub *petty textualism*. Obviously, the connotation is pejorative, and I mean it to be, because this form of textualism is not true to textualist principles, or originalist principles (Blackstonian ones) even if it parades itself as such. It is a spurious form of textualism that rejects the whole text and, as such, can create both a false "plainness" and a false "ambiguity" in statutory interpretation. To those who find the word "petty" insulting, it seems rather mild compared to the insults thrown at legislative evidence (e.g., garbage, ashcans, entrails). Although I have no aim to increase the incivility of our legal discourse, someone wise once said that, if you do not exaggerate, no one will know what you are talking about. Petty textualism is beneath textualism's own aspirations.

"Petty textualism" as method proceeds as follows: the interpreter pulls one or two or five words out of a lengthy statute, holds them up as chunks of text, declares the words plain and, as plain, ends the case. In the act of dissection, the interpreter is doing something apparently innocuous but quite problematic: she is taking text *out of context*. Decontextualization of this kind is not only bad textualism (textualism generally holds as a theory, if not practice, that one must read the whole text), it is also petty textualism. It reduces statutory interpretation to the smallest of terms, in the absolute size of the object of attention and the relative size of the object as compared to the legislature's ends. In a democracy of over 300 million persons, large national projects, markets, justice, and even human life should not depend upon the *picayune*.[23] Petty textualism should be more of a scandal; it makes judges appear pedants and scriveners, fighting over dictionaries and obscure Latin phrases. The great judges of yesteryear—Justice Marshall, Justice Harlan, Justice Holmes—knew justice demanded more than wordplay.

As philosophers of language know, words taken *out of context* have so many meanings they have none—other than the meaning the interpreter assigns. Take a simple example, the word "fifth." One might think that there is an obvious meaning to a number—5—but meanings easily vary with context. If I say "I'll take the fifth" to a group of lawyers, they will assume a legal context—that a witness is refusing to testify under the Fifth Amendment to the Constitution. But what if the context is surgery or a liquor store? The term "fifth" then takes on an entirely different meaning—it could be a fifth scalpel or a fifth of gin. As Professors Goldsworthy and Ekins have written, "*If presuppositions are not grasped*, almost anything we say is open to being misunderstood in unpredictable and bizarre ways."[24] No philosopher of language disputes this proposition. Textualists insist that context is necessary, but their definition of context is vague—an unidentified relevant linguistic community that chameleon-like changes from ordinary persons, to highly educated lawyers, to members of Congress, to judges themselves. As the great contracts scholar Corbin argued, every interpreter uses some extrinsic evidence, even if it is the interpreter's own life experience, and this is truest when the judge asserts that words are "plain and clear."[25] Corbin was only partly right in the case of petty textualism. There is more than the problem of unannounced extrinsic evidence at stake in petty textualism; there is also the question of bias and logical fallacy.

Petty Textualism and Spurious Interpretation

Exhibit One for the claim that textualism has reached extremes are the arguments that propelled the recent health care case, *King v. Burwell*, into the Supreme Court.[26] Political opponents of the health care law based their case on a "petty textualism" argument—by pulling a single word, state, out of a 900-plus-page statute, isolating that word, and proclaiming that its meaning was plain, and plainly contrary to the Act's survival.[27] The opponents' chosen word "state" appears in a tax provision providing the law's tax credits to health care exchanges "established by the State,"[28] when in fact many exchanges had been established by the federal government when the states failed to create such exchanges. To some, my claim might seem odd because the Supreme Court's opinion has been taken to signal the Court's move away from textualism and toward purposivism: the opinion begins with what may be the clearest expression of the Act's plan ever written. But that move was only necessary, as the Court acknowledged, because of the "strong" textualist claim of the law's opponents [29] who pulled "state" and "established by the State" out of context of the rest of the statute. The majority did handsprings to find the words of the tax statute ambiguous so that it could reject the petty textualist claims of the health care law's opponents. In fact, a textualist could have resolved the case quite easily based on the whole text of the statute, in the government's favor.

Petty textualism's method rejects "whole text" readings albeit without justifying its dissection method. First, a word or phrase is taken *out of context*, isolated. The old context—the health care law created in one institution, Congress—is now gone. The word *state* stands in limbo, contextless, capable of any meaning from "state of injury" to "state of play." Second, the word is put in a new context—recontextualized—pulled out of the legislative context where it was constructed and into a new judicial context where it is to be interpreted. Linguists call this "entextualization" because the text is re-embedded in a new context without anyone actually paying attention or specifying the new context.[30] No one announces the shift in context. The result is an important shift in meaning and power from the original context (elected members of Congress) to the new interpretive context (unelected members of the judiciary). Power is most powerful when it shows itself least.

To gain some purchase on the power involved, consider what might happen if the new interpreter were a doctor or a diplomat. A doctor asked about the term *state*, if he were told the law was about health care, might easily think "state of injury." Almost instinctively, he brings his own context—the medical profession—to help him define the term *state*. So, too, a diplomat is likely to think that *state* means a country like Ghana or Germany. An American judge brings his context with him as well, the background assumptions that come with what are essentially stereotypical American legal meanings. The judge will assume that *state* means a political or geographic body, like Iowa, a part of our federal system. That institutional context—the judge's or doctor's or diplomat's job—unconsciously limits the probable and putatively "plain" meanings to those the interpreter takes from repeated, stereotypical problems, in his own institutional context. Background contextual meaning is added, but silently, without thought. The doctor does not say to himself, "I am now in a doctor's office and interpreting *state* to mean 'state of injury' "; the judge will not specify "I am now on a court and think *state* means a governmental body smaller than the nation." The interpreter's institutional context will exist, and *its stereotypical meanings and their implications, the ones used every day, will be added to the text* based on the interpreter's institutional position, but the move will be automatic, silently embedded in judgments of "plainness." Remember that there is a lot at stake in the judgment of plainness, for at that point, the "new textualist" will end the inquiry; no further evidence of Congress's meaning, or even canons of construction, are deemed necessary.

If the interpreter's institutional context adds meaning, albeit silently, one might consider this inevitable: in every statutory case, we move from a context where congressional assumptions about making law are lost to judicial assumptions about interpreting law. But there is something more important about this kind of "petty" decontextualization. First, semantic isolation adds meaning in the sense that it *excludes the rest of the statute as evidence of meaning*. Imagine taking the term "Ishmael" out of the novel *Moby Dick*, trying to understand the meaning of the book and then, worse, stopping yourself from reading the rest of the book because "Ishmael" is plain. This hardly seems like a sound method to understand the full text. Second, semantic isolation adds something more precise—exclusivity. We know from pragmatic approaches toward language that the absence of text can provide important meanings—called implicatures—given background assumptions about the context. For example, to borrow a well-known example, a recommendation letter that only briefly tells us of the candidate's class attendance leads to the implicature (from the absence of further text) that the candidate is not terribly qualified. So, too, here, by excluding the rest of the text, dissecting a piece out of the tax statute, creates the implicature that exchanges could be "created *only* by the state." As we can see from my specification of the added term "only," the cutting out of a few words, the *isolation of text*, may add meaning, implying that states are the only source of a health care exchange.

Of course, if I am correct, this kind of petty textualism assumes, by its method, what it is trying to prove. As students of argumentation have contended, "wrenching text from context" has the potential to create logical fallacies: in this case, meanings logically opposed to the statute's whole meaning.[31] Opponents of the health care law were trying to persuade the Supreme Court that the health care tax credits only applied to state, not federal, exchanges, but their method creates that *interpretation. The isolation of the text*, its displacement from the rest of the statute, implicates exclusivity—that "only" states may create exchanges. Sophisticated linguistic theory supports this claim. The implicature was first emphasized by the linguist Paul Grice who explained that the absence of text—as against an assumed contextual background (see the recommendation letter example above)—can create meaning.[32] More recent work by Professor Levinson highlights implicatures as arising from a default "contrast set" as a restriction on the set of possible implications.[33] When one says "some of the students did well," the implication is that not "all" the students did well, the background unstated contrast set being "some" as eliminating the possibility of "all." In *King v. Burwell*, the unexpressed contrast set is "state versus federal." The phrase "established by the State," taken in isolation, rejects the federal exchange reading by implication from the choice of text. The bottom line: implications are cheap, they are silent, and do not require articulation, even if they invite the interpreter to add meaning, to read "established by the State," as "established *only* by the State."

I call this "spurious" plain meaning because it is the isolating procedure—the wrenching of text from context—that creates apparent but false plain meaning. This "spurious" plain meaning is made all the worse in *King v. Burwell* because the opinion purports to put the text back *into context* to find *ambiguity*. Although the petitioner's plain meaning argument is deemed "strong," the Court acknowledges what I have argued, that its "plainness" comes "when viewed in isolation."[34] As Chief Justice Roberts explains, "if we give the phrase 'the State that established the Exchange' its most natural meaning (the petitioners' meaning as "only" by the State), there would be "*no* qualified individuals on Federal Exchanges,"[35] meaning no one would be getting tax credits on those exchanges. Although "out of context,"[36] the tax statute appears plain, once put back into the statute, ambiguity arises. The savvy interpreter must ask why the word "state" or "established by the State" was taken out of context in the first place. One only needs to find ambiguity if the original decontextualizing move (taking "established by the State" out of the tax provision), is a "strong" plain meaning reading, as the Court reported.[37] Finding the statute ambiguous "in context" was parasitic upon the original decontextualizing move, and thus as spurious a form of ambiguity as the spurious plain meaning upon which it depended.

This interpretive two-step is particularly unwise in complex statutes where one is trying to make sense of the *relationship between several provisions in a law*. The *King* case involved two major structural provisions and one smaller tax provision—the two health market exchange provisions (42 U.S.C. 18031 and 42 U.S.C. 18041), and the tax credit provision, 26 U.S.C. 36B. In isolating a few words from the tax section ("established by the State"), the interpreter risks changing the meaning of the whole text, as we have seen above (to mean "*only* by the state"). Moreover, the very fact of isolation may defeat relationships created in other parts of the statute. The federal exchange statute directed that the federal exchange *substituted* for the state exchange "within the State" when the state failed to create its own exchange.[38] Let us call this the "substitute" relationship—F stands in for S wherever we have an exchange created "within the State" where the state has refused to create an exchange—"within the State" being the language of the federal exchange statute. [39] By focusing on the tax provision's language, without regard to the exchange statutes, the "substitute relationship" text—that providing that the federal government may substitute for a state—is eliminated.

One can see this quite easily by taking "*state means only state*" (the challengers' amendment to the law) and putting it back into the federal exchange statute, which then becomes nonsense.[40] If this does not convince, then simply add two words "or within" into the "sub-sub-sub" provision (the Court's words)[41] of the tax statute ("established *by or within the State*"), and the entire scheme is resolved: tax credits are to be granted in cases of an exchange "established by or within the State." End of case. Yes, I have imported the language "within" from the federal exchange statute, but I have done so to give meaning to all the statute's provisions, not just some. Note as well that I have not made reference to any purpose of the statute, its plan or legislative evidence of any kind, even if the Supreme Court found that necessary. I have simply harmonized the three provisions' text, rather than severed the statute's major provisions from each other. If I am correct, then the case should have been an easy one for the government. The Supreme Court need not have done handsprings about death spirals and statutory "plans" to reach the proper result, even though I applaud the chief justice for his opinion's extraordinary clarity in summarizing the statutory plan. Both the plain text and purpose supported tax credits for all exchanges. The conscientious judge would, of course, check this against the legislative record, but no one should doubt that there are easy statutory cases; they should be more worried that petty textualism makes easy cases into hard ones with a bit of wordplay.

Critics might argue that interpreters always decontextualize, taking individual words or groups of words out of statutes. Even linguists know that ordinary meaning, from a semantic perspective, requires at least a full sentence.[42] Petty textualism's statutory slicing and dicing is a new phenomenon, not an old one. Harmony, not isolation and fixation, is the theme of standard statutory interpretative methodology. Text may be isolated for the provisional purpose of analysis, but the interpreter does not stop there. Petty textualism ends the analysis after dissection; standard textual analysis keeps looking for evidence—the rest of the sentence, the rest of the statute, other statutes, the legislative record. Typically, multiple sources are consulted to seek a convergent meaning. In the real "vehicle in the park" case, *McBoyle v United States*,[43] Justice Holmes asked whether a criminal statute barring the interstate transportation of vehicles included the interstate transportation of an airplane. The specific clause was "any other self-propelled vehicle not designed for running on rails."[44] Justice Holmes identified the clause and the specific word "vehicle." He asked for the prototypical meaning of vehicle—the best undisputed example was a car. He noted that the government's argument could logically apply to airplanes, but that would expand the statute's coverage from its core,[45] and was inconsistent with other federal and state statutes. The "theme" of the statute he said was vehicles on land (looking at specific examples cited in the text). He explained that "[a]irplanes were well known in 1919 when th[e] statute was passed, but it is admitted that they were not mentioned in the reports or in the debates in Congress."[46] He concluded with a reference to "fair notice," that the criminal should know his crime is a crime (a reference to the canon known as "rule of lenity" without the name).[47] In short, the opinion reflected plural statutory modalities, looking for meaning convergence—text, theme (purpose), legislative history, and canon-like, common law, interpretive rules.

McBoyle is very far, however, from the analysis one might expect today, which takes text "out of context." Consider how *McBoyle* would have come out if the new textualist method of *Holy Trinity* were to apply.[48] As we have seen earlier, the question in that case was whether a contract/slave labor statute should include a minister. If the new textualists' preferred reading of *Holy Trinity* is any indication of the proper methodology, one takes "labor" out of the statute, looks to a dictionary, and ends the case. Labor means labor, section 1 of the statute says "labor or service of any kind," and we are done.[49] Notice that an expansionist reading is given to the term "labor"—applying the statute to a larger group of persons other than the undisputed application (manual labor). Notice as well that the new textualist argument that the minister should be included in the 1885 statute was based on a few words from section 1 of the statute ("labor or service or any kind"), ignoring a different definition of laborer in section 4 (much more clearly focused on manual labor, "laborer, mechanic or artisan") and the exclusion in section 5 for a variety of professional groups, including "professional actors, artists, lecturers, or singers."[50] Applying Justice Scalia's now famous *Holy Trinity* critique to *McBoyle* would mean that "vehicle" means anything that can be a vehicle, the extensivist meaning, and that Justice Holmes was wrong in method and result.

Critics might say that petty textualism is rare. This is not the time or place to engage in a full blown study, but it is rather easy to see that analogous examples can be found in well-known "new textualist" Supreme Court opinions. Justice Scalia's lengthy majority opinion in *West Virginia v. Casey* treated the words "attorneys' fees" separately from the term "costs" even though they appeared in the same textual phrase ("attorneys' fees as part of the costs").[51] Treating "attorneys' fees" out of context yields an implicature that it is a separate self-standing category excluding things outside its bounds, and not as the statute says ("as part of") subsumed in a larger category "costs" of the lawsuit. So, too, his dissent in *Chisom v. Roemer* zeroed in upon the meaning of the one word "representatives" in a single sentence to bar vote dilution claims in the case of judicial elections under the voting rights act's 1982 amendments.[52] The dissection suggested exclusivity—only representatives, not judges, were covered by the statute—without regard to competing terms in the same sentence covering "the political process," and "the electorate" suggesting the inclusion of all elections, including judicial elections. Similarly, in *Babbitt v. Sweet Home*, Justice Scalia's dissent focused on the term "take," again isolating it, contrary to the words used to define "take" in the statute (e.g. "harm" among a long list) and a later statutory section covering incidental harm. In all of these cases, statutory and legislative evidence suggested that the statutory dissection was significant, took text out of context, and that the implications of taking that text out of context were erroneous.[53]

If I am correct that something like "petty textualism" exists, then theorists and practitioners of statutory interpretation need to do more on two fronts. First, they need to theorize textualism in practice: in Chapter 2, I argued that every term in a statute can be rendered ambiguous by asserting prototypical (best undisputed application) versus extensivist meaning (all logical applications). Not only does petty textualism fail to grapple with this linguistic reality, it reaches conclusions contrary to textualism's professed aim to read the "whole text." This should cause concern about the consistency of textualist theory with textual method—does textualism profess a holism that it does not perform? Meanwhile, purposivists need to pay more attention to the ways in which textualism is *practiced* if they mean to provide ways for lawyers to argue *against* petty textualism. In analyzing *King v. Burwell*, I have shown textualism of the petty variety trades on decontextualizing moves that the astute textualist lawyer can reverse quite easily by opening the textual frame. *King v. Burwell* should have been an easy case for the government based on the whole text. Finally, both textualists and purposivists need to consider how often this kind of approach mars statutory interpretation. Having identified this phenomenon, I make no claim that I know its pervasiveness; that it has occurred in as important a case as *King v.*

Burwell, and other important "new textualist" opinions, invites further inquiry.

Decontextualization and Cognitive Bias

The problem with this method of interpretive dissection is not simply that it adds meaning, but that it adds a particular context likely to aggravate cognitive bias. No judicial interpreter believes that she should make a statute mean what he or she wants it to mean, but that is precisely the position in which judges stand if they adopt a textualist view which recurs to no evidence, even the whole text, that would disconfirm the interpreter's initial view. Put more insistently, petty textualism is capable of constructing its own judgments of plain meaning and, as a result, raises important questions about bias. Judges, like all interpreters, are subject to cognitive bias. It is easier for them to resort to their own meanings—meanings of an elite judiciary rather than ordinary voters or ordinary members of Congress—and they are likely to do so unconsciously.[54]

Enter the problem of canons—judge-made law created to answer judge-made interpretive questions. Lest one find my argument for "petty textualism" self-interested—the special pleading of one committed to the value of legislative evidence—it is worth considering the empirical evidence that supports both my critique of petty textualism and the likelihood of bias. The strongest empirical work in the field of statutory interpretation shows how the isolation of texts as "plain" increases potential judicial bias. The authors asked over 1,000 students to make judgments about whether a particular statute was ambiguous and their preferred policy result. The stronger the policy bias toward one result, the more likely the student found the statute "plain" rather than ambiguous based on an "internal" judgment of plainness (consulting simply themselves). By contrast, when students were asked whether an ordinary person (someone other than themselves) would find the statute plain or ambiguous, the policy bias disappeared.[55]

Even if judges take a lesson from this empirical "ambiguity" study and look for "ordinary" meaning to avoid policy bias, this does not complete the analysis of cognitive bias in a conflict of interest situation. The plainness/ambiguity study only scratches the surface of the potential problems of cognitive bias posed by petty textualism and canons of construction. All of our minds—not just those of lawyers and judges—are subject to "bounded rationality," and focusing on a few words, without attention to context, our analyses can yield errors. The Nobel-prize winning psychologist Daniel Kahneman dubbed it the "focusing illusion."[56] Decision theorists, cognitive scientists, behavioral economists, and business school professors call it focalism. The basic principle is simple: focusing on one aspect of a problem, the interpreter blinds herself to assumed or background context. Over 40 years, across a variety of disciplines, focalism's failures have proven experimentally and theoretically robust.[57] Although this is not the favorite cognitive bias of law professors, many have spent the past 20 years investigating the effects of similar cognitive errors made by juries, judges, and a variety of legal actors.

Although some doubt the virtues of the "cognitive revolution" in public law fields, no one has bothered to think hard about the ways in which statutory interpretation falls prey to a variety of cognitive biases. Professors Farina and Rachlinski, in a larger work on cognitive bias and governmental process,[58] suggest that the traditional forms of cognitive bias literature suggest that courts should welcome legislative evidence, since it requires transparency and greater deliberation. When judges have to explain their decision about "plain" meaning, that very process will reduce cognitive bias toward a particular position. Alexander Platt has argued that staging the decision procedure—from text to ambiguity to legislative evidence—can operate against confirmation and coherence bias.[59] Professor Schauer has suggested, however, that judges' cognitive bias is endemic to case-by-case adjudication.[60] Without attempting to resolve this debate, let me emphasize one particular aspect of cognitive bias that is not particularly well known in the legal academy, but uniquely aligned with the problems I have identified in "petty textualism," namely the *focusing illusion*.

After decades of assault on the idealized "rational actor," we know our minds are subject to "bounded rationality."[61] One subset of research within "bounded rationality" is "bounded *awareness*"—that we are aware of only some facets of a problem at first glance, which leads to overvaluing one aspect of a problem at the expense of unstated, presumed background context. Studies involving bounded awareness provide robust support for the proposition that we all suffer from some cognitive biases and that these biases involve the risks of blinding ourselves to relevant information.[62] The most famous of such studies involves people asked to watch a basketball game and count how many times a ball passes from players to players; it turns out that over and over again, viewers miss a woman in a gorilla suit who stops, stomps on her chest, and walks through the game. When told that they have missed the woman in the suit, many insist that this could not be possible. That study won the Ig-Nobel for its illumination of an important phenomenon, implicit attentive bias, with humor.[63]

Attention bias is more than political bias or ideological proclivity. Bounded awareness suggests that judges or interpreters are not even aware of the possibility that, in their focus on a particular text, they might miss something rather large, like the gorilla in the room. Even the most well-tempered, apolitical judge could find himself subject to this dilemma. So, unlike the original "realist" attack on statutory interpretation as one about overt policy-bias, this attack highlights implicit, unseen, tendencies toward bias. Consider the following problem. A boy and his father are in a car crash. The father dies. The boy is rushed to the hospital and taken to the operating room. When the boy's face is revealed, the surgeon says, "I cannot operate; this is my son." How can the father die and yet live? Readers struggle to solve the riddle by considering that the surgeon could be a stepfather or an adopted father. Even those of us who should know better fail to consider a simpler explanation: that the surgeon is a mother, not a father. This is not simply a matter of old-fashioned gendered default assumptions. Women as well as men puzzle over the claimed riddle because the mind *focuses* on the father–son relationship and its dramatic severance.[64]

The "focusing illusion" reflects a similar idea: when you focus on a particular element of a situation, you risk overvaluing that subject and undervaluing the surrounding context or competing explanations. Nobelist Daniel Kahneman first developed this insight by asking rather basic questions about whether people believed that they would be happier if they lived in California and concluded that isolating these kinds of factors led to inaccurate judgments about relative well-being. From this simple premise, a vast literature on focusing effects has emerged, supporting Kahneman's finding in much more complex situations.[65] In his more recent work, Professor Kahneman explains the focusing effect as a reflection of a fundamental brain duality: we often make snap judgments based on the most available information (system 1 "fast" thinking), but these judgments are often wrong because they are based on too little information. He calls the principle: "*what you see is all there is.*" So, for example, when information is scarce, the "fast-thinking" system will jump to conclusions based on the available information, seeking out no new information. An investigator asks, "Will Mindik be a good leader? She is intelligent and strong." An answer quickly comes to mind—yes. But if the adjectives were "corrupt and cruel," the fast-thinking system would yield the opposite result. The fast-thinking system is automatic and does not stop to investigate Mindik or list positive leadership qualities. System 2, the slow-thinking system, is lazy; it is fully capable of systematic and careful reasoning, but system 1 is automatic and unconscious, preferring the quick conclusion, leaving us with a bias based on the first impression, and a tendency to jump to conclusions with insufficient information.[66]

Petty textualism has a tendency, as I have shown, to engage in "what you see is all there is"—to jump to conclusions before looking at easily available evidence, or even the whole text. Worse, it blinds the analyst to other information, such as legislative evidence, all the while insisting that this blindness is a virtue. Given the behavioral research revealing our lazy self-congratulatory reasoning processes, this should come as no surprise. Even in much more complex situations, people tend to jump to conclusions precisely because they refuse to engage in the mental effort to consider more information. This is particularly true in cases where the context involves parties who have limited knowledge of other persons or institutions—as exists in the case of judges and Congress. Professor Max Bazerman of Harvard Business School has studied the focusing illusion in complex negotiation settings and has argued persuasively that people tend to focus on the information they know, and systematically fail to make the effort to understand the other party's knowledge and incentives. He and colleagues Avishalom Tor and Dolly Chugh argue that decision making can be improved if negotiators create an active procedure for distrusting their own initial reaction by considering the "rules of the game" from the perspective of the other party. This kind of "de-biasing" technique has been considered a promising approach in limiting focal bias.[67]

As we have seen from the empirical studies in statutory interpretation on "plain" meaning, shifting from the "internal perspective" on plainness to one where the individual stands in as a third party (ambiguity or plainness to an ordinary person), reduces bias. The focusing illusion studies go further and suggest that de-biasing requires one to understand not only something about the other party but also the "rules of the game" governing the other party. The intuition is simple: one cannot win a chess game if one focuses on a particular square or a particular move without responding to the opponents' moves according to the "rules of the game." This provides strong support for what I have called, in Chapter 3, a *decision process approach*—which requires judges to look at legislative evidence and to understand that evidence in the context of Congress's own sequential processes and rules. It also provides support for why petty textualism, focusing too narrowly on a bit of text, can yield dogmatic, but spurious results, even for the committed textualist. As Kahneman explains, overconfidence is one of the greatest problems of "*what you see is all there is*": persons who only see one side of a story are persistently more confident that they are right, seeing their own blindness as virtue rather than vice.[68]

To see how focal bias emerges—even in the most banal of contexts—consider a simple decision-making context repeatedly studied by researchers: the Monty Hall game. The Monty Hall game is patterned after a TV game show in which Monty Hall would show a contestant three doors, and the contestant would have to choose one. The contestant would pick a door, then Monty would open that door, and if it did not reveal the prize, Monty would ask the contestant whether he wanted to switch his choice. As a simple matter of probability, a contestant should always switch at this point, but that's not what happened. (At the start, a player had a 1 in 3 chance of winning; once Monty had opened a failed door, the player had a 2 in 3 chance of winning.) "Years after the show went off the air, statisticians, economists, and journalists noted that contestants tended to make a systematic mistake: they tended not to switch to the remaining unchosen door."[69]

Lest one think that this is a simple probability miscalculation, Chugh, Tor, and Bazerman show that the phenomenon still occurs if you change the rules of the game—if Monty does not open a failed door but points to a door and the contestant is told that Monty is "mean," trying to prevent the contestant from winning. In that case, the contestants should *not* switch, but in fact they do. The point of this scenario change is to show that the cognitive failure is the failure to attend to the incentives and knowledge of the other party. As Bazerman and Chugh explain, "Seeing the importance of Monty's decision rule, and his likely decisions, is the key to the winning strategy. But bounded awareness can prevent individuals from seeing this readily available information."[70]

Similar failures occur in more complex cases used as standard business school problems, like the "Acquiring a Company" problem. In this game, a company seeks to acquire a target. The acquirer knows that if it acquires the target, it will increase the target's value by 50 percent and that the value of the company is equally likely to be between $0 and $100. The target knows the company's value precisely. The same failure appears: the offerors focus on what they know and their probability of gain, without regard to the knowledge of the target and its incentives. The standard offer price is somewhere around $50–$60, but in fact the company could be worth nothing. CEOs and graduate students routinely fail to look at the knowledge and context of the target, focusing instead on their own possible gain.[71] If the target company knows its value, and that value is equally likely to be anywhere from $0 to $100, it is also true that it is equally likely that the value is likely to be less than the average $50–$60 offer.

Focusing failures can lead to very serious decision errors. The *Challenger* space mission killed seven astronauts. The scientists were aware that the launch was occurring at the lowest temperature in NASA history, and they focused on prior launches of O-ring failure at low temperatures; no clear pattern between O-rings and temperature led them to approve the deadly launch. If mission control had run a regression analysis on the prior 17 launches without O-ring failures, that would have led to "an unambiguous conclusion: "the Challenger had more than a 99% chance of malfunction."[72] The information was available and accessible but ignored. There is nothing magical in this idea. Looking for alternate explanations simply replicates the most basic notions of rational inquiry: no assumption counts unless it has been tested against alternative explanations and information.

Statutory Interpretation and the Focusing Illusion

Why are these findings relevant to statutory interpretation? Over the past half century, judges' interpretive gaze has developed an instinct for the capillary, limiting information about the statute's original context, Congress. Statutory interpretation has moved farther and farther away from a method starting with the general purpose of a statute. For decades, purposivism was the dominant mode of analysis. Contrary to textualism, which can find itself mired in the petty word or two, purposivism sees a statute at a more general level. It ascribes a reasonable plan on the theory that a statute is not simply a collection of words but a a form of speech aiming to achieve an end—an action in the real world. But purposivism has been under steady attack for years and is in retreat (largely because of objections to legislative evidence this book aims to counter).

Focalism's lesson is that one must resist stopping at a single bit of information—a word or a phrase, let us say—stamping it as plain and ending the analysis. One must look for *disconfirming* information, information that may falsify one's initial impression of "plainness." This should certainly be true for those who aim to consider the whole text, not simply bits and pieces. But even looking at the whole text can sometimes deceive. Legislative evidence can be powerful disconfirming information. Consider the English case *Pepper v. Hart.*[73] Judges looking at a tax law saw it as "plain," against the taxpayer, because they read the words *cost* and *benefit* as plain, without regard to their larger context. But once the Lords looked at the legislative evidence, the British version of our Congressional Record, they found that the ministry had adopted precisely the opposite view of those terms and that the taxpayer should win the case. The Lords were worried enough about making such a blatant error that they made a drastic change in practice, eliminating a centuries-old rule demanding that they blind themselves to legislative evidence. Implicitly at least, the Lords appear to have recognized that looking at alternate sources of meaning hedged against focalism and cognitive bias.

Pepper v. Hart is far from the only case demonstrating focal errors—the failure to look at relevant and sometimes controlling legislative evidence. Consider the cases we looked at in Chapter 3. In *TVA v. Hill*, the snail darter case, the court and the lawyers focused so much on the environmental statute that they missed a controlling appropriations law with language aimed at resolving the controversy.[74] In *United Steelworkers v. Weber*, the court focused on the deeply ambiguous term *discrimination*, even though there was a more specific provision on quotas, section 703(j), that spoke to the issue and was necessary to the bill's passage.[75] In *Griggs v. Duke Power*, the appellate court failed to trace changes in the statute's text and relied upon legislative statements about a failed amendment.[76] In the timing case, *Amalgamated Transit Union Local 1309 v. Laidlaw Transit Servs., Inc.*, the court of appeals wasted ink on the term "less," an obvious drafting error, resolved easily by recourse to the legislative debate.[77]

If lawyers frame a statutory interpretation problem narrowly on particular words because they are taught that isolating and decontextualizing creates "plain" meanings—and that any other evidence is irrelevant—they invite error. Judges will make the wrong decisions, even as they insist that their method is correct precisely because it focuses! This helps to explain the empirical evidence gathered by Professor Eskridge that a narrow textualism rejecting legislative evidence has increased the statistical likelihood of congressional overrides—Congress's signal to the court that it has made an obvious and important error.[78] The cynical might say that the whole point of petty textualism is to prevent legislation. In a world of legislative complexity, errors and inconsistencies abound, prime fodder for those who would stall the legislative process based on a misplaced preposition. Returning statutes to Congress to fix their grammar not only invites costly litigation about petty claims, but it can destroy a law whose voting coalition no longer exists.

The Canons and Focalism

When most judges and I went to law school, we never learned about interpretive canons, since we were taught that canons led to no determinate result, and the canons had been demolished as tools of construction by a powerful article written by Karl Llewellyn in the 1950s.[79] In that article, Llewellyn attempted to show that, for every canon, there is a counter-canon. So, even though ancient texts said that statutes should not be interpreted in derogation of the common law, they said the opposite as well—that statutes should be interpreted liberally. Canons were make-weights: as Judge Richard Posner has argued, "There is no canon for ranking or choosing between canons; the code lacks a key."[80] Since the 1990s, however, courts have become increasingly enamored with canons; as petty textualism has arisen, so too have canons, as a way to resolve the ambiguities or vagueness of particular statutory terms.

There is no necessary or logical relationship between "petty textualism" and canons. One can, in theory, be a textualist or a purposivist willing to view the whole text with or without canons. In his recent primer on interpretive practice, Professor Eskridge makes the case that canons are a distinct common law interpretive regime.[81] There is a *historical connection*, however, between anti-pluralism, petty textualism, and canon fever. As textualism has become more and more dominant in the courts, more and more intensely focused on bits of text, so too have judicial interpreters become more insistent on applying canons of construction and blinding themselves to legislative evidence. At a high level of generality, the fight is between those who see democratic legitimacy in bits of text, and those who see democratic legitimacy in public debate. At a more prosaic level, it is between those who would make of law the strange latinate practices of the elite bar, and those who make of law respect for the work of members of a representative democracy who are never elected for their linguistic precision, but for their results.

The canon debate matters because it is the claimed alternative to actual evidence of legislative context. Although textualists insist that they look at "context," the use of canons calls this into question. Canons are judicially created rules largely unknown to Congress, much less the ordinary person. Some, like Professor Geoffrey Miller, have argued that canons are basic conversational principles that everyone uses. But Congress, as I have argued, in its debates, is not engaged in conversation; they are engaged in electoral battle. Professor Amy Barrett has argued that the canons can often be justified in terms of constitutional law, the judicial power used to promote judicial values when those values are contravened by legislation. I have no qualms about such a claim, but it is not an interpretive claim; it is a constitutional claim. If the Constitution requires canons as part of a larger enterprise seeking convergent meaning, so be it. The problem I am addressing here is whether to use canons—judicially created presumptions of meaning—as a replacement for actual evidence of legislative context. As measured against that test, canons should fail as an experiment in imagined meaning.

Consider a recent case before the Supreme Court, *Yates v. United States*, a case that seems quite silly, in which the Supreme Court addressed whether the destruction of a *fish* was a crime under a complex financial fraud law, Sarbanes-Oxley (SOX). "John Yates, a commercial fisherman, caught undersized red grouper in federal waters in the Gulf of Mexico. To prevent federal authorities from confirming that he had harvested undersized fish, Yates ordered a crew member to toss the suspect catch into the sea."[82] Yates was properly convicted under a different statute and sentenced to a month in prison, but he was also convicted under SOX's 18 U.S.C. 1519 which could have yielded him a 20-year jail term. Section 1519 of SOX provided that no covered person should destroy a "document, record, or tangible object" to obstruct an investigation. The government took the position of the petty textualist, urging that "tangible object" under section 1519 meant tangible object, including fish. If we focus only on the statutory term *tangible object,* of course, we will pay no attention to the fact that the textual context, and purpose, of the statute was to eliminate *financial fraud* and that there was no financial fraud at issue in the destruction of *the fish*. To any person on the street, this should have been an easy, even laughable, case; one has to wonder why the prosecutor felt compelled to bring such a charge, why the Justice Department wasted its limited resources on such a case, and why the Court took it at all.[83]

The Court not only took the case, but its warring opinions resolved the linguistic issue with large doses of canon fire. The plurality opinion, written by Justice Ginsburg, framed the issue in purposive terms, noting the entirely common-sense notion that the statute was aimed at financial fraud, and citing a Senate report to support its claim that the statute was a "document-shredding" statute. These were but brief notes, however, in a lengthy discussion of "traditional tools of statutory construction"—namely, canons from the rule against surplusage to *noscitur a sociis,* from *ejusdem generis* to "the rule against lenity," all of which led the Court to conclude that fish were out of the picture.[84] Justice Alito concurred in the result, writing his own opinion invoking *noscitur a sociis* and *ejusdem generis,* with much emphasis on the verbs and nouns in the statute.[85] Justice Kagan, writing for the dissent, adopted the government's textualist argument, with its expansivist "any" object reading, finding the term "tangible object" entirely plain, citing Dr. Seuss's *One Fish Two Fish Red Fish Blue Fish* and rejecting the canons invoked by Justices Ginsburg and Alito. As she explained: "This case raises the question whether the term "tangible object" means the same thing in § 1519 as it means in everyday language—*any* object capable of being touched. The answer should be easy: Yes. The term "tangible object" is broad, but clear." [86]

Yates is a text-book analysis of how canons can be used to support diametrically different meanings, as the plurality, concurring, and dissenting opinions each relied upon canons for their position. This is not surprising since even prominent language canons have a logical affinity with their opposites. *Ejusdem generis* and *noscitur a sociis* involve reading a string of words as consistent with a general concept. By moving up a level of generality, however, one necessarily devalues the meaning of particular terms in the statute, and as a result, these canons provoke predictable counter-canon attacks. The savvy canon aficionado will recognize that whenever *ejusdem generis* and *noscitur a sociis* are deployed, it is possible to predict that the use of that canon in effect "reads out of the statute" its more particular terms, invoking the canon against surplusage (that each and every word of a statute should have meaning), or the canon on meaningful variation (that different words in a statute mean different things). So, for example, in *Yates*, by reading tangible object as something like a document, as did the plurality opinion, the interpreter seems to either read out the term "tangible object" or gives it less of a meaningful variation. This canon-counter-canon duel is as predictable as its failure to avoid focal bias.

Notice that while interpreters focus on the canon battle, they pay less attention to the whole text. The government's argument in *Yates* engaged in the "petty textualist" dissection of text, emphasizing the term "any . . . tangible object." This leads to an enrichment of the statutory meaning of "tangible object" as absolutist and expansive. The full text of the statute provides something more narrow. It reads: "Whoever knowingly alters, destroys, mutilates, conceals, covers up, falsifies, *or makes a false entry in* any record, document, or tangible object" may be charged with an offense. As Justice Ginsburg rightly asked, can one really make a "false entry in" a fish? The point is that the government's textual argument is partial. Like the arguments we saw in *King v. Burwell* and other "new textualist" opinions, the government's focus on an abbreviated text assumes the argument it is trying to prove: that the Congress passed a general spoliation of evidence statute. Nothing in the canons, however, leads the dissent to recognize this move, for canons typically lead to counter-canon responses.

The more one focuses on canons, the less one focuses on the *legislative context*. In *Yates*, the legislative evidence disconfirms the dissent's notion that there was only one possible meaning to "tangible object," or that focusing on that term could describe the statutory issue Congress was addressing. The cognitive bias literature tells the judge to consult information from "other parties" (here, Congress) to de-bias her first, gut impression—the apparent plain meaning. As Representative Oxley, the House author of the legislation, told the Court in his amicus brief, Congress was concerned with prototypical examples of financial fraud prominent at the time—section 1519 was an anti-shredding statute, not an anti-fishing statute.[87]

The Oxley amicus brief in *Yates* explains Congress's process in passing the law. The government was hoping, and the dissent would have held, that in SOX, the Justice Department had obtained a general anti-obstruction statute, with a penalty of up to 20 years, that could be applied to every large or small federal crime, from murder to check-kiting. The Oxley brief explained why the government's (and the dissent's) argument was wrong, misreading what Congress had done in contemporary fraud statutes generally and in Sarbanes-Oxley more particularly. There are some ancient general fraud statutes (mail fraud, wire fraud), but in recent years, consistent with committee-centered legislative expertise, and to avoid over-broad applications and unintended consequences of the criminal law, Congress has legislated against specific kinds of fraud, passing laws for health care fraud, securities fraud, and computer fraud. Consistent with that trend, section 1519 was a fraud statute for accountants and lawyers (the target of SOX), not fishermen.[88]

Focusing narrowly on the term "tangible object" and even adding a linguistic canon or two, cannot explain the real interpretive problem with the statute. The Justice Department had argued for some time that the Supreme Court had made its job more difficult by interpreting a different statute, the anti-tampering statute, section 1512, too narrowly in obstruction of justice cases. They also argued that the existing laws on obstruction of justice were a mess. They wanted a general federal obstruction of justice statute. In their *Yates* brief, the government claimed section 1519, the shredding statute, was their long-sought anti-obstruction law. Representative Oxley explained that there were good reasons why Congress did not want to pass a general obstruction statute since such a statute could reach very broadly—throw away a piece of paper with intent to obstruct, and significant jail time (20 years under the section 1519) could result. Rather than giving the government a large new statute, the Congress reversed the narrowing Supreme Court rulings with respect to the anti-tampering statute, section 1512 (in a Senate amendment offered by Senator Lott) and created a new anti-shredding law for financial accountants and attorneys, in section 1519, coupled with a financial record preservation act in section 1520 (in a Senate amendment offered by Senator Leahy). On the day the conference report was passed, after the House had accepted these provisions of the Senate bill, the Democratic chairman of the Senate Judiciary Committee and author of section 1519, Senator Leahy, explained that his amendment "close[d] loopholes and toughen[ed] penalties for shredded documents as we learned had occurred at Arthur Andersen."[89] His fellow Senators, Republicans Hatch and Lott agreed[90]: section 1519 was described as a document-shredding provision, not a general anti-obstruction statute. None of the Supreme Court opinions, however, seemed to find this bipartisan agreement on the meaning of the statute relevant, preferring to selectively cite a committee report, by a divided committee, written before there was any attempt to incorporate section 1519 or 1520 into the general SOX legislation.[91]

This analysis requires the interpreter to understand a broader history of obstruction of justice along with two statutes, one on witness tampering and the other on financial fraud—which is the hard work of statutory interpretation. One never even gets to these questions, if one focuses exclusively on the term "tangible object," as did the dissent. Invoking canons, as we have seen, does not do much better. Mucking about with *noscitur a sociis* and *ejusdem generis* confirms the plurality's few sentences on common sense purpose analysis—this was a shredding statute—but invocation of the canons leads to predictable counter-canon responses. In dissent, Justice Kagan found the same canons led to the notion that the statute was a general obstruction of justice law.[92] This obscures rather than illuminates the real statutory issue: did Congress pass a general anti-obstruction law in section 1519, section 1512, or no general obstruction statute at all? Neither petty textualism nor canons can answer that question;

the only way to answer the question is to look to the best evidence of Congress's actions—the legislative evidence of how section 1519 became law, the debates on the Leahy amendment, and statements on the conference report.

Focal bias is not the problem of a few semantic canons. As Professor Eskridge writes, "Most canons are neither linguistic nor extrinsic source rules but are *substantive* in nature."[93] Although new empirical evidence by Professor Krishnakumar suggests that the Roberts Court has infrequently invoked substantive canons, and they have not played an "outcome-determinative" role, the potential reach of such canons is vast.[94] As Professor Barrett has shown, the canons have an ancient pedigree, including canons for federalism, preemption, and avoiding constitutional questions, as well as canons for sovereign immunity, extraterritorial effect, and retroactive application. There are canons against derogation of the presidents' traditional powers and for Native American tribal immunity; Congress is assumed to pass laws that do not violate treaties or approve federal regulations that intrude on state responsibilities.[95] Such canons operate as substantive default rules, rules that tell courts to weigh ambiguity against particular policy outcomes. They differ in kind from the "linguistic canons" which focus judges on words, phrases, and commas. The argument I am making here says nothing about the wisdom of these default rules as a judicial common law regime, as a method for coordinating courts where there is no legislative evidence, or whether they are consistent with basic democratic principles.

My concern is that substantive, like grammar, canons may exacerbate focal effects and/or petty textualism. If one has committed a focusing error at the start, one may look to substantive canons that are irrelevant or unnecessary. Reconsider the *Public Citizen* case, from Chapter 3, involving the question of how to apply a statute that made a public "advisory committee" of any two persons consulted by the president. The Court focused on the term *utilized* and concluded that Congress had lost its mind, and the statute was absurd;[96] as I jokingly describe it, the term "advisory committee" appeared so broad it might cover a meeting of the president with his children. In fact, there was a fairly easy explanation for the added term that did not involve the assumption that Congress was daffy: *utilize* came in at conference, and under conference committee rules, no member, once it reached the floor, would have interpreted it to make a major change in the statute. A reasonable member of Congress was likely to see it as irrelevant, not absurd. More important for our purposes here, however, Justice Brennan supported his reasoning by use of a substantive canon—avoiding constitutional questions; Justice Kennedy, in concurrence, went further and decided the law was unconstitutional as applied.[97] The substantive canon, not to mention the constitutional judgment, was unnecessary; indeed, it was only made necessary by focusing on the word *utilize*.

Neither substantive nor semantic canons can achieve the third-party perspective legislative evidence offers; in fact, substantive canons may run directly contrary to how Congress looks at the matter. Substantive canons are policy choices that may have no relationship to how Congress legislates, as Professors Gluck and Bressman have shown.[98] As we saw above, in the negotiating scenarios, understanding the "rules of the game"—from the perspective of the other party (here Congress)—is a promising de-biasing strategy. Canons cannot provide that perspective. Consider the infamous snail darter case, *TVA v. Hill*,[99] where the Court had a conflict of two laws and focused on one—the environmental law—protecting the little fish, and not the appropriations laws, which protected the dam. Chief Justice Burger stopped a dam project that had cost hundreds of millions of dollars and had been ongoing for years—a project started before the endangered species law had even been enacted. In *TVA*, a substantive canon was used exacerbating the majority's focus on one law rather than reconciling two laws—or even finding the real law. The majority emphasized the text of the Endangered Species Act (ESA), rejecting evidence that Congress continued to fund the dam in appropriations laws passed long after the ESA became law and long after Congress knew of the snail darter issue. The Supreme Court supported its focus with a substantive canon advising against "repeals by implication,"[100] on the theory that appropriations laws were somehow imperfect expressions of democratic decisions (something no one in Congress would ever think; appropriations are the most, not the least, important laws). The canon, however, was deeply misleading about the actual statutory record. The Court failed to cite the text of a 1977 statute that Congress passed to resolve the matter: that harmonized the ESA and the dam, protecting the snail darter (it thrived once relocated), and appropriate money to continue dam construction. The text of the 1977 appropriations bill for TVA provided "$2,000,000 to relocate endangered or threatened species to other suitable habitats *as may be necessary to expedite project construction.*"[101] This statute was an express resolution of the matter that the Supreme Court ignored, replacing democratically legitimate text supporting the dam and the darter with judicially created canons that supported only the darter.

Critics might argue that there is an inconsistency between legislative decision theory's emphasis on a targeted procedural analysis and my critique of an excessively focused textualism. Equating petty textualism with legislative decision theory because they both "focus" confuses a process that intensifies bias with its opposite: a de-biasing regime. *In one case, the interpreter seeks out more and better information; in the other, relevant information is banished from view.* Focusing errors occur when one refuses to look at other information; there is nothing in legislative decision theory that demands one blind oneself to the whole legislative record if necessary to determine legislative context. In fact, the claims operate from entirely different, even opposed, baselines. In civil procedure, no one confuses the basic elements of the process—motion to dismiss, summary judgment, and jury instructions—with isolating a particular word in a jury instruction. Considering legislative evidence as subject to a general rule sequence is a far cry from focusing on a single word in a statute. To be sure, focusing errors might be made in reviewing legislative evidence if one takes a "petty textualist" view and applies that in one's search for legislative evidence (just as such an approach can intensify bias if applied to canons). For example, in the *Yates* case, if the interpreter limited a search for legislative evidence to the term "tangible object," the legislative evidence would be polluted by the petty textualist method. In any event, it would yield a null set, since this term was not part of the debate on the amendment yielding section 1519, at issue in *Yates*, senators typically referring to the law as an "anti-shredding" statute. [102]

Canon-enthusiasts claim that looking to canons clarifies or confirms plain meaning, thus providing all the restraint necessary for the statutory interpreter, without recourse to the de-biasing effects of legislative evidence. There are reasons to worry about that claim. First, since canons add text, their method seems to run contrary to, rather than in favor of, plain textual readings. Second, since even the Latin, linguistic canons yield counter-canons, there is no assurance that the canons will in fact create a single plain meaning. Third, canons cannot cure the problem of a judge who simply finds meaning "plain," end of story, and never looks to the canons. Finally, even if the canons could be a source of "restraint" as their advocates insist, or a wise guide to ordinary meaning, they do not pull the judge out of her frame of reference sufficiently to operate as a de-biasing procedure; canons are judge-made law and are likely to reinforce judicial bias toward judicial, rather than popular or ordinary meanings. Some canons are simply common sense propositions and I have no objection to using common sense, or grammar, to find prototypical meaning,[103] confirmed by real evidence of legislative meaning. I do have an objection to using canons as a substitute for democracy.

Conclusion

As my colleague Professor Jonathan Molot once wrote, "We are all textualists in an important sense."[104] Justice Scalia was at the forefront of the movement emphasizing the power of the text. This virtue comes with vices, however. Text alone has never been enough without context. Scalia and Garner's *Reading Law* argues that the context to be supplied is the context of judicial canons, not legislative evidence, and that these canons can yield "right answers."[105] This optimism is likely to be wrong on two counts: first, the choice of canons is parasitic on the choice of text, and canons applied to the wrong text, or a wrongly isolated text, may do nothing to cure that error; second, empirical evidence of human cognitive bias supports the likelihood that judges and lawyers jump to hasty conclusions about plain meanings and are likely to do so unconsciously unless they reach out to look at legislative evidence. It is the great ambition of the judiciary to be the author of reason in a system otherwise tempted by emotion and ill humors. If judges aim to be the true authors of that reason, they must reject petty textualism and refuse to honor canons as the only evidence of meaning interpreters may consult.

5

What Is Legislative Intent? Evidence of Context

"Intent is unfortunately a confusing word."

DEAN LANDIS[1]

IF LEGISLATIVE DECISION theory is to persuade lawyers and judges to look to legislative evidence, it must grapple with those who object that legislative evidence depends upon a fantasy called "legislative intent."

For centuries, interpreters have invoked the idea of "legislative intent" to resolve difficult statutory questions. Legislative intent is, however, the most confusing idea in all statutory interpretation theory.[2] Textualists reject the idea, arguing that "we are governed by laws, not by the *intention* of legislators."[3] Purposivists embrace the seemingly equivalent term *purpose*, even if its semantic connotations appear as unfortunately full of putatively imaginary spirits.

In this chapter, I argue that to look to legislative evidence is not to look for intent, but legislative context. It turns out that many of the simple objections to legislative intent are a form of cheap intent skepticism. The search for legislative evidence is just that, a search for evidence, not some ghostly spirit. To paraphrase scientist Alan Turing, the question whether computers think is beside the point; machines do not have minds, nor does Congress—the only important question is "how" they decide.[4] So, too, the question here is not whether Congress has a mind but how it decides and what it means by its decision. No person thinks in zeros and ones, but computers do. Similarly, congressional rules of proceeding amount to a contextual code essential to understand public legislative evidence.

When Congress fails to make its meanings clear, when its textual signals are hopelessly garbled, courts must look to legislative evidence. By legislative evidence, I mean public evidence of context. The context may be small and precise—like the meaning of words in a conference report—or large and consequential—like the filibuster of civil rights legislation. What is important is that one is relying on *evidence* of legislative action and understanding that evidence within a basic understanding of Congress 101, rather than imagining mental states.

Those who refuse to look at legislative evidence (textualists) or who look at it without understanding the legislative context (textualists and purposivists) risk errors. Indeed, the normative price we pay when any interpreter fails to look at context can be high indeed. Rule context is crucial to understand statutory context. If I say "I divorce you" in a cocktail party, no one would think that my statement "I divorce you" would effectuate a legal divorce. As the philosopher John Austin explained, the performative utterance will be "unsatisfactory . . . if certain rules, transparently simple rules, are broken."[5] For example, an opera singer could utter the words of a statute at an opera, and no one would think it was an actual command to the audience. For a statute to be a statute—a valid command—it must be consistent with the procedures by which the people consent to be governed. So, too, as we will see, crediting legislative evidence as the act of Congress, must be consistent with the groups' understanding of legislative context under the rules of Congress's proceedings.

The Metaphysical Objection to Legislative Intention

Intention blankets life and law. Philosophers have debated the question for centuries.[6] So, too, have linguists and literary theorists and intellectual historians.[7] More recently, psychologists and social psychologists have entered the fray, showing that the youngest of children attribute intention to others.[8] Humans are particularly adept at reading others' "minds."[9] If this is correct, we must believe that something "real" is going on when we are searching for intent, but the question remains what that search should entail.

The finest minds have struggled with the question of "legislative intent." Few believe that statutes appear by accident. Votes are not delivered at the point of a gun. Yet, beyond this minimal sense of intentional-as-not-accidental, opinions about legislative intent diverge rather widely. Critics have urged that Congress cannot have an intent because, by logic, groups do not have a mind; "intent" is inherently individual and subjective. In this chapter, I call this the "metaphysical claim." I argue that this claim asks the wrong question. My argument does not reject the notion of intent. Instead, I redefine it as a search for public legislative context.

The Critique

Law professors have been arguing about "legislative intent" since the 1930s. At the time, Professor Max Radin, a left-legal critic, claimed that a group legislature has no intent precisely because of its collective character: "the intention of the legislature is undiscoverable in any real sense. . . . The chances that of several hundred men each will have exactly the same determinate situations in mind . . . are infinitesimally small."[10] Radin's critique has become a classic in statutory interpretation theory. But it is not an outdated objection; in 2014, Professor John Manning repeated it in the *Harvard Law Review*.[11]

The two most prominent theories of statutory interpretation—textualism and purposivism—depend upon the fallout of Radinesque skepticism. In the 1980s and 1990s, Justice Scalia launched "textualism" on a warship aiming to destroy the idea of "legislative intent." There being no collective intent, he argued that text alone should govern.[12] Like textualism, "purposivism" emerged from a struggle with "legislative intent." After World War II, and Hitler's rise, legal academics worried that skeptical positions could lead to lawlessness. In the Hart and Sacks materials, legal process theorists chose the term *purpose* to replace *intent* on the theory that judges' job was to impose, as much as to find, a reasonable statutory purpose, hoping to avoid Radin's skeptical claims.[13]

Despite the ancient pedigree of "legislative intent," reaching back to Blackstone and earlier,[14] textualists seem happy to jettison hundreds of years of history on the theory that "group intent" provides an insuperable *metaphysical difficulty*. For purposivists, the metaphysical difficulty prompted a shift from intent to purpose. The only problem is that the same critique appears to apply there.[15] If there is no collective intent, how can there be a collective purpose? If intent is inherently subjective, is purpose any less subjective, particularly when there are multiple purposes? Does the subjectivity of purpose simply disappear when it is a "reasonable purpose" attributed by a judge to a statute? If we state purpose at a high enough level of generality, is not the purpose of every law to gain justice?[16]

Over time, this puzzle has not disappeared; it has gained prestige. The greats of modern jurisprudence and political science have embraced or grappled with the metaphysical objection. The legal philosopher Ronald Dworkin recapped the argument, calling it the "speakers' meaning" view,[17] worrying deeply about how individual meanings might be collectively joined.[18] Dworkin's successor, Professor Jeremy Waldron, struggled with this problem in more sophisticated fashion. His principal target was constitutional interpretation, but in a long chapter on lawmaking and democracy, he repeated Radin's claims about collectivity as inconsistent with intent.[19] Finally, the great political scientist Kenneth Shepsle gave positive political theory's imprimatur to the "group-intent objection" with the very title of his paper, "Congress Is a 'They,' Not an 'It.' "[20]

Problems with the Critique

The metaphysical critique against legislative intent deserves to be unwound. Let us separate two claims. The first is that intent is inherently subjective and internal—inside someone's mind—and therefore that it cannot be a reliable basis for statutory interpretation. The second claim is that intent is logically impossible because groups cannot have intent—there is no "single mental state" of all members. The problem with these claims, as we will see, is the assumption that intent requires a mental state.

The Subjectivity Objection

Legislative evidence is neither internal nor private. To the extent subjectivity suggests the "internal," it does not apply to the Congressional Record, committee reports, or C-SPAN, all of which can be touched, felt in book form, or googled. Perhaps, of course, "subjectivity" stands in for something else; it is a capacious term of legal opprobrium. Critics may believe legislative history subjective because it reflects the comments of a few, not the entire body. Or perhaps they mean that it is subjective because it is revisable; unlike a law, legislative evidence may change over time. Or perhaps critics believe that legislative history is subjective because it is written by those delegated the task, staffers. If these claims are correct, then the implicit argument is that *subjectivity* means partial, delegated, and revisable.

Now conduct a thought experiment and use these same meanings of *subjectivity* and apply them to Supreme Court decisions. If I apply the standards above, then Supreme Court opinions become just as subjective as legislative evidence. Such decisions are not necessarily the act of the whole group; no one claims that closely divided Supreme Court decisions are not "decisions." Even the hundreds of plurality opinions—opinions where there is no majority—are still considered "decisions."[21] Clerks often draft opinions, and the justices assign opinion-writing to individual members, violating the anti-delegation idea associated with subjectivity. Supreme Court cases appear final in theory, but they really are not; they may be overruled by the Court or overridden by Congress in statutory cases. Yet no one says because Supreme Court decisions are partial, delegated, and revisable, that those decisions are subjective.

It should seem stranger than it does to talk of legislative intents rather than legislative *decisions*. We write easily of Supreme Court opinions as "decisions." That the Supreme Court may change its "mind" (that the Court may overturn its own precedent) does not prevent us from calling its work "a decision." That a Supreme Court decision is partial (e.g., the Court may divide 5–4 or even yield more complex plurality and subplurality opinions) does not prevent us from calling its work "a decision." That Supreme Court justices delegate drafting to their clerks does not prevent us from calling the resulting opinion "a decision." That Congress may override a judicial decision in a statutory case does not mean that it is not a "decision."

It should also seem stranger that Supreme Court decisions are not typically associated with the term *intent.* Lawyers often look behind the meaning of a majority opinion to other opinions to find the central agreed-upon doctrine. In fact, we quickly resort to procedural context to determine meaning when Supreme Court decisions are unclear. So, for example, if a concurring fifth opinion is more persuasive, the opinion of a single justice may become the functional opinion of the Court's majority.[22] That we do not look to the memos of individual clerks reflects the "rules of the judicial game": these are not public documents. Indeed, if earlier chapters have failed to convince that rules are central to contextual meaning, then one need only consider the meaning of a Supreme Court opinion if 8 or 9 votes were required for precedential value. Change the rules of majority voting in the Supreme Court, and you change the meaning of a decision.

If this analysis is correct, there is nothing inherently "subjective" about legislative intent—where *subjectivity* is defined as the partial, the delegated, or the reversible. The semantic equation of "intent" with individual minds has led us astray. We should recognize that *intent* is *often a substitute for a felt-uncertainty of meaning.* Faced with such a situation, we just as easily find ourselves looking for judicial "intent" as for "legislative" intent. Faced with plurality Supreme Court opinions (opinions for which there is no majority opinion), lower court judges must try to find the meaning of the opinion, defined as the "narrowest" possible meaning held by a majority of justices. In some cases, the quandary is made more difficult because concurring and dissenting opinions yield a "cross-cutting" majority, requiring the reader to graph the opinion's parts and subparts to find what we can colloquially call a collective "intent."[23] Whether it is legislative, or judicial, evidence, we search for intent when the rules for communication have failed or the signals are mixed. Any "solution" to the puzzle of intent must then depend upon finding a way to resolve that uncertainty. But before we get there, we must answer the second objection—whether "groups" have intent.

The Collectivity Objection

Is it oxymoronic to search for the legislative intent of a group? For some time now, scholars in jurisprudence, statutory interpretation, and political economy have questioned whether groups such as Congress can possess a collective intent. Philosophers Jeremy Waldron and before him Ronald Dworkin[24] have wrestled with this question, as have Professors Joseph Raz and John Gardner.[25] The result has been a persistent, decades-old skepticism about group intent. Only very recently have contrary voices appeared. Legal philosopher John Ekins defends intent against standard claims.[26] Similarly, philosopher Philip Pettit and political economist Christian List have weighed in against the "group intent" objection, urging that this question is really rather more important than it might seem: to reject a group intent because of the group is to make a rather extravagant claim indicting the ability of vast numbers of social organizations—from Microsoft to Harvard to the Catholic Church—to act as group agents.[27]

If the question of "group *intent*" is contested, very few doubt that groups *act.* When a corporation issues a report or Congress passes a statute, it acts. Acts differ from intents, meanings, and beliefs because they are *observable and do not exist solely in one or more minds.* Putting on one's shoes is different from thinking about putting on one's shoes and telling someone else that you are about to put on your shoes. That an act may take the form of speech or words does not deny it the status of an act as distinct from a mere mental state.[28] An act that the group would recognize as a group action (i.e., authorized by the group or part of that group's organization or procedure) is an exercise of group agency.[29]

If this is correct, then the group intent puzzle becomes how to reconcile the notion of group action with controversies about group intent. To do that, we must think a bit harder about what we mean by intent. Here, I consider three ideal types—mental intent, communicative intent, and pragmatic intent.

MENTAL INTENT—INFERENCE FROM MIND

When lawyers seek "legislative intent," they sometimes mean that they are looking to "reconstruct" the mental state of the members who would have voted on a bill.[30] They are talking of intent as "mental state." In fact, this view of intent is neither necessary nor sufficient to explain the concept. Intent does not require, as a number of philosophers have shown, an "occurrent" mental state or mental picture. One may simply act. Lawyers know this: in arguing about mental states like intent in the criminal law, they do not expect to discover a picture of the brain but to infer intent from action or behavior. Unfortunately, in the field of statutory interpretation, the general view holds to the notion that there is a separate "mental event" associated with the creation of statutory text. This view of intent is unnecessary, and one I reject.

COMMUNICATIVE INTENT—INFERENCE FROM SPEECH

Intent-as-communication is a staple of standard versions of statutory interpretation theory.[31] Dworkin explained this notion (one he disavowed)[32] as the "speaker's meaning" view. This view "assumes that legislation is an occasion or instance of communication." The "ruling model of this theory is the familiar model of ordinary speech."[33] In ordinary speech, as linguists, literary theorists, and others have shown, it is common sense to hold that statements are made with the purpose to communicate. As Stanley Fish, one of the most zealous interpretive defenders of intent-as-communication, explains, "interpretation always and necessarily involves the specification of intention."[34]

Under the idea of intent as "communication," "everyone who is an interpreter," including statutory analysts, is in "the intention business."[35] This view is distinct from the mental state approach because it requires the conveyance of meaning: one can have a mental state (for example, a secret wish) and yet never communicate that internal state to another.[36] This view of intent thus raises the potential for a mistaken attribution of intention, faulty communication of that intention, as well as improper uptake on the part of the listener.[37] This view of communication-as-intent is not sufficient for it fails to grapple with the notion of action and context, as we will see below.

PRAGMATIC INTENT—INFERENCE FROM ACTION

Pragmatic intent focuses on action. Philosophical pragmatism takes the view that one cannot know one's ends without acting to achieve those ends. Intent under such an inference contemplates "present and future *conduct.*"[38] Because pragmatic intent focuses on action, *it does not require a mental state or a communication*; for that reason it emphasizes and *requires* an understanding of context from which to infer meaning.

Contrary to the "snapshot picture"—frozen in time—of mind or communication, under a pragmatic idea of intent, intents may *change over time* as new and relevant information becomes available.[39] Perhaps most importantly, pragmatic intent is not limited to a single individual at a moment in time.[40] It contemplates acting with more than one person over time, specifically allowing for "we-intentions."[41] So, for example, two people can act to tie each other's shoes (in the absence of a joint mental state or a shared agreement). As long as they act to tie each other's shoes, it does not matter whether they had a mental picture contemplating such action or an overt communicative agreement to tie each other's shoes. Pragmatic intent thus lays the groundwork for the claim that group actions reflect a vision of intent that does not require mental state or even overt communication—simply joint action.

Context is important to all forms of intent I have noted but, in the case of pragmatic intent, context is *not optional.* One can think of mental pictures without thinking of the context bringing forth those pictures; one can also think of communicated statements like "take the fifth" without adding context. Adding context helps to understand each of these, which is why philosophers of language typically require context. In the case of pragmatic action, however, we have moved beyond the idea of mental pictures or statements to actions and decisions as core evidence of intent.

Since action is the key, there may be no statements or putative mental states from which to make inferences. For example, consider two people silently playing chess. One cannot understand their collective action without knowing the background context—the rules of chess or the significance of the checkered board. It is not enough that we know the players' mental state or even that they have agreed to play chess if they are playing checkers. In sum, if one can infer intent from action, then it is neither necessary nor sufficient to understand intent either as a state of mind or communication. Action-in-context yields the necessary information to determine meaning.

Radin's Error: Intent as State of Mind

Armed with these ideas of intent, we can return to Professor Radin's realist objection and see that it depends upon assumptions about intent that beg the question he seeks to answer. Radin wrote that "the intention of the legislature is undiscoverable in any real sense. . . ." "The chances that of several hundred men each will have exactly the same determinate situations in mind . . . are infinitesimally small."[42] Radin's claims raise three concerns: unanimity, stasis, and delegation.

The unanimity problem: Radin wants "exactly the same" intents "in mind,"[43] minds that are "uniform," several hundred men with "the same . . . situations in mind."[44] But no one believes that collective entities, whether corporations or universities, only act when everyone shares a unanimous intention or set of factual assumptions.[45] Like Congress, faculties and corporations and churches make decisions all the time in the face of disagreement. We do not hold corporations to account only when all members sign a letter agreeing to the decision. Perhaps more importantly, no one believes that majoritarian decisions are impossible or illegitimate because a majority does not include everyone. Majoritarianism presumes disagreement.[46]

The stasis objection: The second implausible assumption implies the static nature of group agency. The "same intent" objection suggests that representatives share the same intent at the same time. Congress, faculties, unions, and churches make decisions *over time*, not instantaneously.[47] No one says a corporation or university or labor union has not made a decision because of the time it takes to make that decision. Perhaps most importantly, we know that Congress makes decisions through procedures over time.[48] As Professor Waldron has rightly emphasized, these procedures are Congress's "constitution."[49]

The delegation objection: Finally, Professor Radin suggests that there can be no group agency because only a few members draft legislation: a "legislature certainly has no intention whatever in connection with words which some two or three men drafted."[50] Radin is correct that participation in legislating tends to be concentrated on a few who stake their political futures on the difficult course of bill passage.[51] But the few who draft a bill cannot pass it. Senators who write for 2 or 3 people, as opposed to 60,[52] are engaged in a fool's errand.[53] They must anticipate the votes of a supermajority. If drafting is the work of the few, legislating is the work of the many (and, under supermajoritarism, the "super-many").

Ultimately, the claim that a few write the law[54] goes too far: it applies to all collective action. Like Congress, corporations and unions and universities delegate decision making to smaller groups to reduce the transactions costs of decision making. Delegation is considered proper corporate management.[55] If delegation is to be denied, or decried as improper, throughout our society, then Professor Radin's argument is a form of what Professors Pettit and List call "eliminativism,"[56] which is to say all collective bodies and their actions are potentially illegitimate-because-partial. The Radin critic must ask why it is that something that happens every day in corporate America somehow indicts Congress.

The mental state error: The most important point to see about Professor Radin's argument, however, is the idea of intent on which it relies—an individual mental event. Radin writes of "situations *in mind*" and "pictures *in mind*."[57] He muses that legislators have "different ideas and beliefs," specifically equating this with a mental event:

> The chances that of several hundred men each will have exactly the same determinate situations *in mind* . . . are infinitesimally small. The chance is still smaller that . . . the litigated issue, will not only be *within the minds* of all these men but will be certain to be selected by all of them as the present limit to which the determinable should be narrowed.[58]

Lest one think Professor Radin not committed to the idea of intent-as-mental-state, consider his argument that, in an extreme case, "it might be that we could learn all that was *in the mind of the* draftsman." Or his argument that "even if the contents of *the minds* of the legislature were uniform, we have no means of knowing that content except by the external utterances or behavior of these hundreds of men."[59] Given this idea of individual intent, Radin *must be a group skeptic:* if intent lies within the private world of individuals' minds, then it is impossible to conclude that groups have intent. Radin's argument is a self-fulfilling prophecy. Groups do not have minds. Assuming an idea of intent by definition incompatible with group agency, it follows that Radin's argument cannot be anything but a claim against group agency writ large.

Professor Radin's arguments are not substantially improved by the more sophisticated arguments made by Professor Dworkin. He argues, like Radin:[60] "so long as we think legislative intention is a matter of what *someone* has in mind *and means to communicate* by a vote, we must take as primary the mental states of particular people because institutions do not have minds."[61] Even if we imagine that the individual is "communicating," this does not solve the problem of combining individual minds or communications. Indeed, Dworkin is at pains to use the "combining minds" problem as an inherent problem for collective intent.

The "group intent objection" should be rejected as question-begging. If you assume at the start that intent reduces to the occurrent mental state of an individual, or a mental state communicated to another, then groups cannot have intent by definition since they do not have minds. Define intent as *I* (singular), and it cannot be *I* (group)—except in the rare case where each and every member has identical occurrent mental states or, to put it less formally, unless one can show that each person has the same thought "in his or her head" at the same time. Similar arguments can be applied even if we change our idea from intent-as-mental-state to intent-as-communication. If we assume at the start that intent signals a communication from one person to another, then we beg the question in favor of individuals again. Define communication as *C* (singular) and it cannot be *C* (group).

Group Intent Reconstructed

Returning to Alan Turing, let us remember that the question is not whether computers or groups have minds but how groups and computers act. Unlike Radin or Dworkin, I do not deny group intention;

in this sense, I am firmly in the camp of Pettit, List, and Ekins. On the other hand, like Turing, I do not think that these scholars are focused on the right question. Given the variety of meanings of intent I have specified, it is not enough to simply say "intent," full stop. Elsewhere I have urged that intent is a metaphor, and metaphors need referents: if I say the world is a stage, to quote a banal example, I have two concepts in mind—world and stage. That intent is a "metaphor" does not obviously articulate the reference. The referent I propose is legislative context. To recap, group intent is possible because group action is possible, but the more important question is how we find the meaning of group action. In this section, I move from critique to a positive view. I aim to construct a plausible account of group action based on legislative evidence legitimized by the group.

The Virtues of Legislative Context

Let us begin with the basic proposition that actions taken within an organization like Congress cannot be understood without understanding their procedural context—that this is not an optional but a necessary position. To take a simple example, let us say that you want to know the meaning of the statement "go to the floor!" One might assume that this statement means to drop to the floor to do push-ups. But in the congressional arena, it means something else. If a senator asks you to "go to the floor" it means to go to a particular place in the Senate known as "the floor," or the Senate chamber.

Congressional context helps us focus on conduct over time, as decisions change. When views change, they change in the context of a structure leading to conduct—enacting a law. Imagine if we were to freeze-frame the views of senators on civil rights in 1963. Many senators' views, *ex ante*, would appear quite rigidly racist. Now, fast forward to the "longest debate in history," on the 1964 Civil Rights Act.[62] As the debate went on, legislators changed their views. And they changed their views not because their beliefs about race changed but because their views about the wisdom of voting for the bill—action in congressional context—changed. No matter what their personal views, the idea that the voters would punish them at the polls if they did nothing, moved them to vote for the bill.

Context demands knowledge of procedural rules. Statutes emerge from a particular procedural context, not at a baseball game or a theatrical performance (different contexts with different rules).[63] Statutory speech operates in a particularly "formalistic" context, to borrow Professor Waldron's term.[64] Legislative speech does not, emphasis on *not*, rely upon the rules of ordinary speech. Linguistic conventions governing ordinary conversation are mediated, in the legislative context, by congressional rules and proceedings, as well as institutional structure.

As I explained in Chapter 1, politics is essentially conflictual and full of ambiguity. Members are just as often trying *not* to communicate or to communicate to third parties—their constituents. While linguists presume that ordinary speakers provide limited, relevant, and cooperative statements, legislative war suggests precisely the contrary. To the extent that some have thought to rely upon the views of linguists on ordinary conversation, like the brilliant linguist Paul Grice, these assumptions do not easily apply to legislative debate. [65] Indeed, in many cases, congressional procedure suspends the maxims of ordinary speech.

Inferring Group Intent from Group Action

If congressional context is always helpful in finding meaning, it has the added virtue of helping us construct a plausible vision of group intent. Group intent is an inference from group action. Just as moving a pawn in a chess game cannot be understood without the rules of chess, no congressional action can be understood without understanding the rules of the game. As those like law professor Scott Shapiro and philosopher Michael Bratman have emphasized, planning is the essence of decision and that requires, in a large collective body, procedures for how a group plans for the future.[66]

Lest this seem counterintuitive, remember that intent is not inevitably located in a mind or even "embodied." Sometimes when we talk of intent, it seems almost impossible not to imagine a mind. That a group is not "embodied" does not mean that the group does not have the functional equivalent of what we typically see as embodied. So, for example, a wheelchair is not biological material, but it enables bodily movement. So, too, group procedures are not embodied, but they operate, in the legislative context, as the functional equivalent of mind. Just as a wheelchair allows an individual to move, so, too, a group's procedures allow it to plan for the future as a group, to come to decisions, and, in this sense, to have group intent.[67]

The pragmatic modality of intent, by focusing on action and requiring context, allows for "we-intentions" that are more than the sum of individual mental states or communications. These intentions may be shared consciously or not, with or without overt communication between the parties, simply as an inference from action. For example, suppose that a group of senators file a cloture petition. Those senators have signed their name to a document, acting to close debate. From this *action*, we can infer that the members share a we-intention. This does not require that senators communicate with each other or that we know anything about what is inside their heads; they may simply sign without discussion. Nor does it suggest that the signatories have precisely similar "we want cloture" mental pictures in their heads. Signing may be thoughtless. But if the members act in parallel, whether by painting a house or signing a document, even without a mental event or communication, we can infer that they had the we-intention to do the act.[68]

In the legislative context, this is important for two reasons. Principles of congressional action are we-intentions in the *pragmatic sense of the term* "intention." Members act based on rules and procedures. This does not require that all members agree to those procedures, have mental states agreeing to those procedures, have communicated about the procedures, or have even read the procedures. *All they have to do as a group is act according to the procedures.* If the group shows by its actions a we-intention to abide by congressional process, that is enough for the pragmatic modality of intent. Lest this confuse (as *intent* almost immediately forces us into thinking of mental states), there are easy examples of similar coordinated action. For example, we can infer from the actions of chess players who sit down to play the game without a word that they are operating based on a we-intention to play chess.

The we-intention of congressional *procedure* can be conceived as a "meta-intention" in the following sense.[69] It is a we-intention to provide a framework for individual we-intentions in the future.[70] A pragmatic we-intention with respect to congressional *procedure* governs processes for *every* statute.[71] For example, acting pursuant to congressional procedure reflects a pragmatic we-intent that if a majority votes for the statute, that vote prevails for every member in the group—no matter what their mental state or what they have communicated about the bill. The statute's opponents share a pragmatic we-intention with the statute's supporters to *act* as a group "we" on the legislation. Why is this? Because, as even group intent skeptics like Ken Shepsle understand, if there is any core to a group, it is the organization and procedures governing that group.[72]

Like a church, a corporation, or a university, Congress as a group agent depends upon procedures to plan future action. Think of congressional rules as a signpost saying: "any act that follows according to these procedures is now stamped as legitimate group action, and when you (individual representative) act in this way, you have acted with group agency." This applies to all steps within the congressional process legitimated by the rules. There is nothing terribly exotic about this: when we agree to abide by a Supreme Court decision or an election, even if we disagree with the outcome, we do so because we have made a pre-commitment to decision procedures we believe are legitimate. We recognize Supreme Court decisions as legitimate, no matter the number of concurring opinions and whether the vote is 9 to 0 or 5 to 4.

To summarize: as we saw earlier, the problem with the group intent objection is that it imagines intent as the mental state of an individual or communication between individuals. Intent does not require an individual mental state, nor individuals' communication. Action implies intent. So, too, group action implies group intent. Group action happens because of sequential procedures. This is how the group plans for the future. When one looks for "congressional intent," one is *not looking for any special mental state behind text or action*—whether of individuals or groups. Instead, one is looking for crucial context for interpreting group action. In other words, one is looking for legislative evidence—the meaning of public acts done according to the rules. Congress has no mind, but it has the functional equivalent of intent—a way to plan for the future. And that "way" is essential context for understanding its decisions.

Group Agency, Sequential Procedure, and Feedback

Recent work on group agency supports my claims about group intention. Philosopher Philip Pettit and political economist Christian List have recently modeled what they call "group agency" in an attempt to put to rest sophisticated claims made by political economists that groups can never act rationally under the Arrovian cycling theorem.[73] Although that theorem is beyond the purview of this chapter, List's and Pettit's arguments provide substantial analytic support for rejecting the "group intent objection." At the very least, their arguments suggest that the skeptical "cash value" of group intent skepticism—that groups cannot act—is minimal.

Professors List and Pettit argue that group decisions emerge as a result of sequential processes involving feedback. As they explain, "a group's performance as an agent depends on how it is organized: its rules and procedures for forming its propositional attitudes . . . and for putting them into action."[74] Procedures allow decisions that do not correspond to the intentions of any particular member but allow for group agency. Feedback allows individuals to shift from their original preferences to ones that they "judge . . . better, for the group to accept."[75] To embrace this account of group agency, it is important to recognize what the theory does not entail. It does not entail some spectral intent hovering above the group. Pettit and List reject this view of the "group-mind" as a failed legacy of an "emergentist" tradition in which group-think arises in mysterious fashion.[76]

Professors List and Pettit are also quick to explain that their model *does not eliminate individuals.* The formal model uses the concept of supervenience to describe the relationship of individuals to groups.[77] Imagine that we have data points arrayed on a graph, based on particular numerical positions (3 on the horizontal axis, 4 on the vertical axis). Now we add another 100 data points, placing them on the graph based on given coordinates (5,6; 10,3; 4,2; etc.). By the time we are done, we see that the data points create a square shape. The square shape is the group attitude; it is more than the individual data points, but it does not eradicate those individual data points. The bottom line: one does not have to give up methodological individualism, or posit a "group mind," to believe that it is possible for a group to act in ways that no individual member prefers *ex ante* or even *ex post*.

Although Professors List and Pettit make a variety of arguments about group agency, for my purposes, the central point is that sequential procedures are points of preference aggregation and revision.[78] List and Pettit reject the caricatured assumption that "preferences are fixed."[79] In fact, as economists have known for several decades, preferences do change, and they should change with new information, under basic theories of rationality. They also change because new reasons arise about alternative courses of action, including new procedural reasons.[80] Put in other words, rules and procedures may force endogenous preference shifting. As long as preferences cannot yield a result without proceeding through a gauntlet of rules, preferences will shift as a result of those rules or, if not, they will yield no result at all.

List's and Pettit's insights on group agency are more than theoretical—they are also realistic. It is a fact that Congress works through sequential procedures. Those rules would be unnecessary if members could simply sit down and determine, on a moment's notice, how they would vote.[81] That, after all, is the claim made by those who accept a static, internal, notion of intent. In fact, legislation is always beset by the vagaries of time and uncertainty. *Ex ante*, members often do not know the preferences of other members or even their own constituents. That uncertainty is managed by procedural means: voting procedures force members to reveal their preferences. With new information about preferences, other members in turn may change their preferred positions.

To pass legislation, members must obtain the support of others—at least a majority if not a supermajority. Procedures allow for feedback as to how others will vote on a proposal or what bill changes are necessary to secure a member's vote. So, for example, let us say the chair of a committee proposes a bill. That bill is then heard in committee. At the markup, changes are made. The new bill may no longer reflect the preference of any single committee member but does reflect the shared preference to move the legislation to floor debate. If the bill ultimately passes, it may not reflect the individual or additive preferences of individual members. This should not cause dismay because it is inherent in the process of aggregation and required for group action.

Consider the Civil Rights Act of 1964.[82] Prior to bill debate, members' preferences varied greatly. Some would have preferred no bill—it was a long and fierce filibuster.[83] Some wanted a stronger bill. But once faced with the likelihood that the filibuster would fail, and the possibility of electoral consequences once the bill passed, some members' preferences changed.[84] Members who *ex ante* preferred no bill changed their preference to vote for cloture. This example illustrates how procedural processes create occasions for testing preference aggregations reached by subordinate bodies. When the Senate debates a bill,[85] before cloture is achieved, a compromise bill will be "substituted" for the committee bill.[86] In the 1964 civil rights bill, the Mansfield–Dirksen substitute was offered.[87] As the bill moved through the process, procedural rules allowed for what Professors Pettit and List describe as preference aggregation and transformation. *Ex ante* the final bill may not have represented the wishes of any individual member, but because of this internal dynamic, which the rules require, of staged preference aggregation, the law came to be the act of the whole.

Legislative History As Legislative Evidence

If a search for legislative context requires *legislative evidence, what evidence counts?* We can get a purchase on the best evidence based on the rules that make actions legitimate for the group. The best evidence should reflect the group's embrace of a group decision-making process. Bipartisan agreement is the best case. Delegations to subgroups pursuant to rule is fully appropriate. At a minimum, *evidence that violates the rules of group decision should be rejected*; minority views and post hoc manipulations should fail. To the extent that there is a normative hierarchy in legislative history, it is a normative hierarchy determined by Congress's own group proceedings.

Process Tracing and Group Attribution

When there are textual conflicts—when the House wants bill X and the Senate wants bill Y or when committee A wants bill Q and committee B wants bill Z, Congress's rules provide the ways in which the group comes to a decision. For that reason, under legislative decision theory, process tracing is essential. By *process tracing*, I mean tracing the process by which the central language came to exist in the bill. At one level, this means statutory history—the history of how particular text was created. New textualists have no principled objection to statutory history, but their methods—targeting specific terms within a law—tend to see the text as complete in itself rather than as the product of a dynamic process. Process tracing is not confined, however, to statutory history or the granular comparison of bill text. Much insight can be gained, for example, in considering the back-and-forth of provisions in more general terms.

Process tracing can illuminate key texts. In the famous affirmative action case *United Steelworkers v. Weber*, the grand debate was about the meaning of "discrimination," and there were claims made about the legislative history by both the majority and the dissent about the meaning of that term.[88] Process tracing helps us to see, however, that there was more to the textual question than the notoriously difficult-to-define term *discrimination*. The most important and specific statutory provision on affirmative action was section 703(j), added in the Senate prior to cloture—which specifically provided that no company would be "required" to impose quotas.[89] Justice Rehnquist's dissent, as we noted in Chapter 3, relied upon a long legislative history that violated, in essence, Congress's own rules by citing a minority report for the "group" meaning of the bill. Justice Brennan's majority opinion emphasized the bill's undisputed application—to improve the position of African American workers—but left the more specific key text on quotas, section 703(j), to a subordinate provision. Both opinions, liberal and conservative, would have been more succinct had they considered that 703(j) was a more specific, key cloture-induced supermajority compromise text modifying the more general sections referring to "discrimination."

Process tracing can also eliminate the need for long legislative histories and answer questions about seemingly "absurd" texts. As we saw in Chapter 3, in several cases, the central legislative evidence was limited in some cases to a few pages of material. This is not always true; to find the undisputed application of a statute may require a more general review of the legislative evidence. Nevertheless, there are cases where process tracing showed that the key legislative evidence was quite limited: in *Public Citizen* v. *American Bar Association*,[90] the Federal Advisory Committee Act case, comparison of the bills passed by the House and the Senate revealed that "utilize" appeared, for the first time, in the conference report. So, too, in *Green v. Bock Laundry*, the unfathomable term "defendant" showed up, at the end, in the conference report.[91] Finally, in *Griggs* v. *Duke Power*[92] although the testing issue was debated throughout the bill, the final compromise came in a post-cloture floor amendment that sought to alter the Mansfield–Dirsken substitute; senators' live statements on the amendment covered just a few pages.

Legislative Evidence As Legitimate Group Evidence

If group process determines the legitimacy of legislative evidence, group process provides the general principles governing the kinds of legislative evidence courts should accept and reject. Legislative evidence of bipartisan agreement is the highest quality evidence. Legislative evidence barred by the group, or incapable of influencing the group, should be rejected. This explains the theory's insistence that minority views should not be taken as authoritative and existing judicial discomfort with post hoc speeches and statements that are not made "live" on the floor of the chambers. At the same time, it supports some conventional views about the legitimacy of group agents' or leaders' views.

Congress follows rules requiring majoritarian decision making. Losers' statements can be important in some cases, as, for example, when opponents agree with the bill proponents on an undisputed example. Sometimes, they provide key context, but they cannot represent the authoritative meaning of a disputed text, lest courts upend majoritarian rule. Filibustering senators' views should be viewed with great caution and presumptively used only as an indication of what the bill did *not mean*. This is particularly true when members try to manipulate the process. Imagine, for example, had the Supreme Court accepted the statements of the senators in *Hamdan v. Rumsfeld*,[93] who engaged in a fake colloquy, staged to appear as "live" debate, trying to regain what had been lost on a failed amendment, even after the final vote on the bill had taken place. Because such history cannot change the group's decision, it should be rejected.

The group authority principle not only leads to rejecting what most courts, if they noticed, would in fact reject, but also suggests support for some rather conventional views about legislative evidence. Judges should view individual members' statements with caution. A random House member's view on a bill deserves no credit unless those statements are used to show a bipartisan consensus on an undisputed application, or the individual bears delegated group authority. It is the wise and general rule that the bill manager's or author's statements are given weight—because the group has delegated to them important responsibilities to shepherd the bill through the legislative process. So, too, the statements of committee chairs should be given more credence than the isolated statement of a member because chairmen have group authority, at the beginning of the process, to craft compromises and develop expertise on the committee bill. This principle also suggests, consistent with the conventional wisdom, that committee reports should be given weight, as reports are authorized by the group and often deferred to by the group. All of this, however, is subject to a rule of basic sequence: statements by bill managers or committee reports are only relevant on the text that was enacted; if the central text has been altered, or superseded by later events in the legislative sequence, then the authors' group authority may no longer apply to the interpretive question.

After Narrative: Legislative Evidence, *not History*

Purposivists and textualists have assumed, without question, that legislative histories should be be histories—that is narratives. If I am right about the legislative process, we should be looking for decisions and votes, not histories. The making of a statute is not a narrative process; rather, it is a process dominated by conflict, delay, compromise, and digression. As students of narrative know, the secret and perverse logic of narrative operates in reverse.[94] Narrative is created by "a discoverer standing at the *end* of the process, then laid out as a plot leading from beginning to discovery. Earlier events or actions make sense only as their meaning becomes clear through subsequent events."[95]

The only real way to make sense of Congress's decisions is to start at the end, as I have suggested in Chapter 3, to reverse engineer a text that is made sequentially over time. Purposivists have made their work much harder than it has to be by trying to write histories as if the final text reflected a straight narrative line from the first draft (an unrealistic assumption to say the least in today's legislative world). The reality is that bills change over and over again; the final text should be the starting place for any analysis of legislative evidence. From there, the debate on the conference report and the conference report's joint explanation is the best evidence of what happened in the final bill (both houses have to repass the text that the conference report includes). If there is no debate on the conference report, or no conference report, then the floor debate and amendments leading to the text should be consulted. In the Senate, particular attention should be paid to the substitute text needed to obtain cloture and post-cloture debate. After that, one may have recourse to committee reports which may or may not be relevant depending upon whether they are bipartisan and have any relationship to the text that was actually passed.

Purposivists may resist this enterprise, preferring to find general purpose or legislative intent. Legal process theory prizes generality. This affection has led to predictable attacks, however. For decades, critics have argued that there are many purposes to a statute, so that purposivism cannot be a legitimate method for finding "legislative intent" on any particular question. More recently, purposivists' critics have used this multiplicity of purposes to their advantage by picking purposes expounded by those who opposed or even filibustered a bill. Without a more rigorous method of analyzing legislative evidence, at the very least recognizing that there are supporters and opponents to bills, purposivists are left with the possibility that they, too, as I have showed in Chapter 3, will embrace as the purpose of the bill a position that was opposed in real life. At the very least, searching for bipartisanship would add much to purposivists' interpretive repertoire.

There is no logical reason why more rigorous method, and attention to legislative evidence under the rules, tilts in any particular political direction. Looking for undisputed bipartisan evidence prevents one from picking one's favorite purpose and narrows the inquiry to something a good deal more concrete, a real life problem, a paradigm example. Moreover, there is nothing necessarily liberal, in the political sense of that term, about generality. Highlighting specific text, usually preferred by conservatives, in *United Steelworkers v. Weber*, can yield a result liberals favor, upholding a voluntary affirmative action agreement under section 703(j), even if one were not convinced that the best undisputed example focused on workplace prejudice against African Americans. On the other hand, looking closely at legislative evidence can lead to more moderate conclusions, as in *Griggs v. Duke Power Co.*, that the case could have emphasized a bipartisan agreement that tests had to be related to the job, rather than the need to resolve the larger question of disparate impact.

The most important reason to move away from the conventional view of legislative history is to encourage the search for actual *evidence.* Purposivists often claim that their focus on generality is justified because the legislature cannot foresee the many problems that could arise after the statute is passed. That is an empirical question. As we saw in Chapter 3, in *Griggs*, Congress debated the testing question over and over again; there is no excuse in such a case for not paying attention to the legislative evidence. Textualists often claim that they need not look to legislative evidence because any particular piece of text reflects a complex, and unknowable, compromise. That is an empirical question. If laws exist, then both houses agreed upon the text. As we have seen in Chapter 3, there is knowable, and rather short, evidence about the Tower amendment on testing that led to the *Griggs* case and supports a moderate or even conservative reading. If one cares about text, one should presumably be delighted to compare the text of the failed Tower amendment to the Mansfield–Dirksen substitute with the compromised Tower amendment.

Ultimately, purposivists must come to realize that there is no inherent virtue in describing statutes at the most general of levels, other than to give more power to the interpreter and less to Congress. Perhaps this is the idea. Professor John Manning has recently argued that purposivism is a highly non-deferential statute-fixing enterprise running contrary to general deference doctrines in constitutional law.[96] If the idea is to impose normative "coherence" on the law, then of course, invoking general purposes will give more and more power to judges. There is no logical political tilt to generality, however. If the judges lean in a conservative political direction, the coherence is likely to lean toward the conservative; if they are liberal, it is likely to lean toward the liberal.

Textualists are not immune from a similar critique—that their method aggrandizes judicial power. Picking and choosing text without context amounts to interpretation by fiat; as we have seen, a simple term like *fifth* can mean different things, depending upon the context. When a judge picks terms like "state" or "object" out of a complex statute, like a health care or financial fraud law, she makes a choice, and that choice is often untheorized or at least undertheorized. As we have seen in Chapter 4, that choice may yield a question-begging form of textualism that simply proves its argument by the choice of text one puts in quotation marks. Just as the judge's notion of general coherence is likely to be affected by her predilections, her notion of specific plain meaning and proper text is likely to be similarly affected.

There is only one non-judicial antidote to the bias toward judicial power held by both purposivists and textualists—looking at the evidence, the context, which is what we should mean when we look for legislative intent.

Conclusion

Jurisprudential experts have debated the question of "legislative intent" for long enough. That is the wrong question. The question to ask is how Congress makes decisions, and what evidence should count to determine its decisions. The "metaphysical objection" against legislative intent as subjective is based on ideas that would, if applied to a court, make Supreme Court opinions appear, by analogy, as subjective "legislative history" of the Court's vote (after all, even Supreme Court opinions can be hopelessly plural and opaque, are delegated to clerks to draft, and are revisable by the Court or Congress in statutory cases). The "group intent" objection is equally implausible. It depends upon the unlikely assumption that any similar group, such as Microsoft, Harvard, or the Catholic Church, can not *act* as a group and that from those acts we can infer a group "intent" based on the group's rules and proceedings, without recourse to any fantastical notion of a group-mind or even group communication. Judges and lawyers would be better off letting go of the term "legislative intent" to avoid these philosophical debates. The semantic connotations of the term "intent" too often lead us to ask and answer the wrong questions. It is time to stop talking about legislative intent, and start learning how to look for legislative evidence.

6

The Constitutional Argument for Legislative Evidence

Each House may determine the Rules of its Proceedings. . . . Each House shall keep a Journal of its Proceedings, and from time to time publish the same . . .

U.S. CONST., ART. I, § 5.

So taken are we with models derived from ordinary conversation, we are inclined to ignore the formalities necessary for political discourse in a numerous and diverse society.

JEREMY WALDRON[1]

SOME ACADEMICS, AND occasionally Supreme Court justices, argue that citing legislative history is unconstitutional.[2] The good news is that this constitutional skepticism lives in a world where lawyers and judges largely ignore the claim. As a general rule, lawyers proceed to file briefs, as they have for the past century, citing legislative history, without the least worry that they are acting unconstitutionally. To be sure, some judges, theorists, and lawyers, most notably Justice Scalia, energetically criticize legislative history, claiming that its citation by lawyers and judges is unconstitutional, not to mention shameful, illegitimate, and other nasty adjectival complaints. Nevertheless, every recent empirical investigation suggests that the Supreme Court still cites legislative history,[3] suggesting that the Court does not consider this evidence unconstitutional. As even Justice Scalia admitted, "resort to legislative history has been standard judicial practice since the mid-20th century."[4]

In this chapter, I argue that constitutional skepticism about legislative history is unwarranted, even by the skeptics' own theoretical, textualist, standards. Skeptics worry that it is unconstitutional to supplant "law" with "legislative intent," but as we have seen in Chapter 5, no one is replacing "law" with vague mental states. Legislative evidence is all quite public; in 1842, the Supreme Court made clear that congressional documents were in fact very good evidence indeed, writing that "in all public matters, the journals of congress and of the state legislatures are evidence; and also the reports which have been sanctioned and published by [their] authority."[5] No one confuses legislative evidence with law; but it is evidence of context, and without context, one can make rather serious mistakes about text, as textualists admit. The constitutional question, then, is whether the Constitution commands that a court blind itself to legislative evidence of meaning when the text is vague or a choice of texts is involved. My answer is "no."

Legislative evidence has a specific constitutional mandate: the text of the Constitution specifically delegates to each house of Congress the power to create rules of proceeding under Article I, section 5.[6] This constitutional provision rebuts critics' claims that recourse to legislative evidence created by a single house is unconstitutional under the Constitution's text. More importantly, this clause raises serious questions about the major constitutional arguments against legislative history, which rest on the Bicameralism Clause or an implied principle of anti-delegation based on that clause. In the event this does not satisfy, I consider how legislative evidence fares under a richer separation of powers analysis. The bottom line: judges and academics should abandon broad all-or-nothing constitutional arguments against legislative history.

The Constitutional Text

Article I, section 5 of the Constitution lives a vibrant constitutional life in Washington, even if it remains unknown to constitutionalists, untaught in constitutional law courses, and new to the legislative history debate.[7] When members walk into very different chambers on opposite ends of the Capitol, when they debate or defeat bills, when committees meet and members filibuster, Congress acts pursuant to the Constitution's Article I, section 5, the otherwise obscure but important Rules of Proceedings Clause (also known simply as the "Proceedings Clause"). It is an old Washington joke that pundits overestimate the divisions between Republicans and Democrats—the real enemies are the House and the Senate. In part, this reflects the simple fact that the bodies operate with highly different rules and procedures. Put in its starkest terms, the House operates by majoritarian principles, and the Senate operates, because of the filibuster rule, by supermajoritarian principles.[8]

For our purposes, it is important to recognize that legislative evidence has a firmer textual basis in the Constitution than other commonly used interpretive materials. In the average appellate case, the statute is unclear. (If there were no ambiguity, the case would never reach an appellate court.) Then, the question is how to resolve the conflict or ambiguity. Should a court look to canons of construction created by the judiciary when the statute is unclear? Should it look to administrative regulations created by the executive? Or should the court look to legislative evidence? Nowhere in the Constitution are executive regulations or judicial canons mentioned. By contrast, the Proceedings Clause gives explicit authority to the "proceedings" of each house, the proceedings documented in a constitutionally prescribed legislative journal.[9] Because of that specific constitutional authority, legislative evidence should *be given more, not less, constitutional weight than other materials—although this argument runs contrary to conventional wisdom.*

Article I, section 5 authorizes each house to create its own legislative proceedings, proceedings documented as required by the Journal Clause. Legislative proceedings, as we will see, commonly include delegation of tasks to committees and resolution by conference committees, as well as rules for debating and amending bills. Of course, neither the term "legislative history" nor "legislative evidence" appears in the Constitution, but it is not too hard to imagine that if the Constitution delegates to each house the power to regulate their proceedings that this could include everything from rules for committee reports to legislative debate. The Constitution is often sparser than one might expect. Nowhere does the Constitution provide that the Supreme Court may write "opinions," yet few doubt that the Court has the power to issue opinions as a necessary and proper incident of the power to *decide* "cases and controversies."[10] One can certainly decide a case without an opinion; the Court simply votes. It does not follow that Supreme Court decisions are nonauthoritative because justices write an opinion explaining a precedential "history" of the reasons for their vote. Just as Article III's direction to courts to decide cases allows a court to explain its decision, Article I's Proceedings Clause allows each house the power to create rules allowing it to explain its proceedings.

At the very least, the Proceedings Clause demands that statutes be read within the procedural context in which they are created. As we have seen, it may matter if statutory language is asserted as an amendment, changed in committee, or at the conference stage. This is such an obvious proposition, it goes unnoticed. In the Supreme Court, no one would confuse an argument made at the certiorari stage with an argument made at the merits stage; similarly, no one would assume that the writ of certiorari, which starts many constitutional cases, is issued after a full merits decision. The Supreme Court's rules matter for its proceedings, even if the Constitution says nothing about those judicial rules. By contrast, the Congress's Proceedings Clause should make it clear that the rules of each house's proceedings deserve recognition because those proceedings are explicitly recognized in the constitutional text.

This argument should give comfort to the vast number of lawyers and judges who cite legislative evidence. As we will see, the major constitutional objection to citing legislative evidence is based on the Constitution's text; if the skeptics are to be true to their own textual constitutional theory—which demands textual answers—they must have some account for the whole Constitution, including the Proceedings Clause. As we will see, this Clause provides significant difficulties for the claim that the constitutional text bars legislative evidence.

The Rules of Proceedings Clause

The constitutional critique of legislative history is decidedly modern. Since the beginning of this country's history, lawyers have cited legislative documents.[11] Only late in the 20th century did agencies, academics, and judges begin to assert, with increasing stridency, that citing legislative history was unconstitutional. Initially led by Justice Scalia, those who call themselves "textualists" have made legislative history their cause célèbre, going so far as to suggest that citing legislative history is "illegitimate" and even "shameful."[12]

Although relatively few judges or lawyers have embraced this claim, and important congressional conservatives, like the current Chairman of the Senate Judiciary Committee, Senator Grassley, have openly rejected it,[13] constitutional skepticism about legislative history has cast an enormous shadow on the use of legislative evidence in statutory cases. It has yielded lively debate on the Supreme Court, as the justices openly joust at oral argument about the proper use of legislative materials.[14] Dozens of law review articles, and even Supreme Court opinions, grapple with whether legislative history should count and how it should count. Empirical studies abound attempting to determine precisely how many Supreme Court cases cite legislative evidence, ranging from 17 to 75 percent, depending upon the Term and how such evidence is counted.[15] In the past decade, the conventional wisdom has emerged that legislative history use has declined in the Supreme Court because of Justice Scalia's open attacks upon it. Whether true or not, the shadow of constitutional skepticism has changed the way in which the Supreme Court refers to legislative evidence, with the justices virtually apologizing about its use, or claiming it is only used to "confirm" the plain meaning,[16] or added only for those on the Court who "consider [it] relevant."[17] Few, other than the valiant Professor Brudney, have attempted to respond in any sustained way to the constitutional skepticism.[18]

The constitutional argument against legislative history rests on the Bicameralism Clause of the Constitution. That clause provides that "Every Bill . . . shall, before it become a Law, be presented to the President of the United States. If he approve he shall sign it, but if not he shall return it, with his Objections."[19] Although the untutored will recognize this as providing the president with veto authority, Justice Scalia focused on this constitutional provision for proof that "laws" require both houses of Congress to act, and both houses of Congress do not "pass" legislative evidence or history. A judge who credits legislative history is said to "contravene the constitutional requirement of bicameralism and presentment."[20] As the leading textualist in the legal academy explains: "Simply put . . . Article I, Section 7 of the Constitution itself gives the text [of a statute] a greater claim to authoritativeness," under the Constitution.[21] Since legislative evidence has not passed both houses, it fails the Bicameralism Clause and, as a result, does not pass constitutional muster.

The obvious problem with this argument lies in the Constitution itself. If Article I, section 7 provides for bicameral unity, Article I, section 5 provides for precisely the opposite—*bicameral disunity*—when it comes to the creation of legislative evidence. The Proceedings Clause provides a specific textual authorization for each house to create its own rules of proceeding. Congress makes law through these proceedings; Article I, section 5 authorizes each house the power to create its own rules, and the Journal Clause provides that each house's proceedings may be recorded. Given that the Proceedings Clause grants legitimacy to acts of Congress *done in separate houses*, the idea that both houses must act to give legislative proceedings constitutional legitimacy fails under the Constitution's own text.

Critics attempt to reinforce the bicameralism argument by claiming that the text of the statute is the only law to apply under the Bicameralism Clause.[22] Legislative evidence not being law, courts should blind themselves to it. This is overstated: the Bicameralism Clause itself provides that the text emerging from Congress is a bill, and the bill must be approved by the president for it to become law. If one should ignore all that is not law, then presumably one should ignore the bill text as well as the legislative history. (Even textualists refer to bill text.) In fact, if one should ignore all that is not law for bicameralism purposes, then one might as well throw out judicial precedents, canons of interpretation, and administrative regulations, all of which courts regularly use to interpret statutes, and all of which fail the "two house" rule. The bottom line: the bicameralism argument reaches so far that it undermines everything but the text of the statute, including all canons and every other traditional method of statutory interpretation.

Ironically, the framers of the Constitution considered the Proceedings Clause an essential means to enforce *bicameralism.* Without allowing each house to set its own rules, the distinctiveness of each as a legislative body suffers. Just ask anyone on the floor of the Senate if changing the filibuster rule would turn the Senate into the House, and you will see why rules matter to bicameralism.[23] This not only protects each house from the other, it also protects both houses from other departments. The framers understood the dangers of granting this power to another department. Consider, for example, what would happen if the president were given power under the Constitution to set the rules of Congress. He could eliminate the filibuster rule or change the rules necessary for cabinet or judicial nominations. He could even decree that both houses have the same rules, turning a formally bicameral Congress into a functionally unicameral one. Power over the rules of proceedings is Congress's power, a very important power, granted to each house, individually.

Some critics suggest that courts should pay no attention to Congress's rules,[24] basing their argument on an arcane and embattled judicial doctrine called the "enrolled bill doctrine."[25] That doctrine wisely suggests that courts should ignore litigants' arguments that Congress's clerks have made errors in copying the final bill. Even if this judicially created rule were relevant to legislative evidence, such doctrines are incapable of overcoming clear constitutional text. Questioning clerks' transcription skills is a far cry from banishing legislative evidence as unconstitutional. An analogous argument would suggest that since errors may be made in transcribing Supreme Court opinions, the opinions themselves should be ignored. Comity suggests respect for, not ignorance of, coequal branches' processes.

The History of the Proceedings Clause

The Proceedings Clause, as I noted earlier, lives a vibrant life; it is neither the arcane morass seen by some nor the housekeeping matter ignored by others. History reminds us of its importance. The framers understood that the power to set the agenda yields significant power over an institution. The Constitutional Convention began by setting rules for debate and ended by delegating tasks to various committees. The very first Congress created rules for committees and conference committees.[26] The earliest Congress kept a journal, now known as the Congressional Record, acting pursuant to the Constitution's Journal Clause, to "insure publicity and responsibility in all the proceedings of Congress."[27] That journal recorded the kinds of proceedings—amendments, committee reports, votes—that should at a minimum be necessary to interpret legislation under the theory I have propounded. As early as 1792, Elbridge Gerry called for the recording of congressional debates to inform the public, the president, and the courts. Newspaper reporters performed this function as early as 1789; by the 1840s, Congress employed commercial printers and demanded receipt of these published reports.[28]

At the founding, the rules of proceeding were so important that the author of our Declaration of Independence, Thomas Jefferson, as vice president, devoted much energy to writing an important, and still relevant, procedural manual governing legislative proceedings.[29] Jefferson decreed that legislative procedures were a part of Congress's "natural right" of self-governance.

> Every man, and every body of men on earth, possesses the righ[t] of self-government: they receive with their being from the hand of nature. . . . The law of the majority is the natural law of every society of men. When a certain description of men are to transact together a particular business, the times and places of their meeting and separating depend on their own will; they make a part of the natural right of self-government. This, like other natural rights, may be abridged or modified in it's [sic] exercise, by their own consent, or by the law of those who depute them . . . but so far as it is not abridged or modified, they retain it as a natural right, and may exercise it in what form they please.[30]

In 1839, Frances Lieber referred to Jefferson's manual as "of essential importance to liberty itself."[31] Lieber was well aware that the

French Revolution had taught the dangers of chaotic and violent legislatures bound by no settled rules. These men lived in a world where the organization of self-government was palpable and necessary, both to thwart overweening autocrats to control the mob, and avoid the guillotine. Like Jefferson, Lieber wrote eloquently about the evolution of American rules of proceeding, having been brought from England, thus likening them to "the rest of the common law," which became "a most essential part of our Anglican constitutional, parliamentary liberty."[32]

In short, the Proceedings Clause cannot be ignored in any constitutional argument against the use of legislative materials. Of course, one might contend, as have some, that even if these proceedings are entitled to respect, there is no original judicial practice recognizing the legitimacy of congressional evidence. Justice Scalia and Professor Garner cite evidence against such a practice which focuses on the notion that courts should not seek, from legislative evidence, a phantasmic "intent."[33] Leaving aside the question of intent, which as I have argued, is a diversion, there is a good deal of historical evidence that, at the founding, state and federal judges did not blind themselves to legislative proceedings. In 1793, in the Supreme Court of Pennsylvania, Justice M'Kean in *Roach v. Commonwealth*, referred to a "legislative construction" of a series of statutes: "it appears in the *Journals of the Assembly*, page 552 and 555 . . . [in the year 1780] that the Legislature would not charge the officers with the clothes &c furnished them, at the specie price."[34] In 1805, in *United States v. Fisher*, Chief Justice John Marshall explained, "Where the mind labours to discover the design of the legislature, it seizes every thing from which aid can be derived."[35] In 1810, *Fletcher v. Peck* repeats the jury's verdict which includes references to Congress's journals and direct quotations from committee proceedings.[36]

So, too, early Circuit Court and state decisions referred to legislative proceedings, as in the 1801 decision in *Hollingsworth v. Duane*, where it was reported in the opinion that "Mr. Dallas then read the Case of William Smith, from Debates of Congress, fols. 196, 383, 391, and made some observations, with a view to establish his proposition, that birth in the colonies conferred a right of becoming a citizen of the United States."[37] In 1814, in *Commonwealth v. Cushing*, counsel argued before the Supreme Judicial Court of Massachusetts for a statutory construction based on what "appears from the debates and deliberations in the legislature when those bills were pending."[38] This lawyerly practice may have even existed in colonial courts, as a Provincial Court of Maryland in 1771 reports in *Dorsey's Executors v. Worthington*, that the lawyers cited to "debates and proceedings of the upper and lower houses in 1725 and 1726."[39]

In the early Republic, lawyers arguing before the United States Supreme Court invoked statements of individual members and committee reports. In 1803, in *Marbury v. Madison*, Mr. Lee read the "printed journals" of the Senate.[40] In 1814, in *The Venus, Rae, Master*, counsel invoked "Mr. Russell's statement in the report of the committee of congress . . . journal of H. of Rep. . . ."[41] In 1825, *The Antelope* reported counsel's argument referring to "the reports of various committees of Congress" on the slavery question and what they "clearly prove . . ."[42] In 1839, in *Ex Parte in the Matter of Duncan N. Hennen*, counsel discussed proceedings of Congress in the House and cited the "register of debates" on the question of the removal power.[43] This federal practice may well have started as early as 1795, in *Bingham v. Cabot*, when the facts were stated including references to letters and proceedings before the "Commercial Committee of Congress" in the first Congress.[44]

The justices themselves cited the proceedings of Congress in early cases. In 1832, Chief Justice Marshall in *Worcester v. Georgia* stated that "the early journals of congress exhibit the most anxious desire to conciliate the Indian nations."[45] In the 1831 case of *Cherokee Nation v. Georgia*, Justice Baldwin considered "proceedings of the old congress" including the Committee for Indian Affairs and a 1782 congressional report.[46] Justice Thompson, dissenting in that case, wrote: "The journals of congress, from the year 1775 down to the adoption of the present constitution, abundantly establish this fact." He continued: "On examining the journals of the old congress [including proceedings and resolutions] the terms 'nation' and 'tribe' are frequently used indiscriminately. . . ."[47] In 1834, in *Wheaton v. Peters*, Justice Thompson, dissenting, quoted a committee report on the exclusive protection of copyright.[48] By 1874, in *Blake v. National Banks*, the Supreme Court stated that they were "compelled" to resolve an ambiguity in a tax statute "by the journals and records" of Congress.[49]

State Supreme Court justices did not blind themselves to legislative proceedings.[50] In 1825, Justice Gibson, dissenting in *Eakin v. Raub*, a Pennsylvania Supreme Court decision wrote: "I would just as soon resort to the debates in the legislature, for the construction of an act of assembly, as to the debates in the convention, for the construction of the constitution."[51] In 1828, the Pennsylvania Supreme Court in *Commonwealth ex rel. Bache v. Binns*, on the statutory question of holding incompatible offices under Pennsylvania law, the court referred to legislative debates including a committee report: "Mr. Wayne, chairman of the committee to which the subject was referred, brought in an argumentative and able report, denying the right; but this decision of the committee was reversed by the senate."[52] In 1844, in *Hill's Adm'rs v. Mitchell*, the Arkansas Supreme Court stated that "in the construction of all doubtful statutes, and even constitutional provisions, the history of the enactment, as furnished by the rolls of journals, is the very best evidence as to its meaning and intention."[53] That same year, in *Sisk v. Smith*, the Illinois Supreme Court stated that "in [this] case, the intention of the legislature is manifest, and perpetuated by the record of their proceedings in the legislative journals."[54] There are other examples of this practice after the Civil War.[55]

To be sure, there are contrary 19th-century examples. One often cited, is by Chief Justice Taney, of infamous *Dred Scott* fame,[56] writing in 1845 in *Aldridge v. Williams*, that "the law as it is passed is the will of the majority of both houses, and the only mode in which that will is spoken is in the act itself."[57] This position was expanded by Justice Peckham, of almost equally infamous fame for his opinion in *Lochner v. New York*,[58] in the 1897 case of *United States v. Trans-Missouri Freight Ass'n*, that "debates in congress are not appropriate sources of information from which to discover the meaning of the language of a statute passed by that body."[59] No one, including Justice Scalia, who relies on these statements, doubts that these views were eclipsed in the 20th century,[60] and that this coincides with the fact that statutory law, as opposed to judge-made common law, has become the dominant mode of regulation in the 20th century.

To use Professor Eskridge's phrase, today we live in "a republic of statutes."[61] When federal legislation blossomed in the New Deal, so too did the practice of writing lengthy legislative "histories," as Professor Nicholas Parillo has recently recounted in brilliant detail.[62] A full history of "legislative history" is yet to be written. But there is no evidence of which I am aware, that early American courts viewed legislative materials with the kind of disdain our Congress now enjoys from judicial and academic critics who refer to the "ashcans of legislative process,"[63] "the shoddiest unenacted"[64] intentions, and who describe legislative evidence as "entrails,"[65] "fantasy,"[66] mere "legal fiction."[67]

The Bicameralism Paradox

If constitutional skepticism about legislative documents is new, it is not without sophisticated and dedicated academic and judicial adherents. As Professor Manning recognizes, the bicameralism argument seems paradoxical: taken to its logical extreme, it appears to make the courts' own interpretive materials unconstitutional since canons and prior cases and common law are not "passed" by both houses.[68] There is, however, a more sophisticated version of this claim that deserves attention. Legislative history's critics reply that the real problem is not bicameralism as such but something I will dub "self-delegation"—that Congress delegates to itself the power to interpret the law.[69] As Professor Manning has explained:

> It is the very fact of *congressional* involvement in the creation of legislative history that justifies textualists' rejection of such materials. When a court assigns legislative history decisive weight because of the speaker's legislative status, it permits a committee or sponsor to interpret a law on Congress's behalf. This practice effectively assigns legislative agents the law elaboration function—the power to "say what the law is."[70]

Under this account, the *self-* part of *self-delegation* poses the problem. Put in other words, when it comes to legislative history, Congress has a conflict of interest. The argument is ingenious but unpersuasive because it is temporally challenged. It posits that Congress passes a bill and then delegates to a committee the power to interpret that bill. In fact, as Professor Jonathan Siegel has explained, this imagines Congress in reverse. Bills start in committee and proceed from there to floor consideration. Statements made in committee and on the floor are not interpreting a bill that has already passed; they reflect a process that is under way. Legislative evidence shows how a bill is made *ex ante;* it is not a post hoc advisory opinion.

More troubling is the claim that self-delegation represents a serious constitutional problem. The Proceedings Clause *explicitly provides for self-delegation.* The Constitution gives *each house* the power to decide its own rules. To say that the legislative power may not be delegated might be true if it meant *all* the legislative power—if Congress gave Arizona the power to legislate for the nation, for example.[71] But it is explicitly not true of legislative proceedings and evidence of those proceedings. As a matter of constitutional text, it cannot be said that the legislative powers provided in Article I[72]—the "legislative powers herein granted"—do not include that which follows, Article I, section 5, which in fact delegates power to a part of the Congress, each house, to set the rules of its own proceedings.

Constitutional skeptics invoke the Supreme Court's decision in *INS v. Chadha*[73] to suggest that legislative self-delegation is unconstitutional. *Chadha* struck down the legislative veto—a device allowing congressional committees or a single house to veto regulations. Legislative history critics suggest that *Chadha* stands for the proposition that it is wrong to delegate legislative power to a committee.[74] From *Chadha,* it appears to follow that the "part"—the committee—cannot do the work of the "whole" Congress. Of course, if the committee could do the "whole work" of Congress, that would pose a constitutional problem. But the Constitution does not bar delegation of the rules of proceeding: Article I, section 5 delegates legislative power to "parts" of Congress, and it delegates the proceedings power to "each house." *Chadha* cannot erase that text. Whether *Chadha* is right or wrong is irrelevant to the validity of each house's rulemaking power, both as a matter of constitutional text and fact.

Ironically, the metaphor on which the anti-delegation argument trades—that the whole power should not be replaced by a part—supports the claim *for* legislative history, at least in some of the most difficult cases. If textualists are worried about legislative history adopted by the few, they should be just as, if not more, worried about *statutory text adopted by the "few."* Remember *Public Citizen*, discussed earlier, in which 535 members voted for bills the Supreme Court deemed absurd.[75] The whole voted for a bill that covered federal advisory committees that were "established," by the government. That language went to conference. The conference—a much smaller body—added the problematic term *utilize.* Surely, if one is worried about the whole/part problem, one should worry about the same problem when it comes to *text.* In reality, members worry about this all the time, and both houses have created rules to bar members from wholesale rewriting of bills by conference committees.[76] At the very least, recognizing how Congress proceeds provides a better explanation of the statute than the assumption that 535 members of Congress embraced absurdity or lost their minds.

Finally, the nondelegation argument does not solve the bicameralism paradox. Self-delegation, if a problem, occurs throughout the government. Agencies regularly delegate to themselves the power to interpret as well as apply law; they write regulations about their organic statute and then apply those regulations in individual cases. So, too, courts regularly self-delegate. Not only do they create their own "rules of proceeding," they create a vast number of interpretive tools to address statutes: canons of construction number in the hundreds. Congress has never granted the courts the power to create canons of interpretation, yet canons have proliferated in the modern age. Are not these new canons "lawmaking" in the act of "interpretation"? Does not the court have a conflict of interest in delegating to itself the power to create its own judicial rules of interpretation? This explains why "conflict of interest" alone has never been a solid principle to resolve separation-of-powers controversies.[77]

Ultimately, the conflict of interest argument is a consequentialist one: if courts use legislative evidence, Congress will have a greater incentive to put materials in legislative history rather than text. The idea that Congress creates legislative history as a response to courts' actions is likely to strike any member of Congress as amusing. As Judge Katzmann and other astute observers of Congress know, the "first branch tends to give little attention to the large number of statutory opinions of the lower courts."[78] Whatever interpretive approaches courts embrace, Congress will continue to create legislative materials because it needs to create those legislative documents to do its job creating statutes. If nothing else, legislative proceedings are preference aggregation tools necessary to reach collective decisions in a body of 535 members. Every empirical study to date, from my own to others' far more extensive efforts, reveals that legislative history is created because members have to create it, not because courts rely upon it.[79] Just as students do not take notes to please the teacher, members of Congress do not take notes of their decisions to please justices.

To resolve the bicameralism paradox, one must recognize precisely the opposite of the nondelegation argument: *the Constitution itself provides for self-delegation with respect to legislative rules and proceedings.* The legislature as a whole, given legislative power under Article I, section 5, is permitted by the Proceedings Clause to delegate to its subparts, the House and the Senate, the power of explaining the laws they draft and how they proceed through the legislative process. The Constitution thus delegates to parts of Congress a power that the other parts of Congress do not enjoy (the Senate cannot pass rules for the House, for example). The term "proceedings," moreover, clearly implies the kinds of self-delegations common in the early part of our history, involving committees and conference committees. Giving the Proceedings Clause its due helps us solve what Professor Manning has called the bicameralism paradox. The paradox was fueled by the apparent overreach of the bicameral argument: agency rules do not satisfy the Bicameralism Clause, nor do canons or common law. Under an expansive reading of the Bicameralism Clause, the courts' own precedents (as lawmaking) would be unconstitutional. However, if we limit bicameralism to actions taken under Article I, section 5, the Proceedings Clause, the paradox disappears. Only legislative proceedings leading to legislative bills require bicameral approval and, upon approval of the president, become law. That law, however, depends upon the proceedings declared by the House and the Senate under the Proceedings Clause.

The Separation of Powers: Representation versus Adjectives

When all else fails, constitutional skeptics invoke the separation of powers. They write of Congress having aggrandized both *legislative* and *interpretive* functions. Of course, the term *interpretive* does not appear in the Constitution, and even if it did, it would have to be parceled out to all three branches, as they all *interpret* the law in ways that most find perfectly constitutional. When agencies interpret their own organic statute, they are given deference, not a slap on the wrist. Congress surely interprets its own laws in writing new ones. It is long past time that we recognized that courts both interpret and make law. Again, we are back at our seeming paradox—what is good for all other departments is somehow unconstitutional for Congress.

Invoking terms like *interpretive* power suggests that Congress is aggrandizing to itself "judicial" powers by creating legislative evidence. The Proceedings Clause, well embedded in Article I, suggests, to the contrary, that legislative proceedings are just that—legislative. But even if this more precise clause should trump the otherwise unenumerated principle of separated powers, the idea is easily turned around. If Congress is asserting "judicial" power in creating legislative history, are the courts asserting "legislative" power when they reject legislative evidence? As Senator Arlen Specter once put it: "I think when justices disregard that kind of [legislative history], it is just another way to write their own law." Or as Senator Orrin Hatch once explained about legislative history: "text without context often invites confusion and judicial adventurism."[80]

Adjectives, it turns out, are not very helpful in resolving the great constitutional debates about legislative history (or most separation-of-powers debates). The adjectival theory of constitutional construction, which slaps labels on "functions"—such as *interpretive* or *legislative*—cannot solve the structural problem because the adjectives are not unique to any particular department. For example, interpretation and legislation go on in agencies and courts every day in America. Can we say that this mix of functions makes agency interpretation unconstitutional? Adjectival labels cannot supply a firm ground on which to base an argument against legislative materials for much the same reasons the bicameralism argument fails: both are wildly overgeneralized and for that reason fail to distinguish legislative evidence from analogous judicial and executive actions.

Lest this not persuade adherents to the adjectival approach, apply it to the Constitution's text itself. The Constitution itself provides no functional purity. It is often said that the Constitution's vesting clauses—the clauses that appear at the beginning of the first three articles—enumerate types of power and that these types are separated in the document. The idea is that there are three constitutional silos: one legislative, one executive, and the other judicial. In fact, the document does not create such silos. For example, the executive veto exists not in the "executive" silo, Article II, [81] but in the legislative silo, Article I.[82] Similarly, the judicial power to try impeachments does not exist in the "judicial" silo, Article III,[83] but in the legislative silo, Article I.[84] Not all "legislative powers herein granted" under Article I exist in the legislative silo, Article I.[85] Congress's power to "declare the Punishment of Treason"[86] does not appear in the legislative Article I, but in the judicial Article III, just as the legislative power to "make all needful Rules and Regulations respecting" federal property and territories does not exist in the legislative silo, Article I, but in the adjectivally challenged (unnamed) Article IV.[87]

Even if we assume that functional designations play a role in separation-of-powers analyses, such general approaches provide no clear answer with regard to legislative evidence. Indeed, a very sophisticated exchange has occurred between the purposivist Professor William Eskridge and the textualist Professor John Manning. Professor Eskridge argues that the doctrine of the "equity of the statute" is expressly contemplated by the "judicial" power and thus supports purposivist readings.[88] Professor Manning has responded that the history is a good deal more complex and that it is unclear whether the equity doctrine falls within the "judicial" power, as our constitutional structure is in fact different from the British parliamentary model from which the equity doctrine derives.[89]

The arguments are well documented, but precisely for that reason, they have convinced very few that there is a "constitutional prohibition" of legislative evidence to be found in the constitutional term *judicial power.* As a textual matter, surely the Journal Clause or the Proceedings Clause is more specific and therefore should trump the more general notion of "judicial" power. The truth is that, as in many other matters historical, the framers saw no stark line moderns draw. At the time, Blackstone's books were the most important legal texts in America, and those books embraced both the text and, yes, the "spirit"—that is a quotation from Blackstone—of the statute (the "spirit" being precisely what modern textualists oppose).[90]

Elsewhere, I have argued at length about what a real separation-of-powers analysis requires, for I believe that the only thing we can know from the Constitution is that we have a separation of representation as much as a separation of powers.[91] What we know from the Constitution's text itself is that the adjectival theory may be a viable heuristic, but it cannot decide difficult cases at the margin—indeed, it cannot even describe the Constitution we have. If we want to understand the Constitution's structure, the most important words in the Constitution are not the words *executive*, *legislative*, or *judicial*; they are the words creating government by consent of the governed. Article I authorizes people to vote for members of the House of Representatives and the Senate. Article II authorizes the people to vote for a president, through the electoral college. These elected officials then appoint executive officers and Supreme Court justices. These are the central constitutional actions that quite literally "constitute" our government.

Lest one remain attached to the view that the vesting clauses—which appear at the beginning of Articles I through III—create the separation of powers, conduct an intellectual experiment. Strike them from the document. Will the government have no power? Will the president lose his veto power? Will Congress stop making laws? Will the judiciary refuse to issue opinions? No. People will still vote, Congress will still debate, the Supreme Court will still decide cases, and the president will still direct the executive. Now strike the clauses in Article I providing for representation and voting; strike the same clauses in Article II and those providing for the appointment of Supreme Court justices. Now we have no government. The representational and appointment provisions, not the vesting clauses, are the most important in our Constitution.

The Constitution's text distributes the power of representation along geographic lines: the president represents the nation, the senator represents state-defined constituencies, and members of the House represent smaller district constituencies.[92] From these lines, we can reimagine the separation of powers as a form of analysis focusing on the separation of representation. So, for example, when one shifts power from the legislature to the Supreme Court, one shifts it from a highly representational institution—the members in the House and the Senate represent constituencies directly—to one that is not representational at all—the justices have no explicit representational mandate. When we shift power in this way, we reduce the influence of popular constituencies. This is precisely what happens when courts—which have long used legislative evidence—ban it. What was once a practice that involved recourse to popular input now silences the people's voice. To put it more colloquially, as have conservative and liberal senators who have objected to the "no legislative history" rule—such a rule frees judges to write statutes in their own vision, not the people's vision. In other words, a constitutional ban on legislative evidence—even if it could be squared with the Constitution's text—cannot be squared with the very well established principle of legislative supremacy within the separation of powers.

Conclusion

Scholars and lawyers should put to bed the constitutional argument against legislative history. Instead, they should become far more concerned and cautious about particular kinds of legislative evidence raising concerns of democratic legitimacy. Throughout this book, I have offered examples of courts citing legislative evidence that amounts to citing those who opposed, and even filibustered, a bill. We have seen this in opinions embraced by liberals and conservatives alike, in cases well known and obscure. If one is worried about the Constitution, presumably one should worry about a practice that makes winners of losers, upending the Constitution's basic commitment to majoritarianism. At the very least, the notion that courts should avoid constitutional questions cautions against embrace of the legislative history of filibustering and manipulative minorities.

Many scholars have claimed the mantle of providing a so-called democratic theory of statutory interpretation; unfortunately, these claims are often unsatisfactory as there are many ways to define democracy. Here, my claim is simply that one should avoid the constitutional question that would be raised by judicial embrace of a *positively anti-democratic result.* It is not the job of judges to enforce the meanings of a filibustering minority, or the job of the court to rewrite the law in favor of legislative losers. This is a minimalist claim at best, for it rests upon a settled definition of democracy: few would argue that law's legitimacy resides in minority rule. As Thomas Jefferson once wrote, the "law of the *majority* is the natural law of every society of men."[93] At a minimum, this is what respect for Article I's Proceedings Clause should mean. If legislative supremacy means anything, it means that popular voices must count. Courts should not alter that principle by giving a meaning to a statute propounded by those who *lost* the debate.

This problem is magnified in some cases when those who lost the debate seek to relitigate their position in the Supreme Court. With legislators filing amicus briefs in the Supreme Court, particularly legislators who opposed or filibustered bills, the risk has increased that the same legislators will seek to use the justices to promote legislative evidence Congress as a group has rejected. In fact, we saw this in *Hamdan v. Rumsfeld*,[94] discussed in Chapter 3. Those who lost the battle engaged in a fake colloquy staged to appear as a "live" debate, then filed briefs based on the fake colloquy (a gambit only revealed by reviewing the C-SPAN video). As we have seen in the health care case, *King v. Burwell*,[95] briefs written by the bill's opponents sometimes fool the Court into adopting accounts of legislative proceedings that the record cannot support. In my view, the Supreme Court should not rely on legislative evidence proffered in amicus briefs authored by members who cannot claim to act on behalf of Congress because they openly opposed a bill. Presumably, if textualists are true to their theory that, in case of a conflict of interest, self-delegation is inappropriate, amicus briefs written by members who do not in any way act on behalf of the group—i.e. devoted bill opponents—should be treated with extreme skepticism unless offered to show a bipartisan consensus.

It is time, then, to make fewer grand claims that all legislative evidence is unconstitutional. The constitutional arguments have never been strong, and have been ignored by the average lawyer and judge. The Proceedings Clause protects legislative evidence, but it also supports understanding those proceedings well enough to appreciate the basic rules of Congress 101. The question for the future of statutory interpretation is not whether, but how, courts use legislative evidence. It is not whether its use is unconstitutional, but whether courts may continue to interpret statutes without a better understanding of what the Constitution recognizes as legitimate—each house's rules and proceedings.

Epilogue

COURTS AND CONGRESS AS FAITHFUL AGENTS OF DEMOCRACY

MUCH OF THIS book has been about Congress, that entity most lawyers, and perhaps most citizens, view as strange, full of dangerous political energy, and likely to be making sausage. This contempt is relatively modern. Thomas Jefferson and others viewed Congress as essential to liberty and self-governance. It should seem odder that lawyers and judges hold such a dark view of the legislature when, at the same time, they claim to act as the *faithful agents* of democracy. The rhetorical paradox of dark Congress/bright democracy entices me, in a final note, to consider the most important aspects of the judicial role in statutory interpretation—the faithful agent as democratic fiduciary—and to set forth ways that Congress might help judges perform that role.

Courts' Duties as Democratic Fiduciaries

There is no more frequent statement about a judge's proper interpretive role than the ancient claim that it is the job of judges to be a "faithful agent" of the legislature. This claim of fidelity sits uncomfortably with the dark Congress idea. Surely, one who has faith—is faithful to Congress or, even more broadly, democracy—does not look with contempt at its charge and would, as any good lawyer with a dubious client, zealously represent him or her against charges of failure or corruption. Put in other words, faithfulness as a legislative agent seems to put contempt for Congress out of the question. How can one respect an entity one disdains?

Scholars have debated for some time the meaning of faithful agency, some urging a proactive judicial role, others veering toward an ideal of judicial self-erasure. Professor Bill Eskridge has given a powerful argument for what he calls a "relational" agent. Playing off the ancient Lieber example "go fetch the soup meat," Eskridge asks whether a "faithful agent" told to go fetch all of the ashtrays in a building would, in fact, pull them off the wall. He argues that courts stand as partners to judges in making law.[1] Professor John Manning and others reject this claim, urging that judges have no business "reshaping" law as partners with courts;[2] to be a "faithful agent," one must respond to Congress's semantic command. If the language fails the judicial ideal of plainness, Congress, not the courts, should fix it. Courts are to obey like a faithful soldier, not to question the commander's text. Let the ashtrays come off those walls!

These arguments proceed from two very different fears. Eskridge worries that the judge will lose her common sense, will fail to apply the proper context (ashtrays on walls) to the interpretive problem. Manning, on the other hand, is fearful of judicial aggrandizement; he would rather the agent pull the ashtrays off the walls (cause real damage in the world) than see judges gain too much power. I confess I am with Eskridge on the question of context: one need not accept Ronald Dworkin's idea that courts "improve" statutes or even Eskridge's idea that judges are partners with Congress to accept that context matters in understanding meaning. I have, of course, devoted an entire chapter to this claim (see Chapter 4).

What, then, of the fear that judges will aggrandize their power by filling statutory gaps? Although this appears a gesture of humility and restraint, it worships at the feet of a false idol. Implicit in this notion of fidelity is Congress as Herman Melville's Bartleby the Scrivener—a copyist trying to erase his own role in writing. No person elects members of the Senate or the House for their linguistic precision; people elect members to get things done in the world. Not only is the scrivener view wrong about Congress, its implications should be rejected by judges. Presumably, if Congress saw itself that way, it would privilege clarity over action and hire lots of lawyers in expert drafting offices to write clear statutes. And, if that were true, there would be nothing for courts to do in statutory cases, for all statutes would always be plain, and all circumstances would have been foreordained.

The scrivener theory of Congress yields a very odd view of judging. For if the scrivener view is correct, courts have erased themselves from the statutory picture; if statutes are clear, there is no statutory business to do, and the courts are left to happily contemplate the vagaries of the ancient common law. Of course, those who assert this view most assiduously also know that the common law is dead, so that the claims of erasure cannot be real. The erasure is false humility: the kind of law-making courts do has no parallel to the power of the president or Congress; relatively, the judiciary is a weak and passive institution, with no money, no army, and no way to make law unless someone happens to bring a lawsuit. The judiciary cannot make law in the sense that the president or Congress does. Filling holes in a wall, or patching over an odd-looking screw is entirely different than building a fortress.

Judicial humility has, from the very beginning of our country, been used to assert judicial power. In *Marbury v. Madison*,[3] Chief Justice Marshall famously asserted the judiciary's power not only against Congress (by holding legislation unconstitutional) but also against the president (by writing an unnecessary opinion about why the president was not above the law)—moves made in the name of humility, the inability to exercise jurisdiction. So, too, textualists' claims of humility hide an extraordinary assertion of judicial power. Congress does not play with dice; real people live and die depending upon what laws say, and members of Congress are elected or unelected based on that premise, not on the premise that their job is to debate canons or dot *I*'s and cross *T*'s. If something goes wrong with a statute, the representatives will be held responsible, not the members of any special drafting bureau.[4] It is the people, not Congress, who suffer if the court, seeing itself as disciplinarian of a bad copyist, imposes such a view on democracy, thwarting the people's ends—their dams and bankruptcy and health care—simply because language was imprecise.

All the debate about the faithful agent ideal has confused us not only about the true author of statutes (the people) but also about the true nature of the inter-branch encounter we know as statutory interpretation. *The truth is that courts and Congress are interpretive competitors; their interests are not aligned.* Each institution has an incentive to assert its power to determine the final meaning of statutes and the methods of proper interpretation. Like judicial deference ideals more generally, *the faithful agent ideal is not a description of reality but an attempt to counteract a reality*, to protect against the kind of self-interested bias from which all persons and institutions suffer. The faithful agent rule tells courts to try to put themselves in the position of a rival institution to avoid the risk that the judiciary will see the world in their own image.[5]

In a sense, too little weight in the "faithful agency" debates has hinged on the notion of *faithfulness* and too much on the notion of agency. The language of "faith" is the language of fidelity, of the fiduciary, not the simple agent. Courts have a duty to put their own self-interested ideals, their own love of textual precision, and their own tools such as canons and common law, to the side, and do the hard work of finding "what Congress meant." Judges will think like judges, and members of Congress will think like members of Congress. That gap cannot be bridged, however, if one starts from the position of institutional disdain. One must be faithful to the democratic ideal, that a statute is not the stuff of scriveners and pedants, a linguistic puzzle, but aimed to do something in the world. To be a faithful agent, then, is to act as a fiduciary—to rise above courts' own self-interested views of statutes as linguistic puzzles.

At a minimum, to be a faithful agent is not to remake the law, to broaden it in the image of a heroic herculean judge, or narrow it in the image of a libertarian scrooge, *but to reject disdain of its authors*, even when one is asked to interpret laws that one considers vile or language that seems unthinkable. Judges should hesitate and look to the evidence before they assume that there are gaps, before they assume that each piece of text amounts to a compromise, before they assume that meaning is plain, before they declare absurdity or pick one text over another—at least long enough to look at the evidence—the public records of Congress's decisions. The interpretive spirit must be one of inquiry, of discovery rather than disdain, about the only evidence of meaning the people's representatives can give—the record of Congress's proceedings. In short, even if one has contempt for Congress, a judge cannot have contempt for the real authors of legislation, the people. One must put ideas of sausage aside, reject a false erasure of judicial duty, and take responsibility for finding the best evidence of meaning one can find outside the judge's own head.

Judges owe that duty to democracy not because they are the direct agents of the people but because the rule of law cannot be a rule *against the people.* Judges have special skill, expertise, and knowledge about legal matters, and when they deploy that skill, they owe it to the people to explain and implement the government's great objects, its ends, in the clearest possible way. This is the great merit of the purposivist ideal—not to impose the norms of judges, but to respect the people's norms. Of course, purposivism can just as easily be deployed to embrace unjust and illiberal ends if purposivists do not understand how to read Congress. If this book leaves any impression, it should be that neither textualism nor purposivism is panacea, that either theory can lead to outcomes that are democratically perverse, the precise opposite of a judge's duty as a faithful agent, as democratic fiduciary.

Congress's Democratic Fiduciary Duties

If I am right that legal education failed the judges on the bench today, then as many have said, from Judge Posner to Judge Katzmann, they must reach out and get it. As with learning e-discovery or multi-district litigation, the Judicial Conference is fully capable of finding experts capable of teaching the basics of legislative evidence and procedure. In an earlier generation, federal judges were often members of Congress, so such education was not necessary. Fewer and fewer judges come to the bench with legislative backgrounds, however. The organized judiciary, through the Judicial Conference, needs to step in and encourage teaching Congress 101 to new appointees and should also urge Congress to help provide them the tools that would make it far more simple to do what Congress believes necessary: to teach judges how to read the legislative record the way an elected member of Congress would read the record.

First, Congress has done wonderful work with Congress.gov, but it could do a lot more to increase the intelligent consumption of the

Congressional Record. And if Congress is not willing to do it, I suspect that the competing "for profit" databases, which are excellent, like ProQuest, Westlaw, or Lexis, would increase their users if they simplified the process of finding legislative evidence. First, bill texts should be easier to find. Second, the "substitute" bill voted on before Senate cloture should be highlighted in the databases. This is a key procedural move and point of compromise. Third, the Congressional Record should be annotated; every member's speech should indicate a "bill vote" and an "amendment vote" so that the reader knows whether the speaker is a supporter or opponent of the amendment or bill. So, too, the majority and minority leaders, the ranking members, and committee chairs and ranking members should be identified in the record. These are all easy fixes.

Second, Congress should delegate to the Congressional Research Service, or the expert drafting legislative counsel's offices, the power to summarize the process of all major legislation in an "official" nonpartisan timeline for bill "text." Bill summaries are not enough. Bill texts and key dates on votes are central to finding legislative evidence. This bipartisan timeline would appear in reverse order providing text proposed by the conference committee, the Senate bill text, the House bill text, the pre-cloture Senate substitute, and the bills as they emerged from committee. A list of key dates and pages of the Congressional Record for debate and votes would be attached to these texts. For complex bills, texts of floor amendments and pages for relevant debates should also be included. This would reduce the cost of finding both text and legislative evidence. In addition, Congress should attempt to create new rules, or enforce existing rules, to avoid abuse. The Senate should bar the filing of committee reports *after* a bill has been passed. The Senate and House should also bar colloquies post-enactment intended to influence judicial processes.

Third, to gain respect, one must show respect. Just as courts need to understand Congress, Congress needs to understand that courts are struggling with massive caseloads on matters that are not politically controversial but could be easily resolved with the tiniest of legislative effort. Default rules for attorneys' fees and expert witnesses, statutes of limitation, extraterritorial effect, and similar matters could be very helpful to limit litigation. I recognize, and have said before, that I believe that any attempt to enact "rules of statutory interpretation" highly unlikely, that Congress has far more important things to do. But I also believe that there are many good, cost-saving reasons supporting a limited set of codified bipartisan default rules. Call it an "Act to Prevent Costly Litigation," hardly a position either party should reject in principle. As with the Federal Rules of Evidence or the Rules of Civil Procedure, Congress could delegate this job to a distinguished committee of experts in legislative procedure and appellate practice. If most of the states have such defaults, if they have said that their courts can fix grammatical errors, so too can Congress, rather than having multiple appellate courts wasting their time deciding what amount to silly cases that only enrage judges and fuel their contempt for bad legislative drafting. If Congress does not act, then the organized Bar should act on its own, either through the American Bar Association or the American Law Institute, to propose a limited set of bipartisan default rules arising from concrete problems repeatedly encountered by the appellate courts.

Finally, the judicial confirmation process—the only point where many judges encounter the Congress—must be regularized in ways that are more "law-like" and "nominee-friendly," which is to say that there must be general bipartisan timelines and procedures, not to mention transparency, for all nominees about the nature of the process. If there is bipartisan agreement that legislative evidence is relevant, then senators of both parties should stand up for Congress's prerogatives; they should encourage judicial education on basic legislative procedure. Most importantly, senators must insist, in appellate and Supreme Court and other nomination hearings, that nominees pledge not to blind themselves to legislative evidence. No one ever said our form of government was easy; it is a republic, if we can keep it. It cannot be kept, however, if judges read the law against the people.

Notes

Acknowledgments

Index

Notes

Prologue

1. Conversation in 2008 with the author.

2. *King v. Burwell*, 135 S. Ct. 2480, 2492 (2015).

3. *Lockhart v. United States*, 2015 WL 7188394 (U.S.), 26 (U.S. Oral. Arg., 2015).

4. Richard A. Posner, "The Incoherence of Antonin Scalia," *New Republic*, Aug. 24, 2012, https://newrepublic.com/article/106441/scalia-garner-reading-the-law-textual-originalism.

5. Transcript of oral argument, *Arlington Central School v. Murphy*, 548 U.S. 291 (2006).

6. Jonathan Adler, "Kagan Discusses Statutory Interpretation at Law School," *The Harvard Crimson*, Nov. 18, 2015, http://www.thecrimson.com/article/2015/11/18/kagan-talk-law-school/.

7. Henry M. Hart, Jr., and Albert M. Sacks, *The Legal Process: Basic Problems in the Making and Application of Law*, ed. William N. Eskridge, Jr., and Philip P. Frickey (St. Paul, MN: The Foundation Press, 1994), 1378. The book is actually longer, since it includes significant prefatory material. Chapter 5 on legislative process includes long discussions of the American Law Institute and specific kinds of legislation, from food safety to disaster relief, an outdated history of committees and congressional members, but scant material on actual process. See ibid. at 724–726 (summarizing procedure); ibid. at 975–978 (conference committees); ibid. at 1004–1007 (appropriations).

8. Antonin Scalia and Bryan Garner, *Reading Law: The Interpretation of Legal Texts* (St. Paul, MN: Thomson/West, 2012).

9. Posner, "The Incoherence of Antonin Scalia."

10. Stephen Breyer, *Active Liberty: Interpreting Our Democratic Constitution* (New York: Vintage Books/Random House 2005), 85.

11. William N. Eskridge, Jr., *Dynamic Statutory Interpretation* (Cambridge, MA: Harvard Univ. Press, 1994).

12. David R. Mayhew, *Congress: The Electoral Connection* (New Haven, CT: Yale Univ. Press, 1974), 16.

13. Barbara Sinclair, *Unorthodox Lawmaking: New Legislative Processes in the U.S. Congress*, 4th ed. (Washington, DC: CQ Press, 2012), 86–87.

14. Orrin Hatch, "Legislative History: Tool of Construction or Destruction," *Harvard J. Law and Public Policy* 11 (1988), 43.

15. Joan Biskupic, "Scalia Takes a Narrow View in Seeking Congress's Will," *Cong. Q. Wkly. Rep.* 48 (1990) (quoting Senator Specter).

16. Senator Chuck Grassley (R-Iowa), "Transcript: Day Three of the Roberts Confirmation Hearings," *Washington Post*, Sept. 14, 2005 ("Justice Scalia is of the opinion that most expressions of legislative history . . . are not entitled to great weight. . . . Now, obviously, I have great regard for Justice Scalia, his intellect and legal reasoning. But, of course, . . . I don't really agree with his position.").

17. *Rector of Holy Trinity Church v. United States*, 143 U.S. 457 (1892) (contract labor case); *Griggs v. Duke Power Co.*, 420 F.2d 1225, 1239–1240 (4th Cir. 1970), rev'd in part, 401 U.S. 424 (1971) (racial employment discrimination); *United Steelworkers of Am. v. Weber*, 443 U.S. 193, 209 (1979) (affirmative action); *Public Citizen v. U.S. Dep't of Justice.*, 491 U.S. 440 (1989) (judicial nominations); *King v. Burwell*, 576 U.S. 135 S. Ct. 2480 (2015) (health care).

18. *See generally* Daniel Kahneman and Robert Sugden, "Experienced Utility as a Standard of Policy Evaluation," *Envtl. and Resource Econ.* 32 (2005), 161.

19. See Avishalom Tor and Max Bazerman, "Focusing Failures in Competitive Environments: Explaining Decision Errors in the Monty Hall Game, the Acquiring a Company Problem, and Multiparty Ultimatums," *J. Behav. Dec. Making* 16 (2003), 353.

20. Turing's classic paper started out by shifting the question from one of "mind" to whether a computer could win a game. My strategy is similar here, to shift from "mind-reading" to looking for evidence of how Congress works. Some law professors have questioned how I can argue that group intention is a coherent idea and then say that we should jettison the use of the word *intent*. Intention is a fascinating philosophical topic, but since one can eliminate the term and still talk coherently about meaning, it hardly seems necessary to statutory interpretation. Put in other words, I concur with those who believe that group intention is possible as a philosophical matter; I simply disagree on its pragmatic value.

CHAPTER 1 Congress Is Not a Court

1. Lest this seem the account of legally ignorant staffers, it is worthwhile noting that the chief counsel had been a distinguished Supreme Court clerk and top graduate of the Harvard Law School. I had already argued cases in the courts of appeals for the Bush 41 Justice Department.

2. John F. Manning, "Textualism and Legislative Intent," *Virginia Law Rev.* 91 (2005), 431–432.

3. Henry M. Hart and Albert M. Sacks, *The Legal Process: Basic Problems in the Making and Application of Law*, tent. ed. (Cambridge, MA: Harvard Univ. Press, 1958), 1278.

4. The term *positive political theory* is a broad one indeed. I make no attempt in this book to treat all positive political theory, only the variants cited.

5. I believe my approach is in fact a "positive" theory because it describes important rule-based aspects of congressional practice that are real and account for the kind of agenda setting that prevents legislative chaos.

6. I am hardly the first to recognize this. *See*, e.g., William N. Eskridge, Jr., *Dynamic Statutory Interpretation* (Cambridge, MA: Harvard Univ. Press, 1994), 7 (noting the importance of "theories of legislatures"); ibid. ("The 'study of statutory interpretation' . . . demands a theory of Congress. . . ."); ibid., 14 ("Traditional legal writers have no theory of legislatures in general.").

7. Jeremy Waldron, *The Dignity of Legislation* (Cambridge: Cambridge Univ. Press, 1999). Even those who critique simplistic views of legislative supremacy recognize that it is a widely held principle, even "intellectual boilerplate." *See*, e.g., William N. Eskridge, "Spinning Legislative Supremacy," *Georgetown Law Journal* 78 (1989), 319.

8. Jerry L. Mashaw, *Greed, Chaos & Governance: Using Public Choice to Improve Public Law* (New Haven, CT: Yale Univ. Press, 1997), 2.

9. A minimalist theory is based on empiricism, but parsimonious empiricism. Like a description of a chess game that does not include the rules of chess, recent empirical work on legislative drafting (including my own) can yield a superfluity of data that fails this principle of parsimony. *See*, e.g., Victoria F. Nourse and Jane S. Schacter, "The Politics of Legislative Drafting: A Congressional Case Study," *New York Univ. Law Rev.* 77 (2002), 575. Abbe Gluck and Lisa Bressman, "Statutory Interpretation from the Inside: An Empirical Study of Congressional Drafting, Delegation, and the Canons: Part I," *Stanford Law Rev.* 65 (2013), 901.

10. *See*, e.g., Max Radin, "Statutory Interpretation," *Harvard Law Rev.* 43 (1930), 863, 870.

11. Among academics, "decision theory" may suggest an entirely different literature; by using the term, I mean no disrespect. Adrian Vermeule, *Judging under Uncertainty: An Institutional Theory of Legal Interpretation* (Cambridge, MA: Harvard Univ. Press, 2006), 171 ("In economics, philosophy, and elsewhere, 'decision theory' is the branch of rational choice that studies decision making by rational actors subject to various constraints.").

12. I borrow the phrase from Thomas Nagel, although for different purposes. Thomas Nagel, *The View from Nowhere* (New York: Oxford Univ. Press, 1986).

13. John Ferejohn, "Practical Institutionalism," in *Rethinking Political Institutions: The Art of the State*, ed. Ian Shapiro, et al. (New York: New York Univ. Press, 2006), 72–88.

14. Graham Allison and Philip Zelikow, *The Essence of Decision*, 2d ed. (New York: Longman, 1999). *See* Rufus E. Miles, Jr., "The Origin and Meaning of Miles' Law," *Pub. Admin. Rev.* 38 (1978), 399.

15. K. Patricia Cross, "Not Can, but *Will* College Teaching Be Improved?" *New Directions Higher Educ.* (Spring 1977), 10. The literature is vast and reaches back decades. *See*, e.g., Daniel Kahneman and Amos Tversky, "On the Psychology of Prediction," *Psychol. Rev.* 80 (1973), 237, 249 ("People are prone to experience much confidence in highly fallible judgements. . . ."). A useful lay compilation appears in Rolf Dobelli, *The Art of Thinking Clearly*, trans. Nicky Griffin (New York: Harper, 2013).

16. The term *electoral connection* is David Mayhew's. David R. Mayhew, *Congress: The Electoral Connection*, 2d. ed. (New Haven, CT: Yale Univ. Press, 2004).

17. Gina Misiroglu, *The Handy Politics Answer Book* (Detroit: Visible Ink Press, 2003), 331 (citing John Stuart Mill, *Considerations on Representative Government* (Harper & Brothers 1862), 115–116).

18. Charles L. Black, Jr., "The Working Balance of the American Political Department," *Hastings Const. Law Q.* 1 (1974), 13, 16–17.

19. Richard L. Hall, *Participation in Congress* (New Haven, CT: Yale Univ. Press, 1996), 3.

20. R. Douglas Arnold, *The Logic of Congressional Action* (New Haven, CT: Yale Univ. Press, 1990), 5.

21. Mayhew, *Congress*, 5–6; John W. Kingdon, *Congressmen's Voting Decisions*, 3d ed. (Ann Arbor: Univ. of Mich. Press, 1989), 29–71; Barry R. Weingast, "A Rational Choice Perspective on Congressional Norms," *Amer. Journal Pol. Sci.* 23 (May 1979), 245, 249; Richard F. Fenno Jr., *Home-Style: House Members in Their Districts* (Boston: Little, Brown, 1978), 31; Donald R. Matthews, *U.S. Senators and Their World* (Chapel Hill: Univ. of North Carolina Press, 1960), 218–242; Morris P. Fiorina, *Congress: Keystone of the Washington Establishment*, 2d ed. (New Haven, CT: Yale Univ. Press, 1989), 7; Keith Krehbiel, *Pivotal Politics: A Theory of U.S. Lawmaking* (Chicago: Univ. of Chicago Press, 1998); Lewis A. Froman Jr., *Congressmen and Their Constituencies* (Chicago: Rand McNally, 1963), 9.

22. *See*, e.g., Robert A. Bernstein, *Elections, Representation, and Congressional Voting Behavior: The Myth of Constituency Control* (Englewood Cliffs, NJ: Prentice Hall, 1989), 104. On the failure of this kind of study to account for the intensity of preference and measure activity, see Richard Hall, *Participation in Congress* (New Haven, CT: Yale Univ. Press, 1996), 58 ("To the extent that a member believes that her district has an interest in an issue that comes before her, the more involved in the legislative action she is likely to become.").

23. Mayhew, *Congress*, 40.

24. Hall, *Participation in Congress*, 57–65.

25. Arnold, *The Logic of Congressional Action*, 10–11.

26. Contrary to conventional wisdom, the vast majority of legislation never sees the inside of a courtroom. Scholars who take the contrary view are typically starting with a sample of cases biased toward interpretive issues, namely those cases ending up in appellate courts. Positive political theorists rightly argue that the players do anticipate horizontal moves (what a president or court will do), but as I argue later, the vertical dimension can easily dominate horizontal strategic concerns.

27. James Madison, *The Federalist Papers*, No. 51, ed. Lawrence Goldman (New York: Oxford Univ. Press, 2008), 482.

28. James Madison, *The Federalist Papers*, No. 52, ed. Lawrence Goldman (New York: Oxford Univ. Press, 2008), 490.

29. Nelson W. Polsby, "Legislatures," *Handbook of Political Science: Governmental Institutions and Processes*, vol. 5, ed. Fred I. Greenstein and Nelson W. Polsby (Reading, MA: Addison-Wesley Pub., 1975), 277–296.

30. Norman Ornstein, "Freedom Paper No. 3: The Role of the Legislature in a Democracy," in *Freedom Papers 3*, ed. Wayne Hall, et al. (Washington, DC: U.S. Dept. of State, 1992).

31. Ibid.

32. Polsby, *Handbook of Political Science*, 277.

33. Ornstein, "Freedom Paper No. 3." As James Q. Wilson once noted, this is reflected in the very terms used to describe these institutions: the word *parliament* derives from the French word *parler* ("to talk"), whereas the root of the word *congress* is the Latin *congressus* ("to come together or assemble"). *See* ibid.

34. Jeremy Waldron, "Vagueness in Law and Language: Some Philosophical Issues," *Cal. Law Rev.* 82 (1994), 509, 510.

35. Press Release, Senator Olympia Snowe, "Snowe Urges Transparency during Health Care Reform Negotiations" (Jan. 7, 2010) (discussing a letter from Sen. Snowe and other Republican senators to Senator Harry Reid).

36. 136 Cong. Rec. 14,564 (1990) (statement of Sen. Biden).

37. 145 Cong. Rec. 25,443 (1999) (statement of Sen. Wellstone).

38. *Citizens United v. FEC*, 558 U.S. 310, 346 (citations omitted).

39. Jeremy Waldron, *Law and Disagreement* (New York: Oxford Univ. Press, 1999), 10 (emphasis omitted).

40. Mayhew, *Congress*, 106.

41. Niccolo Machiavelli, *Discourses on Livy*, Bk. I, trans. Harvey C. Mansfield and Nathan Tarcoy (Chicago: Univ. of Chicago Press 1996), 16.

42. John Locke, *Two Treatises of Government*, ed. Thomas I. Cook (New York: Hafner Publishing 1947), 229.

43. John Stuart Mill, *Considerations on Representative Government* (Auckland: Floating Press, 1861), 105.

44. *See* Jane S. Schacter, "Accounting for Accountability in Statutory Interpretation and Beyond," in *Issues in Legal Scholarship*, Article 5 (Dec. 2002), http://www.bepress.com/cgi; *see also* Jane S. Schacter, "Digitally Democratizing Congress: Technology and Political Accountability," *Boston Univ. Law Rev.* 89 (2009), 641, 643.

45. *See*, e.g., Mark Tushnet and Larry Yackle, "Symbolic Statutes and Real Laws: The Pathologies of the Antiterrorism and Effective Death Penalty Act and the Prison Litigation Reform Act," *Duke Law Rev.* 47 (1997–1998), 1, 2–3.

46. Some might argue that state elected judges are differently situated, but in fact all judges, elected or not, are constrained by the structure of their institution in the sense that they are limited by the cases and controversies brought to them. They have no general jurisdiction to initiate decisions; they are passive entities that must await the problems that come to them on an individualized

basis in case-by-case form. See Neil K. Komesar, *Imperfect Alternatives: Choosing Institutions in Law, Economics, and Public Policy* (Chicago: Univ. of Chicago Press, 1994), 126.

47. I recognize that there is a wide political science literature suggesting that courts are roughly responsive to democratic concerns. The attitudinal school of thought suggests that there is nothing to judging other than politics. This reduction of law to politics, for anyone who has worked in both, as I have, is a fundamental category mistake.

48. *See* Fred Strebeigh, *Equal: Women Reshape American Law* (New York: W. W. Norton, 2009), 309–444.

49. Violence Against Women Act (VAWA), S. 11, 103rd Cong. § 302(e)(l) (1993); *see* Victoria F. Nourse, "Where Violence, Relationship, and Equality Meet: The Violence Against Women's Act Civil Rights Remedy," *Wis. Women's Law J.* 11 (1996–1997), 111 ("random acts of violence unrelated to gender").

50. Meir Dan-Cohen, "Decision Rules and Conduct Rules: On Acoustic Separation in Criminal Law," *Harv. Law Rev.* 97 (1984), 625.

51. Antonin Scalia, *A Matter of Interpretation: Federal Courts and the Law* (Princeton, NJ: Princeton Univ. Press, 1997), 17.

52. Aharon Barak, *Purposive Interpretation in Law*, trans. Sara Bashi (Princeton, NJ: Princeton Univ. Press, 2005), 97.

53. *See* William N. Eskridge, Jr., "Vetogates, Chevron, Preemption," *Notre Dame L. Rev.* 83 (2007–2008), 1441, 1444–1448; David W. Brady and Craig Volden, *Revolving Gridlock: Politics and Policy from Jimmy Carter to George W. Bush*, 2d ed. (Boulder, CO: Westview Press, 2006); McNollgast, "Legislative Intent: The Use of Positive Political Theory in Statutory Interpretation," *Law and Contemp. Probs.* 57 (1994), 3, 11 ("It is difficult and time-consuming to change most prior legislative bargains.").

54. For those confused by this reference, the House Rules committee issues a "rule" for the debate of bills. The rule typically prescribes the time for debate and the amendments to be debated.

55. U.S. Const., art. I, § 7, cl. 2.

56. Sanford Levinson, *Our Undemocratic Constitution: Where the Constitution Goes Wrong (and How We the People Can Correct It)* (Oxford: Oxford Univ. Press, 2006); Robert A. Dahl, *How Democratic Is the American Constitution?* 2d ed. (New Haven, CT: Yale Univ. Press, 2003); Keith Krehbiel, *Pivotal Politics: A Theory of U.S. Lawmaking* (Chicago: Univ. of Chicago Press, 1998); *see also* Brady and Volden, *Revolving Gridlock*.

57. Victoria F. Nourse and Jane S. Schacter, "The Politics of Legislative Drafting: A Congressional Case Study," *New York Univ. Law Rev.* 77 (2002), 575, 615.

58. Ibid.; *see also* Abbe Gluck and Lisa Bressman, "Statutory Interpretation from the Inside: An Empirical Study of Congressional Drafting, Delegation, and the Canons: Part I," *Stanford Law Rev.* 65 (2013), 901, 996–998.

59. Nourse and Schacter, "The Politics of Legislative Drafting," 575, 615.

60. Eskridge, *Dynamic Statutory Interpretation*, 10–11.

61. Ibid., 9–10.

62. William N. Eskridge, Jr., and John Ferejohn, "The Article I, Section 7 Game," *Georgetown Law J.* 80 (1992), 523.

63. *See* Joseph A. Grundfest and A. C. Pritchard, "Statutes with Multiple Personality Disorders: The Value of Ambiguity in Statutory Design and Interpretation," *Stanford Law Rev.* 54 (2002), 627.

64. McNollgast, "Positive Canons: The Role of Legislative Bargains in Statutory Interpretation," *Georgetown Law J.* 80 (1992), 705, 715.

65. *See*, e.g., Tim Groseclose and Nolan McCarty, "The Politics of Blame: Bargaining before an Audience," *Amer. Journal of Pol. Sci.* 45 (2001), 100, 101 ("Almost all models of bargaining ignore the possibility that the two primary negotiators want to send signals to a third party."). In the international arena, *see*, e.g., James D. Fearon, "Domestic Political Audiences and the Escalation of International Disputes," *Amer. Political Sci. Rev.* 88 (1994), 577.

66. Why does the congressperson care about the vertical market (the constituency) more than the horizontal market (the court/agency)? In part, the answer is timing. A representative's electoral fate depends upon the claim that she has done something; a court may undo that, but the judicial intervention is most likely to occur long after the election. In part, the answer is the power of the vertical market to trump the horizontal market. Even if the court rules against the representative, that might not yield a bad electoral outcome: it might simply add to the salience and importance of the position taking of the representative. More people might vote for her precisely because the court rejected her position.

67. *Teague v. Lane*, 489 U.S. 288 (1989).

68. Author's personal recollection.

69. 110 Cong. Rec. 13,492 (1964).

70. Ibid., 13,503–13,504 (statement of Sen. Case: "I object to the amendment suggested by the Senator from Texas because, first, it is unnecessary. . . . The amendment is unnecessary"); *see* ibid., 13,504 (statement of Sen. Humphrey: "These tests are legal. They do not need to be legalized a second time."); ibid. (statement of Sen. Humphrey: "That is why I said I did not think the proposed new language was necessary.").

71. 110 Cong. Rec. 13,504 (1964).

72. *See*, e.g., 420 F. 2d 1225 (4th Cir. 1970), rev'd *Griggs v. Duke Power Co.*, 401 U.S. 424 (1971). For a more complete explanation of the legislative history, see Chapter 3.

73. H.R. Rep. No. 93–1597 (1974) (Conf. Rep.).

74. *Green v. Bock Laundry Machine*, 490 U.S. 504, 505 (1989).

75. Ibid., 510.

76. For a fuller discussion of this case, see Chapter 3.

77. Krehbiel, *Pivotal Politics.*

78. For a devastating critique of interest group theory, *see* Jerry Mashaw, *Greed, Chaos & Governance: Using Public Choice to Improve Public Law* (New Haven, CT: Yale Univ. Press, 1997), 87–96; see also Jack M. Beermann, "Interest Group Politics and Judicial Behavior: Macey's Public Choice," *Notre Dame Law Rev.* 67 (1991), 183.

79. *See*, e.g., E. E. Schattschneider, *Party Government* (New York: Holt, Rinehart & Winston, 1942) (party model); David W. Rohde, *Parties and Leaders in the Postreform House* (Chicago: Univ. of Chicago Press, 1991) (conditional party model); Duncan Black, *The Theory of Committees and Elections* (Cambridge: Cambridge Univ. Press, 1958) (median voter model).

80. *See* Krehbiel, *Pivotal Politics*, 8–13; ibid., 9 ("While U.S. parties adopt platforms in national conventions, their platforms are usually amorphous, frequently identical on many provisions, and hardly ever serve effectively as constraints during the campaign or after the election."); ibid., 12–13 (median voter theory predicts that winning voting coalitions are "usually small . . . near minimum-majority size . . .").

81. *See* ibid., 13–14. As Krehbiel writes, "consider . . . all votes on final passage of laws enacted by the 102d and 103d Congresses (1991–1994). The average size of the winning coalition on these 324 votes is 79 percent." Ibid., 6; *see also* David R. Mayhew, *Divided We Govern: Party Control, Lawmaking, And Investigations, 1946–2002*, 2d ed. (New Haven, CT: Yale Univ. Press, 2005), 121–123, 222–223 (reporting large coalitions for significant bills). Even among positive political theorists addressing legislative matters there is dispute about the meaning or viability of Arrow's theorem, *see infra* Chapter 2, Part 3. Compare McNollgast, "Legislative Intent: The Use of Positive Political Theory in Statutory Interpretation," *Law and Contemp. Probs.* 57 (1994), 3; Kenneth A. Shepsle, "Congress Is a 'They,' Not an 'It': Legislative Intent as an Oxymoron," *Int'l Rev. of Law and Econ.* 12 (1992), 239–256.

82. Krehbiel, *Pivotal Politics*, 3–19.

83. Kenneth A. Shepsle and Barry R. Weingast, "Positive Theories of Congressional Institutions," in *Positive Theories of Congressional Institutions* (Ann Arbor: Univ. of Michigan Press, 1995), 5, 7 ("[In] no sense was there evidence that majority cycling was a constant companion of legislative life."). McNollgast, "Legislative Intent," 20 ("The structure and process of legislative decision making, once established, leads to policy choices that are structurally stable.") (citing Kenneth A, Shepsle, "Institutional Arrangements and Equilibrium in Multidimensional Voting Models," *Amer. Journal of Pol. Sci.* 27 (1979), 23); *see also* Gerry Mackie, *Democracy Defended* (Cambridge, UK: Cambridge Univ. Press, 2003), 156 ("The Arrow theorem is a great piece of work. It is a logical exercise, it does not describe the real world.").

CHAPTER 2 Statutory Interpretation Theories Misunderstand Congress

1. 15 Cong. Rec. 5358 (1884) (emphasis added).

2. 16 Cong. Rec. 1633 (1885). These are excerpts taken from the congressional debate about one of the great canonical cases of statutory interpretation, *Rector, Church of the Holy Trinity v. United States*, 143 U.S. 457 (1892), a case made famous by Antonin Scalia, "Common-Law Courts in a Civil-Law System: The Role of United States Federal Courts in Interpreting the Constitution and

Laws," in *A Matter of Interpretation: Federal Courts and the Law*, ed. Amy Gutmann (Princeton, NJ: Princeton Univ. Press, 1997), 3.

3. I limit myself to three of the most widely cited theories of statutory interpretation with analogues in judicial practice. Textualism and purposivism are the dominant modes. Positive political theory is included because textualism was at one time considered supported by its claims and because both share an inclination toward contract theory, which is well known among judges and lawyers. There are, of course, a number of academics who have offered their own theories. I engage with a broader range of academic theories at various points in the text and footnotes, given that the audience for this book is not only academics but also lawyers and judges.

4. Scalia, "Common-Law Courts in a Civil-Law System," 3–47.

5. William Eskridge, Jr., "Textualism, the Unknown Ideal?" *Mich. Law Rev.* 96 (1998), 1509, 1511.

6. William N. Eskridge, Jr., "The New Textualism," *UCLA Law Rev.* 37 (1990).

7. Scalia, "Common-Law Courts in a Civil-Law System," 20.

8. Scalia, "Common-Law Courts in a Civil-Law System," 13.

9. Ibid., 31.

10. Ibid., 17 (emphasis added).

11. Ibid., 31 (emphasis added).

12. William N. Eskridge, Jr. "Textualism, the Unknown Ideal?," *Michigan Law Rev.* 96 (1998), 1514.

13. Jonathan Molot, "The Rise and Fall of Textualism," *Columbia Law Rev.* 106 (2006), 1, 36.

14. *See* Chapter 3's notes for recent case examples. For a recent empirical study, *see generally* Abbe Gluck and Lisa Schultz Bressman, "Statutory Interpretation from the Inside: An Empirical Study of Congressional Drafting, Delegation, and Canons: Part I," *Stanford Law Rev.* 65 (2013), 901, 965 ("Our findings suggest that many of the assumptions on which this critique [of legislative history] relies are unfounded. Perhaps most importantly, legislative history was emphatically viewed by almost all of our respondents—Republicans and Democrats, majority and minority—as the *most important* drafting and interpretive tool apart from text."); James Brudney and Corey Ditslear, "Liberal Justices' Reliance on Legislative History: Principle, Strategy and the Scalia Effect," *Berkeley J. of Employment and Labor Law* 29 (2008), 117; *see also* Abner J. Mikva and Eric Lane, "The Muzak of Justice Scalia's Revolutionary Call to Read Unclear Statutes Narrowly," *Southern Methodist Univ. Law Rev.* 53 (2000), 121, 123 ("The Supreme Court, other federal courts, and state courts throughout the country continue to use legislative history to interpret statutes.").

15. *Rector, Church of the Holy Trinity v. United States*, 143 U.S. 457 (1892).

16. Ibid., 458 (citing Act of Feb. 26, 1885, ch. 164, 23 Stat. 332 (repealed 1952)).

17. Ibid., 459.

18. Ibid., 472.

19. Scalia, "Common-Law Courts in a Civil-Law System," 20.

20. Ibid., 21.

21. Miranda McGowan, "Do As I Do, Not As I Say: An Empirical Investigation of Justice Scalia's Ordinary Meaning Method of Statutory Interpretation," *Mississippi Law J.* 78 (2008), 129, 143 (citing Scalia, *supra* note 2, at 17–18).

22. This is apparently filtered through the eyes of Judge Friendly, who once reported that when Justice Frankfurter was still teaching, he urged his students to follow a three-pronged rule for statutory interpretation: (1) read the statute, (2) read the statute, and (3) read the statute. *See* Henry J. Friendly, "Mr. Justice Frankfurter and the Reading of Statutes," in *Benchmarks* (Chicago: Univ. of Chicago Press, 1967), 196, 202.

23. John F. Manning, "Textualism and Legislative Intent," *Virginia Law Rev.* 91 (2005), 419, 431, 438 ("tortuous"); ibid., 423, 430 note 34, 431, 444 note 84, 450 ("opaque"); ibid., 424, 429 note 30, 430, 438 note 64, 448 note 96, 450 ("complex"); ibid., 423, 426 note 23, 431 ("cumbersome"); ibid., 432 note 43 ("strategic"); ibid., 431, 432 note 43 ("arbitrary"); ibid., 420, 425, 445 ("awkward"); ibid., 431, 432 ("nonsubstantive"); ibid., 431 ("highly intricate").

24. Jane Schacter, "Metademocracy: The Changing Structure of Legitimacy in Statutory Interpretation," *Harvard Law Rev.* 108 (1995), 593, 644–645.

25. Mikva and Lane, "The Muzak," 137 ("He seems to frequently argue despite what seems to be evident ambiguity that a statute is clear.").

26. Scalia, "Common-Law Courts in a Civil-Law System," 32 (emphasis in original).

27. Mikva and Lane argue that there is a political tilt to new textualism that "is directed at limiting statutory scope rather than expanding it." Ibid., 123; *see also* Frank B. Cross, *The Theory and Practice of Statutory Interpretation* (Stanford, CA: Stanford Law Books, 2009), 27–57, 163 (arguing that Judge Easterbrook's "Statutes·Domains" approach (*Univ. Chicago Law Rev.* 50 (1983), 533) is openly anti-regulation as it would limit construction to cases in which a case was clearly covered by the statute). In fact, as I argue below, there is nothing terribly libertarian about textualism as a matter of logic; in *Holy Trinity*, for example, the new textualist view *expanded* the application of the statute from the baseline prototypical meaning of manual labor.

28. *See*, e.g., John Manning, "Textualism as a Nondelegation Doctrine," *Columbia Law Rev.* 97 (1997), 673, 685 (attributing reliance on Arrow's theorem to Judge Easterbrook).

29. On the pervasive and unfortunate influence of cycling theory within political science, *see* Gerry Mackie, *Democracy Defended* (New York: Cambridge Univ. Press, 2003).

30. Manning, "Textualism," 431 note 25.

31. Even before the economic collapse now called the Great Recession and his recantation of some portions of law and economics, one of its founders, Judge Posner, wrote that he believed that the "economic approach to legislation" was "incomplete," and he disagreed with those who had pushed the interest group "line hard." Richard A. Posner, "Legislation and Its Interpretation: A Primer," *Nebraska Law Rev.* 68 (1989), 431, 434. More recent work by positive political theorists has questioned some of the premises of strict application of economic assumptions to the political world. *See*, e.g., John Ferejohn, "Practical

Institutionalism," in *Rethinking Political Institutions: The Art of the State*, ed. Ian Shapiro, et al. (New York: New York Univ. Press, 2006), 72, 73–74 (rejecting basic economic assumption that preferences are exogenous to institutions). Even the work in political science on structure-induced equilibria shows the power of institutions to correct the more extreme predictions of Arrovian theory. Kenneth A. Shepsle and Barry R. Weingast, "Positive Theories of Congressional Institutions," in *Positive Theories of Congressional Institutions*, ed. Kenneth A. Shepsle and Barry R. Weingast (Ann Arbor: Univ. of Michigan Press, 1995), 22.

32. U.S. Const., art. I, § 7, cl. 2.

33. Victoria F. Nourse and Jane S. Schacter, "The Politics of Legislative Drafting: A Congressional Case Study," *New York Univ. Law Rev.* 77 (2002), 575, 614–615; *see* Gluck and Bressman, "Statutory Interpretation, Part I," 901; Abbe Gluck and Lisa Schultz Bressman, "Statutory Interpretation from the Inside: An Empirical Study of Congressional Drafting, Delegation, and Canons: Part II," *Stanford Law Rev.* 66 (2014), 725.

34. Dakota Rudesill, Comment, "Closing the Legislative Experience Gap: How a Legislative Law Clerk Program Will Benefit the Legal Profession and Congress," *Washington Univ. Law Rev.* 87 (2010), 699, 702 ("On the most prestigious law faculties, only 5 percent of professors have worked for a legislative institution—local, state, federal or international.").

35. David R Mayhew, *Congress: The Electoral Connection* (New Haven, CT: Yale Univ. Press, 1974).

36. As Professor Bill Eskridge notes, "the first definition of the term "labor" listed in the 1879 and 1886 editions of Webster's Dictionary was "physical toil or bodily exertion." William N. Eskridge, Jr., Abbe R. Gluck, and Victoria F. Nourse, *Statutes, Regulation, and Interpretation: Legislation and Administration in the Republic of Statutes* (St. Paul, MN: West Publishing, 2014), 310. Most of the debate about the statute in *Holy Trinity* assumes "manual labor" as the prototypical object of the legislation. 15 Cong. Rec. 5349–5371 (1884) (House debate and passage); 15 Cong. Rec. 6057–6067 (1884) (Senate postponement of bill to next session). For a fuller treatment of *Holy Trinity, see* Chapter 3.

37. Lawrence M. Solan, "The New Textualists' New Text," *Loyola of Los Angeles Law Rev.* 38 (2005), 2027, 2041–2042.

38. *Holy Trinity* at 472. *Holy Trinity* is typically known as an "absurdity" case, but one way of thinking about absurdity is to view it as arising when there is a strong conflict between legalist meaning (all workers) and prototypical meaning (manual labor or service). Compare, for example, standard examples of "absurdity": "blood-letting" (prototypical meaning = fight; legalist meaning = any bloodletting, including by a surgeon); "prison escape" (prototypical meaning = escape to flout law; legalist meaning = any escape, even if to escape fire).

39. 16 Cong. Rec. 1782 (1885) (statement of Sen. Platt).

40. There is an analogy here to HLA Hart's famous distinction between core and penumbral meaning in distinguishing between easy and hard cases. H. L. A. Hart, *The Concept of Law* (Oxford, UK: Clarendon Press, 1961), 607–615. Of course, there is a certain irony in using the word *penumbral* to describe textualism as textualism is associated with conservatism, and Justice Douglas's use of *constitutional penumbra* has made him the object of conservative ridicule.

41. William N. Eskridge, Jr., *Dynamic Statutory Interpretation* (Cambridge, MA: Harvard Univ. Press, 1994), 4 (quoting *Eyston v. Studd*, 2 Plowden 459, 465, 75 Eng. Rep. 688, 695 (K. B. 1574) (reporter's commentary)).

42. John Locke, *An Essay Concerning Human Understanding*, ed. Alexander Campbell Fraser (Oxford, UK: Clarendon Press 1894), 131; William Blackstone, Commentaries on the Laws of England I (Chicago, IL: Univ. of Chicago Press, 1979), 61 ("The most universal and effectual way of discovering the true meaning of a law . . . is by considering the reason and spirit of it . . .").

43. Frederick Schauer, *Thinking Like a Lawyer: A New Introduction to Legal Reasoning* (Cambridge, MA: Harvard Univ. Press 2009), 151–158 (discussing this debate).

44. Manning, "Textualism," 434–435 note 25.

45. Molot, "The Rise and Fall," 48 note 8.

46. Thomas Merrill, "Textualism and the Future of the *Chevron* Doctrine," *Washington Univ. Law Qrtly*. 72 (1994), 351, 372.

47. Molot, "The Rise and Fall," 46 note 8 (citing Richard J. Pierce, Jr., "The Supreme Court's New Hypertextualism: An Invitation to Cacophony and Incoherence in the Administrative State," *Columbia Law Rev.* 95 (1995), 749, 752).

48. Manning, "Textualism,"435, note 25 (footnote omitted).

49. *Chisom v. Roemer*, 501 U.S. 380, 404 (1991) (Justice Scalia, dissenting) (emphasis added). In the constitutional context, he is even more insistent; *see District of Columbia v. Heller*, 554 U.S. 570, 576–577 (2008).

50. McGowan, "Do As I Do," 149 note 22.

51. Cross, *Theory and Practice*, 66 note 28.

52. Ward Farnsworth, Dustin F. Guzior, and Anup Mulani, "Ambiguity about Ambiguity: An Empirical Inquiry into Legal Interpretation," *Journal of Legal Analysis* 2 (2010), 257. Farnsworth, Guzior, and Mulani usefully distinguish between plain meaning as an "internal view" and "ordinary meaning" as external. Whereas the question "is this meaning plain?" tends to elicit views correlated with strong ideological positions (the internal view), the question "would an ordinary person think this meaning is plain?" (the external view) does not.

53. Molot, "The Rise and Fall," 36, note 8 ("So long as textualism is on the attack . . . little attention is devoted to the interpretive methodology textualism offers to replace strong purposivism or variations within the textualist movement.").

54. *See*, e.g., Adrian Vermeule, "Legislative History and the Limits of Judicial Competence: The Untold Story of *Holy Trinity Church*," *Stanford Law Rev.* 50 (1998), 1833, 1852–1853.

55. Cross, *Theory and Practice*, 82–83 note 28 (summarizing this evidence and relying on Daniel J. Bussel, "Textualism's Failures: A Study of Overruled Bankruptcy Decisions," *Vanderbilt Law Rev.* 53 (2000), 887, 909–910; William N. Eskridge, Jr., "Overriding Supreme Court Statutory Interpretation Decisions," *Yale Law Journal* 101 (1991), 331, 350 table 8; and Michael E. Solimine and James L. Walker, "The Next Word: Congressional Response to Supreme Court Statutory Decisions," *Temple Law Rev.* 65 (1992), 425); *see also* Matthew R. Christiansen and William N. Eskridge, Jr., "Congressional Overrides of Supreme Court Statutory Interpretation Decisions, 1967–2011," *Texas Law Rev.*

92 (2014), 1317; Victoria F. Nourse, "Overrides: The Super Study," *Texas Law Rev.* 92 (2014), 205.

56. *See* John Manning, "Textualism and the Equity of the Statute," *Columbia Law Rev.* 101 (2001), 1, 16 note 64 ("Successful communication depends on meanings shared by interpretive communities" (quoting *Continental Can Co. v. Chi. Truck Drivers & Helpers & Warehouse Workers Union (Indep.) Pension Fund*, 916 F.2d 1154, 1157 (7th Cir. 1990))). *See generally* Stanley Fish, *Is There a Text in This Class? The Authority of Interpretive Communities* (Cambridge, MA: Harvard Univ. Press, 1980), 338–354.

57. Textualists are not alone in this claim; it arises frequently in game theory analyses of statutory interpretation. *See* Daniel B. Rodriguez and Barry R. Weingast, "The Positive Political Theory of Legislative History: New Perspectives on the 1964 Civil Rights Act and Its Interpretation," *Univ. of Pennsylvania Law. Rev.* 151 (2003), 1417.

58. Henry M. Hart, Jr., and Albert M. Sacks, *The Legal Process: Basic Problems in the Making and Application of Law*, ed. William N. Eskridge, Jr., and Philip P. Frickey (St. Paul, MN: West Publishing,1994), 1374–1380.

59. *Holy Trinity*, 143 U.S. 457, 463.

60. I recognize that this quotation is from one of the bill's major opponents, but as I argue in Chapter 3, it is a concession against interest; both opponents and proponents agreed that the core 'mischief' applied to the contract manual labor system. It is a concession against his interest because Morgan opposed the bill because it was too broad and yet conceded that lecturers on religious topics were not covered.

61. Carol Chomsky, "Unlocking the Mysteries of *Holy Trinity*: Spirit, Letter, and History in Statutory Interpretation," *Columbia Law Rev.* 100 (2000), 901; Vermeule, "Legislative History," 1833; Eskridge, Gluck, and Nourse, *Statutes*, 310–311 note 38.

62. Vermeule, "Legislative History," 1850–1851 note 61.

63. Chomsky, "Unlocking," 923 note 61.

64. Hart and Sacks, *The Legal Process*, 1374–1378.

65. Robert A. Katzmann, *Judging Statutes* (New York: Oxford Univ. Press, 2014), 55.

66. Schauer, *Thinking Like a Lawyer*, 167.

67. Nourse and Schacter, "The Politics of Legislative Drafting," 615, note 35.

68. Mary Douglas, *How Institutions Think* (Syracuse, NY: Syracuse Univ. Press, 1986).

69. *See* James B. Thayer, "The Origin and Scope of the American Doctrine of Constitutional Law," *Harvard Law Rev.* 7 (1893), 129, 142.

70. *See* Gerald MacCallum, "Legislative Intent," *Yale Law J.* 75 (1966), 754, 771–772.

71. The suit was ultimately brought by a railroad financier. *See* Chomsky, "Unlocking," 910 note 61 ("John Stewart Kennedy, a prominent banker, financier, and railroad director").

72. 15 Cong. Rec. 5358 (1884) (statement of Rep. O'Neill).

73. Bargaining theorists would tend to say that, in such a situation, the "deal" should be honored, the language "labor or service of any kind" interpreted

broadly, or the lecturer exemption to be interpreted narrowly, because that was the price of bill passage. In fact, this is a highly speculative conclusion. Even if true, it should not result in a legalist/peripheral interpretation of labor. In fact, given the audience costs at stake, precisely the opposite rule should hold true. To honor the bargain as the game theorists might suggest is to give the minority opponents precisely the victory that they could not obtain because the audience costs were too high to openly oppose the bill (who was for slave labor in an era that still remembered the civil war?). Indeed, applying bargaining theory in this way can elevate the loser's claims to winner's status.

74. Compare Cass R. Sunstein, "Beyond the Republican Revival," *Yale Law J.* 97 (1988), 1539, with Jerry L. Mashaw, "As if Republican Interpretation," *Yale Law J.* 97 (1988), 1673.

75. *See* Barbara Sinclair, *Unorthodox Lawmaking: New Legislative Processes in the U.S. Congress*, 4th ed. (Washington, DC: CQ Press, 2011).

76. *See* prologue to this chapter (Sen. Mitchell example).

77. For example, in *Public Citizen v. American Bar Association*, 491 U.S. 440 (1989), the best undisputed example, based on the legislative record, was a committee established by the President or any agency; in *McBoyle v. United States*, 283 U.S. 25 (1931), the original "vehicle in the park" case, the best undisputed example was a car. In *United States v. Yates*, 135 S. Ct. 1074 (2015), the recent fish coverup case, the best undisputed example was shredding financial documents. In the more controversial case, *United Steelworkers of Am. v. Weber*, 443 U.S. 193, 209 (1979), I would contend that the best undisputed example of a program "required" by the government was one ordered by the EEOC or other federal agency.

78. Purposivists might also worry that this sounds like the "expected application" view in constitutional originalism. "Expected application" originalism suffers from problems not shared by modern statutory interpretation—such as the quality of 200-year-old evidence, a problem that does not plague last year's Congressional Record. Moreover, the idea of "expected" applications is different from undisputed applications. Expected to whom? The public, the framers, their opponents? The best undisputed application is one that would not be denied by supporters or opponents in the legislature, if asked whether the statute covered that application.

79. *See* Frank H. Easterbrook, "Statutes' Domains," *Univ. Chicago Law Rev.* 50 (1983), 533, 537.

80. For more elaboration of "paradigm cases," *see* Jed Rubenfeld, *Freedom and Time* (New Haven, CT: Yale Univ. Press, 2001), 178–195; Jed Rubenfeld, "The Paradigm-Case Method," *Yale Law Journal* 115 (2006), 1977.

81. *See* Joseph A. Grundfest and A. C. Pritchett, "Statutes with Multiple Personality Disorders: The Value of Ambiguity in Statutory Design and Interpretation," *Stanford Law Rev.* 54 (2002), 627, 652–653.

82. *See*, e.g., William N. Eskridge, Jr., and John Ferejohn, "The Article I, Section 7 Game," *Georgetown Law J.* 80 (1992), 523.

83. McNollgast, "Legislative Intent: The Use of Positive Political Theory in Statutory Interpretation," *Law and Contemp. Probs.* 57 (1994), 3; McNollgast, "Positive Canons: The Role of Legislative Bargains in Statutory Interpretation,"

Georgetown Law J. 80 (1992), 705; McNollgast, "The Theory of Interpretive Canon and Legislative Behavior," *Int'l Review of Law and Econ.* 12 (1992), 235; John Ferejohn and Barry Weingast, "Limitation of Statutes: Strategic Statutory Interpretation," *Georgetown Law J.* 80 (1992), 565.

84. When textualists cite positive political theorists as allies, they are typically citing that strain of positive political theory that Gerry Mackie calls the "irrationalist" thesis, following William Riker's work, with emphasis on Arrow's theorem. Mackie, *Democracy Defended*, at 23, 156 note 31.

85. There is some difference on this issue among positive political theorists; *see*, e.g., Kenneth A. Shepsle, "Congress Is a 'They,' Not an 'It': Legislative Intent as an Oxymoron," *Int'l Review of Law and Econ.* 12 (1992), 239, 241–256.

86. In this book, I define positive political theory in a narrow fashion to include only those who are using game theory models to describe statutory interpretation. In fact, such theory casts a shadow wider than statutory interpretation itself. *See* Daniel A. Farber and Philip P. Frickey, "Foreword: Positive Political Theory in the Nineties," *Georgetown Law J.* 80 (1991), 457–463 (discussing various meanings of PPT relative to public choice and Arrow's theorem).

87. *See*, e.g., Richard Posner, "Statutory Interpretation—In the Classroom and in the Courtroom," *Univ. of Chicago Law Rev.* 50 (1983), 800, 817.

88. McNollgast, "Legislative Intent," 7.

89. Daniel B. Rodriguez and Barry R. Weingast, "The Paradox of Expansionist Statutory Interpretations," *Northwestern Univ. Law Rev.* 101 (2007), 1207, 1220.

90. McNollgast, "Legislative Intent," 9.

91. Ibid.

92. Ibid., 5.

93. Ibid., 11 note 23.

94. Ibid., 25.

95. McNollgast, "Positive Canons," 708.

96. Ibid., 710.

97. Ibid., 711–712.

98. Rodriguez and Weingast, "Paradox," 1427.

99. Rodriguez and Weingast, "Paradox," 1215, 1218.

100. Ibid., 1220–1221 (emphasis added).

101. McNollgast, "Legislative Intent," 21.

102. Keith Krehbiel, *Pivotal Politics: A Theory of U.S. Lawmaking* (Chicago: Univ. of Chicago Press, 1998); *see also* David W. Brady and Craig Volden, *Revolving Gridlock: Politics and Policy from Jimmy Carter to George W. Bush*, 2d ed. (Boulder, CO: Westview Press, 2006).

103. This is too simplistic a calculus, as the concessions extorted may be completely unrelated to the bill in question or the text. As we will see below, one of the problems with contract-based models is that there is no guarantee that bargaining occurs on questions of text at all or whether the bargaining occurs across bills.

104. *See* Hugh Davis Graham, *The Civil Rights Era: Origins and Development of National Policy, 1960–1972* (New York: Oxford Univ. Press, 1990), 142 ("Hard

bargaining for Senate cloture dominated the next three months, and necessarily involved some trade-offs in response to Dirksen's artful probes."); John G. Stewart, "Thoughts on the Civil Rights Bill," in *The Civil Rights Act of 1964: The Passage of the Law That Ended Racial Segregation*, ed. Robert D. Loevy (Albany, NY: State Univ. of New York Press, 1997), 93, 113 (notes of John G. Stewart, an important congressional staff member, stating that "no agreements will be made until the quid pro quo has been established; namely, that we get cloture activity from Dirksen"); Stewart, "Thoughts on the Civil Rights Bill," 117 ("In short, we want cloture on the whole bill . . . and if Dirksen is not willing to go this route then there is really no business to talk to him about his amendments."); *see also* Stewart, "Thoughts on the Civil Rights Bill," 141 ("Those few amendments which were adopted after cloture resulted from the persistent efforts of their sponsors and from Humphrey's willingness to be accommodating and helpful wherever he could."). The Mansfield–Dirksen substitute was introduced on May 26; the cloture vote occurred on June 10. Stewart, "Thoughts on the Civil Rights Bill," 129. The first Tower amendment was offered on June 11. 110 Cong. Rec. 13,492 (1964). The second Tower amendment was agreed to by voice vote on June 13. 110 Cong. Rec. 13,724 (1964).

105. 110 Cong. Rec. 13,503–13,504 (1964); *see also* ibid., 13,503–13,504 (statement of Sen. Case: "I object to the amendment suggested by the Senator from Texas because, first, it is unnecessary. . . . The amendment is unnecessary"); ibid., 13,504 (statement of Sen. Humphrey: "These tests are legal. They do not need to be legalized a second time . . . That is why I said I did not think the proposed new language was necessary"). Senator Miller asked the managers whether the right to give tests was already authorized under subparagraph (h) of the then extant bill: "I believe that during the development of the amendment [the substitute] amendment, the question of its not being an unfair labor practice for an employer to provide for the furnishing of employment [testing] pursuant to a bona fide . . . merit system . . . was discussed. Would not a test such as is covered by the amendment have to be included in the concept of such a system." Ibid., 13,504 (Sen. Humphrey replied, "That is correct.").

106. Rodriguez and Weingast, "Positive Political Theory," 1507 (recognizing that Tower was an "ardent opponent of the Act"); ibid., 1508 (recognizing that "Tower and his ardent-opponent colleagues would vote against the Civil Rights Act"); *but see* 1504 note 59 (linking Senator Tower to pivotal moderate legislators).

107. The original Tower amendment would have allowed almost any testing, no matter how discriminatory by allowing professionally developed tests to determine whether the individual was "suitable" for a position (suitability being code at the time for discriminatory reasons). For example, a coal handler could be rejected if he failed an I.Q. test. The amendment provided a new section to the Mansfield–Dirksen substitute.

> On page 35, after line 20, insert the following new subsection:
>
> (h) Notwithstanding any other provision of this title, it shall not be an unlawful employment practice for an employer to give *any professionally developed* ability test to any individual seeking employment or being

considered for promotion or transfer, or to act in reliance upon the results of any such test given to such individual, if—

(1) in the case of any individual who is seeking employment with such employer, such test is designed to determine or predict whether such individual is *suitable or trainable* with respect to his employment in the particular business or enterprise involved, and such test is given to all individual seeking similar employment with such employer without regard to the individual's race, color, religion, sex, or national origin, or

(2) in the case of any individual who is an employee of such employer, such test is designed to determine or predict whether such individual is *suitable or trainable* with respect to his promotion or transfer within such business or enterprise, and such test is given to all such employees being considered for similar promotion or transfer by such employer without regard to the employee's race, color, religion, sex, or national origin."

110 Cong. Rec. 13,492 (1964) (emphasis added).

The second Tower amendment modified the "bona fide qualification" language in the statute to provide for challenges to tests that were "used" to discriminate:

> On page 44, line 15, insert the following after the word "origin"; nor shall it be an unlawful employment practice for an employer to give and to act upon the results of any professionally developed ability test provided that such test, its administration or action upon the results is not designed, intended, or used to discriminate because of race, color, religions, sex, or national origin.

110 Cong. Rec. 13,724 (1964).

The resulting statute reads:

> *Seniority or merit system; quantity or quality of production; ability tests; compensation based on sex and authorized by minimum wage provisions.*
>
> Notwithstanding any other provision of this subchapter, it shall not be an unlawful employment practice for an employer to apply different standards of compensation, or different terms, conditions, or privileges of employment pursuant to *a bona fide seniority or merit system*, or a system which measures earnings by quantity or quality of production or to employees who work in different locations, provided that such differences are *not the result of an intention to discriminate* because of race, color, religion, sex, or national origin, nor shall it be an unlawful employment practice for an employer to give and to act upon the results of any professionally developed ability test provided that such test, its administration or action upon the results *is not designed, intended or used to discriminate* because of race, color, religion, sex or national origin. . . .

42 U.S.C. § 2000e-2(h) (2012) (emphasis added).

108. *Griggs v. Duke Power Co.*, 401 U.S. 424, 426 (1971) (citing the statute).

109. Tim Groseclose and Nolan McCarty, "The Politics of Blame: Bargaining Before an Audience," *American Journal of Political Sci.* 45 (2001), 100, 101. In the international arena, *see also* James D. Fearon, "Domestic Political Audiences and the Escalation of International Disputes," *American Political Sci. Rev.* 88 (1994), 577 (discussing vertical and horizontal considerations of democratic states conducting foreign policy).

110. Ferejohn, "Practical Institutionalism," 74.

CHAPTER 3 A Legislative Decision Theory of Statutory Interpretation

1. Richard A. Posner, "Book Review," *Virginia Law Rev.* 74 (1988), 1567.

2. Robert A. Katzmann, *Judging Statutes* (New York: Oxford Univ. Press, 2014), 8.

3. Sometimes textualists suggest that legislative history might be consulted to determine Congress's meanings in cases of apparent absurdity. *Green v. Bock Laundry Mach. Co.*, 490 U.S. 504, 527 (1989) (Justice Scalia, concurring: "I think it entirely appropriate to consult all public materials, including . . . the legislative history of [Rule 609's] adoption, to verify that what seems to us an unthinkable disposition . . . was indeed unthought of.").

4. Legislative history, whether followed or not, remains a staple of federal court practice. A Westlaw search conducted on April 24, 2016, for the term "legislative history" *at least four times in a single case* in the all federal case database over the past 10 years yielded more than 10,000 cases. *See also* Abbe Gluck and Lisa Schultz Bressman, "Statutory Interpretation from the Inside—An Empirical Study of Congressional Drafting, Delegation, and Canons: Part I," *Stanford Law Rev.* 65 (2013), 901, 970 (finding that more than 90 percent of respondents "confirmed the conventional judicial and scholarly assumptions that legislative history is used by drafters to explain the purpose of the statute, to indicate the meaning of particular statutory terms, and to influence judicial interpretation of statutory ambiguities and contested terms."). For recent examples of courts invoking legislative history, *see Arizona State Legislature v. Arizona Independent Redistricting Commission*, 135 S. Ct. 2652 (2015); *Zivotofsky v. Kerry*, 135 S. Ct. 2076 (2014); *DePierre v. United States*, 131 S. Ct. 2225 (2011); *Bruesewitz v. Wyeth LLC*, 131 S. Ct. 1068 (2011); *Los Angeles County v. Humphries*, 131 S. Ct. 447 (2010); *Bilski v. Kappos*, 130 S. Ct. 3218 (2010); *Recovery Group, Inc. v. Comm'r*, 652 F.3d 122 (1st Cir. 2011); *Cohen v. United States*, 650 F.3d 717 (D.C. Cir. 2011). *See also* cases cited Chapter 6, note 3.

5. *Legislative decision theory* differs from some usages of the term *decision theory*. For example, this chapter does not offer a welfarist cost–benefit analysis of decision making. *See* Thomas W. Merrill, "Faithful Agent, Integrative, and Welfarist Interpretation," *Lewis & Clark Law Rev.* 14 (2010), 1565, 1574 (characterizing Adrian Vermeule's theory as an "institutional choice" welfarist approach); Caleb Nelson, "Statutory Interpretation and Decision Theory," *Univ. Chicago Law Rev.* 74 (2007), 329, 334–335 (reviewing Adrian Vermeule, *Judging under Uncertainty: An Institutional Theory of Legal Interpretation* (Cambridge, MA:

Harvard Univ. Press, 2006), and describing its cost–benefit approach as a "decision theory").

6. Judges and scholars have noted their concern that lawyers lack sufficient experience or knowledge of congressional practice. See Vermeule, *Judging under Uncertainty*, 113 (questioning whether parties and judges "lack the comprehensive background knowledge of the legislative process necessary to assess the significance and weight of the sources."); Katzmann, *Judging Statutes*, 8 ("There has been scant consideration given to what I think is critical as courts discharge their interpretative task—an appreciation of how Congress actually functions."); *see also* Dakota S. Rudesill, "Closing the Legislative Experience Gap: How a Legislative Law Clerk Program Will Benefit the Legal Profession and Congress," *Washington Univ. Law Rev.* 87 (2010), 699, 706–708 (empirical study showing what the author calls a "virtual non-existence of legislative work experience" among judges and top legal faculty members). There are notable judicial exceptions on the "experience" score, such as Justice Stephen Breyer, Judge Robert A. Katzmann, and former Judge Abner Mikva, but these judges learned the legislative process long before the "new normal."

7. Kenneth A. Shepsle, *Analyzing Politics: Rationality, Behavior, and Institutions*, 2d ed. (New York: W. W. Norton, 2010), 374 ("Procedures are required to cut through all this instability," given that "there is no equilibrium to majority voting."); *see* Kenneth A. Shepsle and Barry R. Weingast, "Positive Theories of Congressional Institutions," in *Positive Theories of Congressional Institutions*, ed. Kenneth A. Shepsle and Barry R. Weingast (Ann Arbor, MI: Univ. of Michigan Press, 1995), 5, 7; Kenneth A. Shepsle, "Institutional Arrangements and Equilibrium in Multidimensional Voting Models," *American J. Pol. Science* 23 (1979), 27 (offering a model of legislative behavior that results in "equilibrium"). Although the statutory interpretation literature often emphasizes Arrow's theorem, which predicts that Congress, when faced with multiple alternatives, cannot reach a coherent policy choice, few political scientists accept this theory as consistent with empirical reality. Legislative rules and institutions permit coherent policy choices. Second-generation textualism has moved away from this line of attack, as Professor Manning has argued. *See* John F. Manning, "Second-Generation Textualism," *California Law Rev.* 98 (2010), 1287, 1315 ("Second-generation textualism seems to embrace the legislative process, with all its foibles.").

8. Jeremy Waldron, *Law and Disagreement* (New York: Oxford Univ. Press, 1999), 77.

9. Jerry L. Mashaw, "The Economics of Politics and the Understanding of Public Law," *Chicago-Kent Law Rev.* 65 (1989), 123, 152.

10. Abbe R. Gluck, Anne Joseph O'Connell, and Rosa Po, "Unorthodox Lawmaking, Unorthodox Rulemaking," *Columbia Law Review* 115 (2015), 1001; *see also* Gluck and Bressman, "Statutory Interpretation, Part I," 901.

11. The House and Senate rules can be easily found online on Senate.gov. *See also Senate Manual Containing the Standing Rules, Orders, Laws, and Resolutions Affecting the Business of the United States Senate*, S. Doc. No. 113–1 (2014), http://www.gpo.gov/fdsys/pkg/SMAN-113/pdf/SMAN-113.pdf. It is important to note that the term *rules* used in this chapter refers to the standing rules of the House and Senate cited above, not to specific "rules" created by the House of

Representatives Rules Committee to regulate debate on particular pieces of legislation.

12. McNollgast, "Legislative Intent: The Use of Positive Political Theory in Statutory Interpretation," *Law and Contemp. Probs.* 57 (1994), 3, 5; *see* McNollgast, "Positive Canons: The Role of Legislative Bargains in Statutory Interpretation," *Georgetown Law J.* 80 (1992), 705, 741; Daniel B. Rodriguez and Barry R. Weingast, "The Positive Political Theory of Legislative History: New Perspectives on the 1964 Civil Rights Act and Its Interpretation," *Univ. Pennsylvania Law Rev.* 151 (2003), 1417, 1442–1448; Daniel B. Rodriguez and Barry R. Weingast, "The Paradox of Expansionist Statutory Interpretations," *Northwestern Univ. Law Rev.* 101 (2007), 1207, 1219–1222.

13. For a well-known example in which a court found the legislative history helpful in finding the meaning of the text, *see*, e.g., *Pepper v. Hart*, [1993] A. C. 593 (HL) (concluding that the "plain meaning" of cost was not "plain" once Hansard—the British version of the Congressional Record—was considered).

14. *King v. Burwell*, 135 S. Ct. 2480, 2492 (2015).

15. *Church of the Holy Trinity v. United States*, 143 U.S. 457 (1892); *United Steelworkers of Am. v. Weber*, 443 U.S. 193, (1979); *Green v. Bock Laundry Machine Co.*, 490 U.S. 504, (1989); *TVA v. Hill*, 437 U.S. 153 (1978); *Public Citizen v. American Bar Association*, 491 U.S. 440 (1989).

16. *Amalgamated Transit Union Local 1309 v. Laidlaw Transit Servs., Inc.*, 425 F.3d 1140 (9th Cir. 2006).

17. John F. Manning, "Textualism and Legislative Intent," *Virginia Law Rev.* 91 (2005), 419, 423, 431–432.

18. Vermeule, *Judging under Uncertainty*, 149 ("Empirical questions about legal interpretation are inescapable. . . ."); *see also* ibid., 109 (positing that "legislative history is distinctively voluminous and heterogeneous in comparison with other interpretive sources.").

19. The principal cases I discuss—*Public Citizen v. U.S. Dep't of Justice*, *Green v. Bock Laundry*, *TVA v. Hill*, *Holy Trinity Church v. United States*, *United Steelworkers of America v. Weber*, *Griggs v. Duke Power*, are particularly well known in the scholarly literature and in casebooks. *See* William N. Eskridge, Jr., *Dynamic Statutory Interpretation* (Cambridge, MA: Harvard Univ. Press, 1994), 44–47 (discussing *Bock Laundry*), ibid., 74–80 (discussing *Griggs*); ibid., 208–210 (discussing *Holy Trinity*); ibid., 219–225 (discussing *TVA v. Hill*); Antonin Scalia, "Common Law Courts in a Civil-Law System: The Role of United States Federal Courts in Interpreting the Constitution and Laws," in *A Matter of Interpretation: Federal Courts and the Law*, ed. Amy Gutmann (Princeton, NJ: Princeton Univ. Press, 1997), 3, 21–22 (discussing *Holy Trinity*); Vermeule, *Judging under Uncertainty*, 87–117 (discussing *Holy Trinity*); ibid., 28–29 (discussing *TVA*); John F. Manning, "Clear Statement Rules and the Constitution," *Columbia Law Rev.* 110 (discussing *Public Citizen*), 399, 415–417; John Manning, "Federalism and the Generality Problem in Constitutional Interpretation," *Harvard Law Rev.* 122 (2009), 2011–2013 (discussing *Holy Trinity*); John F. Manning, "The Absurdity Doctrine," *Harvard Law Rev.* 116 (2003), 2387, 2479–2480 (discussing *Bock Laundry*); Rodriguez and Weingast, "Positive Political Theory of Legislative History," 1501–1510 (discussing *Griggs*); ibid., 1517–1521 (discussing

Weber). They also appear prominently in major casebooks in the field; *see*, e.g., John F. Manning and Matthew C. Stephenson, *Legislation and Regulation*, 2d ed. (St. Paul, MN: Foundation Press, 2013), 4–17 (reprinting *TVA*); ibid., 36–39 (reprinting *Holy Trinity*); ibid., 81–88 (reprinting *Public Citizen*).

20. *Green v. Bock Laundry Machine Co.*, 490 U.S. 504, 528 (1989) (Justice Scalia, concurring: offering a reading of a statute based on "ordinary usage" and "most compatible with the surrounding body of law into which the provision must be integrated—a compatibility which, by a benign fiction, we assume Congress always has in mind").

21. *King v. Burwell*, 135 S. Ct. 2480, 2492 (2015).

22. *King v. Burwell*, 135 S. Ct. 2480, 2492 (2015) (citing Cannan, "A Legislative History of the Affordable Care Act: How Legislative Procedure Shapes Legislative History," *Law Lib. J.* 105 (2013), 131, 163).

23. *King v. Burwell*, 135 S. Ct. 2480, 2492 (2015) (citing Felix Frankfurter, "Opinion of the Court: Some Reflections on the Reading of Statutes," *Columbia Law Rev.* 47 (1947), 527, 545).

24. Professor Pam Karlan wrote a brilliant article on judicial disdain for democracy, the very topic of this book, but on this one thing, her editors at the *Harvard Law Review* let her down, citing news sources rather than legislative materials. *See* Pamela S. Karlan, "Foreword: Democracy and Disdain," *Harvard Law Rev.* 126 (2011), 45 notes 264–271 (Congress used the "procedural emergency exit" of the budget reconciliation process).

25. Megan Suzanne Lynch, Cong. Research Serv., No. R40480, *Budget Reconciliation Measures Enacted into Law: 1980–2010* (Sept. 2, 2010) (listing 20 major uses of reconciliation).

26. As reprinted in the Congressional Record, the text of the reconciliation bill in its entirety was 156 Cong. Rec. 2153–2167 (2010), or 14 pages. As for the precise length of the health care bills, see William N. Eskridge, Jr., Abbe R. Gluck, and Victoria F. Nourse, *Statutes, Regulation, and Interpretation: Legislation and Administration in the Republic of Statutes, 2015 Supp.* (St. Paul, MN: West Publishing, 2015), 18.

27. A finer-grained analysis of the debate appears in Eskridge, Gluck, and Nourse, *Statutes*, ibid., 15–17 (*Supplement 2015*).

28. Brief of Amici Curiae Senators John Cornyn et al. at 19, *King v. Burwell*, 135 S. Ct. 2480 (2015) (No. 14-144), 2014 WL 7474064.

29. Ibid., 13. For discussion of "behind closed doors," see Eskridge, Gluck, and Nourse, *Statutes*, ibid., 15–17 (*Supplement* 2015).

30. *See* Sanford Levinson, *Our Undemocratic Constitution: Where the Constitution Goes Wrong (and How People Can Correct It)* (New York: Oxford Univ. Press, 2006), 49–62.

31. *E.g.*, Rodriguez and Weingast, "Paradox," 1220 (distinguishing between cheap talk and costly signaling and explaining that all legislators are subject to these rhetorical incentives).

32. *United Steelworkers of Am. v. Weber*, 443 U.S. 193, 209 (1979).

33. Ibid., 197–199.

34. Ibid., 231–254 (1979) (Justice Rehnquist, dissenting).

35. Philip P. Frickey, "Wisdom on Weber," *Tulane Law Rev.* 74 (2000), 1169,

1183 ("There was force to Justice Rehnquist's heated assertions that the majority opinion was an example of Orwellian doublespeak. . . ."); ibid., 1195 ("Justice Rehnquist had the better of those arguments," referring to arguments based on "statutory text and legislative intent").

36. Cloture was voted on June 10, 1964, *see* 110 Cong. Rec. 13,327 (1964); § 703(j) is reprinted in the pre-cloture bill at 110 Cong. Rec. 13310, 13314–13315 (1964). Standing Rules of the Senate, Rule XXII, in S. Comm. on Rules & Admin., *Senate Manual Containing the Standing Rules, Orders, Laws, and Resolutions Affecting the Business of the United States Senate*, S. Doc. No. 88–1, at 24 (1963) (providing for the closing of debate upon a vote then two-thirds of the Senate present and voting).

37. *Weber*, 443 U.S. at 231 (Justice Rehnquist, dissenting). (House minority report); ibid. at 235 (Senate filibusterers).

38. § 703(j) provided that nothing contained within Title VII required an employer or union to "grant preferential treatment to any individual or to any group because of . . . race . . . in comparison with the total number or percentage of persons of such race . . . in any community, State, section, or other area." 42 U.S.C. § 2000e-2(j) (2012). H. R. Rep. No. 88–914 (1963).

39. Lest this seem like an old or odd example, see *Boumediene v. Bush*, 553 U.S. 723, 828 (2015) (Scalia, J. dissenting)(relying on "minority report").

40. The citation of loser's history is not a partisan affair; it can be found in the opinions of liberals as well as conservative judges. *See*, e.g., *Mont. Wilderness Ass'n. v. U.S. Forest Serv.*, No. 80–3374 at 9–10 (9th Cir.) (Judge Norris, rejecting the statement of the Senate author of a bill's nationwide application for a House member who opposed that interpretation), rev'd, 655 F.2d 951 (9th Cir. 1981) (Judge Norris, reversing the original decision based on a conference report on a different bill).

41. *Griggs v. Duke Power Co.*, 420 F.2d 1225, 1239–1240 (4th Cir. 1970), rev'd in part, 401 U.S. 424 (1971).

42. *Griggs*, 420 F.2d at 1234 (Boreman, J. relying on Senator Tower's statements with respect to the first failed Tower amendment).

43. In *Motorola*, a hearing examiner in Illinois ruled that a general ability test for assembly line jobs was discriminatory on the theory that the test was unfair to "culturally deprived and . . . disadvantaged groups." *Myart v. Motorola, Inc.*, No. 63C-127 (Ill. Fair Emp't Practices Comm'n Feb. 27, 1964), reprinted in 110 Cong. Rec. 5662–5664 (1964) (reprinting the text of *Myart* and a letter from the executive director of the Illinois Fair Employment Practices Commission).

44. *See United States v. Turkette*, 452 U.S. 576, 586–87 (1981) (relying upon the statements of Representative Mikva, who opposed RICO, to support the extent of the statute without acknowledging their opposition); *see also* Abner J. Mikva, "Reading and Writing Statutes," *Univ. Pittsburgh Law Rev.* 48 (1987), 627, 632 (describing how he voiced his opposition to RICO in "hyperbolic terms" and that those "remarks have been used ever since as legislative history to prove the broad scope of RICO.").

45. *Griggs*, 420 F.2d at 1234–1235, rev'd, 401 U.S. 424 (relying on Senator Tower's statements with respect to the first failed Tower amendment, the Clark-Case Memorandum drafted two months prior to the amendment, and Senator

Humphrey's statement on the second amendment passed on June 13, 1964); ibid., 1242–1243 (Judge Sobeloff, concurring in part and dissenting in part) (citing the Clark-Case Memorandum and Senator Tower's statements on the first failed Tower amendment).

46. The original bill and the two Tower amendments appear in full in the notes to Chapter 2. The Supreme Court framed the issue as whether a subjective test of discriminatory intent should apply since the Fourth Circuit found no such intent. The statute, however, does not require "intent" in the section governing testing, barring tests "used" to discriminate. The Supreme Court did not emphasize this language, however, but concluded that the act as a whole prevented "practices fair in form, but discriminatory in operation." *Griggs v. Duke Power Co.*, 401 U.S. 424, 431 (1971). Senator Tower's original amendment (the failed one) was cited as supporting "job-relatedness." Ibid. at 436 note 12. In fact, Tower's original amendment, as we have seen in Chapter 2, used language that would have permitted more room to discriminate than the underlying bill.

47. Adrian Vermeule, "Legislative History and the Limits of Judicial Competence: The Untold Story of *Holy Trinity Church*," *Stanford Law Rev.* 50 (1998), 1833.

48. Carol Chomsky, "Unlocking the Mysteries of *Holy Trinity*: Spirit, Letter, and History in Statutory Interpretation," *Columbia Law Rev.* 100 (2000), 901.

49. Vermeule, "Legislative History," 1854–1857; Scalia, "Common Law Courts in a Civil-Law System," 20–21.

50. Scalia, "Common Law Courts in a Civil-Law System," 19–20.

51. Chomsky, "Unlocking the Mysteries," 929–930 (quoting Senator Blair).

52. Ibid., 927.

53. Vermeule, "Legislative History," 1849–1850 (citing 16 Cong. Rec. 1633 (1885))

54. Vermeule, "Legislative History," 1849 (citing Senator Morgan's comments as the meaning of the bill, one accepted by the statute's authors). It is one thing if the statute's authors actually did accept that meaning, but as can be seen from the response, bill supporters made a standard evasive move when met with this objection: if "that class of people are liable" to be imported as slave labor, then "the bill applies to them." *See* ibid., 1850 (citing Senator Blair's response). Supporters thought the opponents were raising "technicalities," eventualities that would never happen (store clerks imported en masse in the hold of a ship). They wanted the bill drafted broadly to cover skilled labor (part of the strong impetus for the legislation), but they were afraid that the more narrow the definition, the more likely it would be subject to constitutional challenge, just as the opponent Morgan suggested, as "vicious" and "class legislation." 16 Cong. Rec. 1632 (1885) (statement of Sen. Morgan). Remember, the bill opponents were urging that the bill should cover all labor.

55. For the distinction between legalist and prototypical meanings, see Victoria F. Nourse, "Two Kinds of Plain Meaning," *Brooklyn Law Rev.* 76 (2011), 997.

56. *See*, e.g., Chomsky, "Unlocking the Mysteries," 927 (noting that Rep. Kelley objected to the language but nevertheless supported the "spirit of the

bill" because it protected labor from "importation of cheap labor in the persons of the worst classes of the least enlightened states of Europe").

57. Ibid., 927.

58. Ibid., 930–931 (quoting Sen. Morgan); ibid., 930 (quoting Sen. Hawley); ibid., 929–930 (quoting Sen. Blair); ibid., 933 (quoting Sen. Platt); *see* 16 Cong. Rec. 1839 (1885) (showing that Sens. Butler, Groome, Hampton, Hawley, Maxey, Morgan, Saulsbury, Vance, and Williams voted against the bill).

59. *See*, e.g., 16 Cong. Rec. 1795 (1885) (statement of Sen. Morgan) ("I think it is one of the duties of the Senate to make laws that are so plain in their meaning that they cannot be misunderstood."); ibid., 1787–1788 (statement of Sen. Saulsbury, characterizing the bill as "very sweeping" and "too sweeping"); ibid., 1789 (statement of Sen. Maxey) ("According to the first section it applies to every character of labor"); ibid., 1834 (statement of Sen. Butler, agreeing with Senator Morgan that the bill was overbroad and would cover individual contracts).

60. 16 Cong. Rec. 1632 (1885) (statement of Sen. Morgan); Vermeule, "Legislative History," 1849.

61. 16 Cong. Rec. 1839–1840 (1885).

62. Chomsky, "Unlocking the Mysteries," 911–915 (quoting the *New York Times*).

63. Gluck and Bressman, "Statutory Interpretation, Part I," 901.

64. *See*, e.g., *Parker v. Franklin Cnty Cmty. Sch. Corp.*, 667 F.3d 910, 917 (7th Cir. 2012) (using Sen. Tower's attempt to limit the reach of the Civil Rights Bill as an element of context).

65. "People who can instruct us in morals and religion and in every species of elevation by lectures . . . are not prohibited." 16 Cong. Rec. 1633 (1885) (statement of Sen. Morgan). A positive political theorist is likely to consider this a costly signal.

66. *In re Silicon Graphics Inc. Sec. Litig.*, 183 F.3d 970, 977 (9th Cir. 1999); accord *Nw. Forest Res. Council v. Glickman*, 82 F.3d 825, 835 (9th Cir. 1996) ("A congressional conference report is recognized as the most reliable evidence of congressional intent because it 'represents the final statement of the terms agreed to by both houses'" (quoting *Dep't of Health & Welfare v. Block*, 784 F.2d 895, 901 (9th Cir. 1986))).

67. *See* Barbara Sinclair, *Unorthodox Lawmaking: New Legislative Processes in the U.S. Congress*, 4th ed. (Washington, DC: CQ Press, 2011), 98 ("By the time legislation gets to conference, many people, and especially many of the conferees . . . have a considerable stake in the legislation's enactment.").

68. Senate Rule XXII provides for the closing of debate after a cloture motion. The cloture rule is the only formal procedure that Senate rules provide for breaking a filibuster. *Senate Manual*, 20–21.

69. 443 U.S. 193 (1979).

70. *Bock Laundry*, 490 U.S. 504 (1989).

71. In *Weber*, the central text was § 703(j), added after the original bill was introduced as a clarifying limit on §§ 703(a) and (d). 443 U.S. at 205–208. Similarly, in *Bock Laundry*, the central text was "the credibility of a witness," passed

by both houses, with the term "defendant" being added in conference. *Bock Laundry*, 490 U.S. at 520.

72. *Weber*, 443 U.S. 193, 231–254 (1979) (Justice Rehnquist, dissenting).

73. *Weber*, 443 U.S. at 231.

74. § 703(j) provided that nothing contained within Title VII required an employer or union to "grant preferential treatment to any individual or to any group because of . . . race . . . in comparison with the total number or percentage of persons of such race . . . in any community, State, section, or other area." 42 U.S.C. § 2000e-2(j).

75. Cloture was voted on June 10, 1964; *see* 110 Cong. Rec. 13,327 (1964); § 703(j) is reprinted in the pre-cloture bill at 110 Cong. Rec. 13,315 (1964). At the time, cloture required 67 votes. Standing Rules of the Senate, Rule XXII, in S. Comm. Rules & Admin., *Senate Manual Containing the Standing Rules, Orders, Laws, and Resolutions Affecting the Business of the United States Senate*, S. Doc. No. 88–1, at 24 (1963) (providing for the closing of debate upon a vote then two-thirds of the Senate, present and voting).

76. 110 Cong. Rec. 13, 315 (1964) (reporting substitute bill, including 703(j)).

77. *Weber*, 443 U.S. at 232–234 (Justice Rehnquist, dissenting).

78. Eskridge, Gluck and Nourse, *Statutes*, 37.

79. *Weber*, 443 U.S. at 235 (Justice Rehnquist, dissenting).

80. Sen. Morse moved to refer the bill to the Judiciary Committee, 110 Cong. Rec. 6454–6455 (1964), but the motion was tabled, 110 Cong. Rec. 6455. *See* ibid. at 6442 (statement of Sen. Long explaining that those who sought to send the bill back to committee were only seeking delay).

81. There is also a good bit of evidence in the pre-cloture debate that supports Justice Rehnquist but, as even he notes, this debate quieted down substantially after the insertion of § 703(j). This suggests that 703(j) resolved the problem. Of course, the "problem" itself may remain contested; Justice Brennan would argue that the problem was the federal government *requiring* a balanced workforce, and Justice Rehnquist would argue that it was any balanced workforce, "voluntary" or not.

82. Some supporters are using the term *discriminate* to mean "any difference in treatment," and others are using it to mean "differences in treatment caused by prejudice against minorities." *See* Frickey, "Wisdom on Weber," 1179–1180 (discussing this essential ambiguity in the term *discrimination*).

83. Fed. R. Evid. 609.

84. *Bock Laundry*, 490 U.S. at 509–510.

85. *Bock Laundry*, 490 U.S. at 511–516; *see also* ibid., 527–528 (Justice Scalia, concurring: "four-fifths of [the majority's] substantive analysis is devoted to examining the evolution of Federal Rule of Evidence 609, from the 1942 Model Code of Evidence, to the 1953 Uniform Rules of Evidence, to the 1965 *Luck* case and the 1970 statute overruling it, to the Subcommittee, Committee, and Conference Committee Reports, and to the so-called floor debates on Rule 609").

86. For another case in which the Court relied upon non-legislative materials, see *Exxon Mobil Corp. v. Allapattah Services, Inc.*, 545 U.S. 546, 569–570

(2005), which rejected a committee report for the views of the Federal Courts Study Committee. *See also* ibid., 575 (Justice Stevens, dissenting, referring to the House report as a "virtual billboard of congressional intent").

87. *See Bock Laundry*, 490 U.S. at 528 (Justice Scalia, concurring).

88. The reference here is to the Judge Levanthal quip that those who look to legislative history tend to look for their friends. *See* Patricia M. Wald, "Some Observations on the Use of Legislative History in the 1981 Supreme Court Term," *Iowa Law Rev.* 68 (1983), 195, 214 ("Legislative history is still . . . akin to 'looking over a crowd and picking out your friends.'" (quoting a conversation with Judge Harold Levanthal)).

89. H. Conf. Rpt. No. 93–1597 at 9–10 (1974) (joint explanation of changes to Rule 609). Although the joint explanation refers to the term *defendant* and even *criminal defendant*, there are far more references to witnesses and parties. *See* ibid., 9 ("The House bill provides that the credibility of a witness. . . . The Senate amendment providing that a witness' credibility . . ."); ibid. ("The Conference Amendment provides that the credibility of a witness, whether a defendant or someone else . . ."); ibid. ("the danger of prejudice to a nondefendant witness"); ibid. ("prejudice to a witness other than the defendant"). In subsection (b), which covered the age of convictions, the joint explanation focuses on parties. Ibid., 10 ("The Conference adopts the Senate amendment with an amendment requiring notice by a party . . . in order to give the adversary a fair opportunity . . ."); ibid . . . (Failure to give notice may "impair the ability of a party-opponent"). None of these references are limited to criminal defendants. At one point in the joint explanation, it is clear that the authors are using the term *accused* to stand in for the much larger category of witness or party. No one doubted that the rule covered impeachment by all *crimen falsi* (false statement crimes), but the joint explanation describes the rule as covering any crime "bearing on the accused's propensity to testify falsely."

90. *See* Victoria F. Nourse, "A Decision Theory of Statutory Interpretation: Legislative History by the Rules," *Yale Law J.* 122 (2012), 70, 102, 128.

91. H. R. Rep. No. 93–1597, at 9 (1974) (Conf. Rep.).

92. Ibid., 2 (1974) (showing the textual amendment added by the conference committee). Ibid., 9–10 (joint explanatory statement of one-and-a-half pages on Rule 609). In the text, I am referring to the one-and-a half page part of the "joint explanation" to the conference report.

93. *Public Citizen*, 491 U.S. 440 (1989).

94. 5 U.S.C. app. 2 § 3(2)(B).

95. For the sake of full disclosure, as an appellate litigator at the Department of Justice, I was involved in briefing FACA cases in the courts of appeals at the time. Later, I was interviewed by the ABA, accorded a "well qualified" rating, and recommended by the Justice Department to sit on the Seventh Circuit Court of Appeals.

96. *Public Citizen*, 491 U.S. at 477–478 (Justice Kennedy, concurring in judgment).

97. Ibid., 453.

98. *See* ibid., 462–463.

99. Ibid., 452–453 (noting that how "utilized" is interpreted could create absurd results); ibid., 465–467 (addressing the issue of constitutional avoidance). *But see* ibid., 482 (Justice Kennedy, concurring, applying FACA to the ABA would be a "plain violation of the Appointments Clause of the Constitution."). On the absurdity canon, see Linda Jellum, "Why Specific Absurdity Undermines Textualism," *Brooklyn Law Rev.* 76 (2011), 917; and Manning, "Absurdity Doctrine."

100. *Public Citizen,* 491 U.S. at 461 ("The Senate bill that grew into FACA defined 'advisory committee' as one 'established or organized' by statute, the President, or an Executive agency." (quoting S. 3529, 92d Cong., §§ 3(1), (2) (1972))).

101. Ibid., 459 ("The House bill which in its amended form became FACA applied exclusively to advisory committees 'established' by statute or by the Executive, whether by a federal agency or by the President himself." (quoting H. R. 4383, 92d Cong § 3(2) (1972)). H. R. 4838 was passed by the House in May of 1972 and sent to the Senate, which struck the entirety of the bill after the enacting clause and substituted the text of S. 3529. It went to conference in September, the Senate agreed to the conference report on September 19, and the House agreed to the conference report on September 20.

102. House Rule XXII(9), in *House Rules and Manual,* 929 ("The introduction of any language presenting specific additional matter not committed to the conference committee by either House does not constitute a germane modification of the matter in disagreement."); Senate Rule XXVIII(3)(a), *Senate Manual,* 53 ("Conferees shall not insert in their report matter not committed to them by either House, nor shall they strike from the bill matter agreed to by both Houses.").

103. Senate Rule XXVIII "prohibits new components of legislation from being inserted into a conference report." David Primo, *Rules and Restraint* (Chicago: Univ. of Chicago Press, 2007) ("Congress limits [the conferees'] authority to the differences between the House and Senate versions of the bill . . . by allowing points of order on both the House and Senate floors against conference reports that exceed that scope.").

104. Senate Rule XXVIII 3(b), in *Senate Manual,* 53 ("If matter which was agreed to by both Houses is stricken from the bill a point of order may be made against the report, and if the point of order is sustained, the report is rejected or shall be recommitted to the committee of conference if the House of Representatives has not already acted thereon."); Senate Rule XXVIII 3(c), in *Senate Manual,* 53 ("If new matter is inserted in the report, a point of order may be made against the conference report and it shall be disposed of as provided under paragraph 5"); House Rule XXII(10)(a)(1), in *House Rules and Manual,* 932 ("A Member, Delegate, or Resident Commissioner may raise a point of order against nongermane matter, as specified in subparagraph (2), before the commencement of debate on—(A) a conference report. . . .").

105. It is sometimes said that this rule is quite often flouted, typically in the context of appropriations bills. See Sinclair, *Unorthodox Lawmaking,* 117–120 (discussing earmarks and misconceptions about earmarks). The bill may be lit

up like a Christmas tree with earmarks, *see* Rebecca M. Kysar, "Listening to Congress: Earmark Rules and Statutory Interpretation," *Cornell Law Rev.* 94 (2009), 519, and there will be little incentive for members to object because each has his or her own individual earmark and thus his or her own violation of the rule. Whether Congress does in fact, on occasion, violate its rules does not undermine the idea that faithful agents of Congress should assume that Congress follows its rules. Certainly, if we assume members know the surrounding body of law, we should assume that they know their own rules.

106. U.S. Const., art. I, §5, cl. 2.

107. My claim is not that Congress must follow its rules or that courts should make Congress follow its own rules. My claim is that, when faced with a difficult case of ambiguity, courts use members' own interpretive principles. By assuming that a member of Congress reading the conference report was entitled to assume that "utilize" did not substantially change "establish," the court defers to Congress without the need to engage in complex statutory or constitutional analyses.

108. *Public Citizen v. U.S. Dep't of Justice*, 491 U.S. 440, 462 (1989) (concluding that the phrase "or utilized" "appears to have been added simply to clarify that FACA applies to advisory committees established by the Federal Government in a generous sense of that term, encompassing groups formed indirectly by quasi-public organizations such as the National Academy of Sciences 'for' public agencies as well as 'by' such agencies themselves.")

109. Statutory history is the history of a statute's text as opposed to any committee report or floor statement commenting on the text.

110. H. R. Conf. Rep. No. 92–1403 (1972). As the Supreme Court noted, the rather short conference report supports the notion that the conferees could not have meant "utilize" in the ordinary sense since the conferees explicitly exempted contractors. Ibid., 10, quoted in *Public Citizen*, 491 U.S. at 462 ("The Act does not apply to persons or organizations which have contractual relationships with Federal agencies nor to advisory committees not directly established by or for such agencies."). There are also indications that the Conference may have added "utilize" to cover presidential transitions. This would, in fact, reconcile the majority reading with an interpretation of "utilize" which gives it a meaning (transitions are covered), but rejects the extensive meaning of "utilize."

111. Vermeule, *Judging under Uncertainty*, 115.

112. *Public Citizen*, 491 U.S. at 471 (Justice Kennedy, concurring: "I believe the Court's loose invocation of the 'absurd result' canon of statutory construction creates too great a risk that the Court is exercising its own 'WILL instead of JUDGMENT,' with the consequence of "substitut[ing] [its own] pleasure to that of the legislative body." (quoting *The Federalist* No. 78)).

113. Although a systematic study must wait, there is at least anecdotal evidence that courts misunderstand (or are unaware of) the rules governing conference reports. *See*, e.g., *Small v. United States*, 544 U.S. 385, 406–407 (2005) (Justice Thomas, dissenting, indicating that the conference committee change was significant enough to cover foreign convictions even though the language passed by the House and the Senate stated "federal" and "state" offenses); *Am. Fed'n of Gov't Emps. v. Gates*, 486 F.3d 1316, 1325 (D.C. Cir. 2007) (interpreting the

last-minute conference change as a "statutory elephant (in the sense of having a huge impact)" on the law). At the very least, some courts appear to ignore Congress's rules when interpreting language added in conference (as in *Public Citizen*). *See*, e.g., *Chem. Mfrs. Ass'n v. Natural Res. Def. Council, Inc.*, 470 U.S. 116 (1985) (interpreting a new provision added in conference without regard to conference rules); *Sec. of the Interior v. California*, 464 U.S. 312, 322 (1984) (interpreting language added in conference without regard to conference rules).

114. *See generally* George A. Costello, "Average Voting Members and Other 'Benign Fictions': The Relative Reliability of Committee Reports, Floor Debates, and Other Sources of Legislative History," *Duke Law J.* (1990), 39, 41 (recounting the standard hierarchy).

115. Eskridge, *Dynamic Statutory Interpretation*, 222 (presenting proposed hierarchy based on the 1982 Supreme Court).

116. Vermeule, "Legislative History," 1833, 1880.

117. For example, in the standard hierarchy, committee reports are given great weight (*see* Costello, "Average Voting," 43), but legislative decision theory suggests that this may be untrue if the text has been significantly modified after the report.

118. Note that specificity and proximity need not be conjoined; for example, there may be cases where the most specific legislative history on the issue appears earlier rather than later in the process, as, for example, when a committee report speaks directly to the question being litigated. Professor Vermeule ("Legislative History," 1874) suggests that courts may overvalue specific information. In fact, I think the opposite is likely to happen since courts tend, today, to look for "purposes," and so they tend to gravitate toward general statements. It is possible that some specific sources should be rejected because they violate the rules set out here—lack of proximity to a final textual decision or attributable to the "losing" side in the debate—but if one is looking for a decision, rather than an intention or a purpose more generally, specificity should count in favor of, not against, legislative evidence.

119. Vermeule, "Legislative History," 1843–1844.

120. Ibid., 1845.

121. Vermeule, *Judging under Uncertainty*, 96–97 (describing how the committee report was attached to a bill which died in the first session of the 48th Congress and that in the second session of that Congress, "other amendments" were made to "critical sections" of the bill, ibid., 97).

122. *See*, e.g., *Blanchard v. Bergeron*, 489 U.S. 87 (1989). In *Blanchard*, the question was whether a contingent fee agreement would cap attorneys' fees under 42 U.S.C. § 1988. The Court relied upon a Senate committee report proximate to the floor debate which spoke to the question of contingent fee agreements, at least to the extent of citing district court cases on that topic. Ibid., 91–92. The Senate report, S. Rep. No. 94–1011 (1976), dated June 29, 1976, was the most specific committee report on the issue, *see* ibid., 6, but not the last report, *see* H. Rep. No. 94–1558 (1976), which was dated Sept. 15, 1976. Nor was the committee report the "last act" on the bill, as there was a debate in the Senate, a filibuster, 122 Cong. Rec. 31471, 31487 (filing a cloture motion) (Sept. 21, 1976); more debate from Sept. 21, 1976 through Sept. 27, 1976, 122 Cong. Rec.

32383, 32388, 32394, 32405 (Sept. 27, 1976); followed by House acceptance of the Senate bill after debate, 122 Cong. Rec. 35578 (Oct. 1, 1976).

123. *Amalgamated Transit Union Local 1309 v. Laidlaw Transit Servs., Inc.*, 435 F.3d 1140 (9th Cir. 2006).

124. 28 U.S.C. § 1453(c)(1) ("a court of appeals may accept an appeal from an order of a district court granting or denying a motion to remand a class action to the State court from which it was removed if application is made to the court of appeals not less than 7 days after entry of the order.")

125. Jacob Scott, "Codified Canons and the Common Law of Interpretation," *Georgetown Law J.* 98 (2010), 341.

126. *Amalgamated Transit Union Local 1309, AFL-CIO v. Laidlaw Transit Servs., Inc.*, 448 F.3d 1092, 1093 (9th Cir. 2006); *LaPritchett v. Office Depot Inc.*, 420 F.3d 1090, 1092 (10th Cir. 2005); *Miedema v. Maytag Corp.*, 450 F.3d 1322, 1326 (11th Cir. 2006); *Spivey v. Vertrue, Inc.*, 528 F.3d 982, 985 (7th Cir. 2008).

127. *Spivey v. Vertrue, Inc.*, 528 F.3d 982, 984 (7th Cir. 2008).

128. S. Rep. No. 109–114 (2005). *See Tanoh v. Dow Chem.*, 561 F.3d 945, 954 n.5 (9th Cir. 2009); *Blockbuster, Inc. v. Galeno*, 472 F.3d 53, 57–58 (2d Cir. 2006).

129. 151 Cong. Rec. S1105 (daily ed. Feb. 8, 2005) (statement of Sen. Charles Grassley, sponsor of the bill: "We placed reasonable time limits on the appellate review of remand orders in the bill.") See summary of compromise bill inserted in the record by Sen. Dodd, 151 Cong. Rec. S1078–S1079 (Feb. 8, 2005). See also debate in the summer of 2004 on a negotiated class action bill that was filibustered. 150 Cong. Rec. S7706 (daily ed. July 7, 2004) (statement of Sen. Chris Dodd); 150 Cong. Rec. S7567 (daily ed. July 6, 2004) (statement of Sen. Charles Grassley).

130. Some courts maintained that the report was submitted to the Senate on February 3, 2005. See *Estate of Pew v. Cardarelli*, 527 F.3d 25, 32–33 (2d Cir. 2008); *Lowery v. Alabama Power*, 483 F.3d 1184, 1206 n. 50 (11th Cir. 2007) (citing 151 Cong. Rec. S978–01 (daily ed. Feb. 3, 2005)). In fact, the language they are citing is to a report of the *bill text* to the floor of the Senate, not a committee report. Special thanks to Janessa Calvo-Friedman, Georgetown class of 2014, for discovering the facts and congressional procedure supporting these claims. As she writes, the committee report itself indicates that it was to be printed on February 28, 2005, S. Rep. No. 109–114 at 1 (2005). It also included dissenting views indicating that the report was filed after the bill was passed. *Id.* at 79.

131. Katzmann, *Judging Statutes*, 21 ("In conference committee, the pressure to come to closure and produce a law can compromise technical precision."); *see also* ibid., 96 (quoting Judge James Buckley of the D.C. Circuit, a former Senator, "with time often the enemy . . . mistakes are made in the drafting of statutes.").

132. *See*, e.g., *Cont'l Can Co. v. Chi. Truck Drivers, Helpers & Warehouse Workers Union*, 916 F.2d 1154, 1156 (7th Cir. 1990) (noting that the conference report included no reference to the interpretive question, as if this indicates significance or absence of information); ibid., 1156 ("Section 4203(d)(2), language common to the two versions, was not mentioned in the Conference Committee's report.").

133. Senate Rule XXII(2), in *Senate Manual*, 21 ("Except by unanimous consent, no amendment shall be proposed after the vote to bring the debate to a close, unless it had been submitted in writing to the Journal Clerk by 1 o'clock P.M. on the day following the filing of the cloture motion if an amendment in the first degree, and unless it had been so submitted at least one hour prior to the beginning of the cloture vote if an amendment in the second degree.").

134. *TVA v. Hill*, 437 U.S. 153 (1978).

135. Ibid., 190 (quoting *Morton v. Mancari*, 417 U.S. 535, 550 (1974)); ibid., 192–193.

136. A 1977 appropriations bill limited TVA's appropriation by providing "$2,000,000 to relocate endangered or threatened species to other suitable habitats as may be necessary to expedite project construction." Pub. L. 95–96, tit. IV, 91 Stat. 797, 808 (1977). *But see TVA v. Hill*, 437 U.S. at 189 ("There is nothing in the appropriations measures, as passed, which states that the Tellico Project was to be completed irrespective of the requirements of the Endangered Species Act.") My thanks to Emily Lanza, Georgetown University class of 2013, for discovering the 1977 appropriations statute.

137. Bill Heniff, Jr., "Overview of the Authorization-Appropriations Process," in *Congressional Authorizations and Appropriations*, ed. Bill Heniff, Jr., Sandy Streeter, et al. (Alexandria, VA: Capitol.Net, 2010), 1, 4. For exceptions to the practice, see Robert Keith, "Examples of Legislative Provisions in Annual Appropriations Acts," in *Congressional Authorizations and Appropriations*, ed. Bill Heniff, Jr., Sandy Streeter, et al. (Alexandria, VA: Capitol.Net, 2010). Although in 1995, by ruling of the chair, the Senate appeared to allow certain legislative provisions on appropriations (known as the "Hutchison" precedent), this was overruled in 1999 by the Senate as a whole. S. 160, 106th Cong. (1999).

138. See the text of the 1977 appropriations bill, which limited TVA's appropriation by providing "$2,000,000 to relocate endangered or threatened species to other suitable habitats as may be necessary to expedite project construction." Pub. L. 95–96, tit. IV, 91 Stat. 797, 808 (1977). Note that this does not violate the rule about legislating on appropriations because it limits the appropriations.

139. *TVA v. Hill*, 437 U.S. 153 (1978).

140. Steven N. Tomanelli, *Appropriations Law: Principles and Practice* (Vienna, VA: Management Concepts, 2003), 30–31. Echoing Karl Llewellyn's view that for every canon there is a counter-canon, Karl N. Llewellyn, "Remarks on the Theory of Appellate Decision and the Rules or Canons about How Statutes Are to Be Considered," *Vanderbilt Law Rev.* 3 (1950), 395, 401, there is a counter-canon to this one: the doctrine of "ratification by appropriation," by which Congress ratifies by appropriation "an agency action that may have been questionable" at the time made. The mere appropriation can signal ratification. Tomanelli, *Appropriations Law*, 27–29.

141. There may be good reason for the use of this canon to control executive abuses of power—when, for example, the executive branch claims authority based on appropriations which, in fact, contravene other laws. Special thanks to Professor Dakota Rudesill for pointing out the difficulties with executive branch use of the ratification canon.

142. Mathew D. McCubbins and Daniel B. Rodriguez, "Canonical Construction and Statutory Revisionism: The Strange Case of the Appropriations Canon," *J. Contemp. Legal Issues* 14 (2005), 669, 671 (remarking upon the appropriations canon's "impoverished analysis of the appropriations process," and concluding that it was "unjustified as a matter of positive political theory").

143. According to Professor McCubbins and Dean Rodriguez, the Supreme Court in *TVA* mistakenly believed that "legislatures do not deliberate adequately when they are occupied with appropriations" (ibid., 687–688), and therefore appropriations laws should not be accorded the respect of "legislation" (ibid., 688–689.). This violates what most political scientists believe about appropriations: not only are such bills legislation, they are very powerful legislation. *See* ibid., 689–690, 695–708 (arguing that the Supreme Court in *TVA* misunderstood and devalued the appropriations process based on controversial normative and positive assumptions about Congress).

144. Ibid., 697 (arguing that the stakeholders—members, voters, and interest groups—"are engaged, active, and participate in the process by which Congress expends money during the regular appropriations process."); ibid. ("The institutional design of Congress reflects a strong interest on the part of all legislators, and particularly the majority party who sets the congressional agenda, to manage and monitor the critical appropriations process.")

145. *King v. Burwell*, 135 S. Ct. 2480, 2492 (2015).

146. It is generally agreed that, under the Rules of Proceedings Clause, U.S. Const., art. I, §5, cl. 2, Congress may set its own rules and as a result may abrogate those rules, although under the rules, doing so would require a two-thirds majority in the Senate. On the entrenchment question and the Rules of Proceedings Clause, *see* Aaron-Andrew P. Bruhl, "Using Statutes to Set Legislative Rules: Entrenchment, Separation of Powers, and the Rules of Proceedings Clause," *Journal of Law and Pol.* 19 (2003), 345. Professor Bruhl's piece also shows how Congress has in fact "added" to its rules through what he calls "statutized rules," whereby statutes provide various procedures, such as fast track procedures for trade agreements. Ibid., 346–347.

147. *See*, e.g., McNollgast, "Positive Canons," 716.

148. One of the classic "folk tales" of conference committees is that members routinely "air drop" language unavailable to other members. This folk account comes, I suspect, from the practice involving *appropriations bills*, which are must-pass legislation and which, under the Budget Act, are not subject to filibuster. Even if this were true, it would provide no reason for a court not to hold Congress to its rules, as one of the salutary side benefits of such an approach might well be that there would be less contravention of the rules.

149. 109 Cong. Rec. S14,256 (daily ed. Dec. 21, 2005) (statement of Sen. Carl Levin: "Senator Warner and I strongly objected to a procedure so totally destructive of bedrock legislative process."). *See also* 151 Cong. Rec. 30,744 (2005).

150. McNollgast, "Positive Canons," 716.

151. Vermeule, *Judging under Uncertainty*, 112.

152. Ibid., 119 ("The judiciary, like Congress, is a 'they,' not an 'it.' That mistake produces the critical and erroneous assumption that coordinated judicial

adoption of some particular approach to legal interpretation is feasible and desirable.")

153. Vermeule, "Legislative History," 1863–1865.

154. *See*, e.g., *West Va. Univ. Hosps., Inc. v. Casey*, 499 U.S. 83, 88–89 and note 4 (1991) (resolving whether "attorneys' fees" under 42 U.S.C. § 1988 includes expert fees by comparing § 1988 with a host of other fee statutes, the assemblage of which certainly requires time and expense).

155. William Eskridge, "Overriding Supreme Court Statutory Interpretation Decisions," *Yale Law Journal* 101 (1991), 348 (finding that the Congress is "much more likely to override 'plain meaning' decisions than any other type of Supreme Court statutory decision").

156. Einer Elhauge, "Preference-Eliciting Statutory Default Rules," *Columbia Law Rev.* 102 (2002), 2162, 2248–2257.

157. Vermeule, *Judging under Uncertainty*, 118.

158. Victoria F. Nourse and Jane S. Schacter, "The Politics of Legislative Drafting: A Congressional Case Study," *New York Univ. Law Rev.* 77 (2002), 575 (empirical study suggesting that Congress does not pay attention to judicial rulings in any consistent way).

159. *See*, e.g., Katzmann, *Judging Statutes*, 96–98 (detailing the history of projects to try to keep Congress informed of appellate decisions and noting that initial efforts revealed that "committee staff did not know about judicial opinions concerning technical aspects of the statutes under the committee's jurisdiction," although they knew about broad policy decisions that had been brought to their attention by a "losing party with influence" in Congress).

160. Ibid., 47.

161. Nicholas Quinn Rosenkranz, "Federal Rules of Statutory Interpretation," *Harvard Law Rev.* 115 (2002), 2085, 2089 (arguing that Congress should pass a set of federal rules of statutory interpretation).

162. Sinclair, *Unorthodox Lawmaking*, 53–54 (explaining the time pressure in the Senate).

163. I call this the "Coasian" principle of legislative instability: Congress will circumvent even the most carefully wrought and complex administrative structures when electoral pressures appear significant. A simple example of this phenomenon is the passage of mandatory minimum sentences after the creation of the complex Sentencing Commission scheme. Paul G. Cassell, "Too Severe? A Defense of the Federal Sentencing Guidelines (and a Critique of Mandatory Minimums)," *Stanford Law Rev.* 56 (2004), 1017 (criticizing the mandatory minimum laws passed by Congress as "redundant" of the Sentencing Guidelines).

164. My position here is not inconsistent with the general claim that there is a large barrier in communication between Congress and the courts; as a general rule, senators and representatives have no incentive to pay attention to courts unless their rulings are politically salient. This is not to say that a repetitive pattern of rulings, or at least a perception of a repetitive pattern, which has become politically salient, may have an effect upon congressional action. *See* Rodriguez and Weingast, "Paradox" (arguing that expansionary progressive readings by courts may inhibit passage of progressive legislation by Congress).

165. This may come as a surprise to some decision theorists, but they should consider that sequential decision making may be a form of preference aggregation preferable to voting or ideological scores. Recent work in philosophy suggests that preference aggregation functions can be achieved by other means, such as "a premise-based or sequential priority procedure." Christian List and Philip Petit, *Group Agency* (New York: Oxford Univ. Press, 2013), 58. For criticisms of standard voting-based models, see Jerry L. Mashaw, *Greed, Chaos, and Governance: Using Public Choice to Improve Public Law* (New Haven, CT: Yale Univ. Press, 1997), 99, describing positive political theorists' approach as "enormously information demanding" and offering "a tool that [judges] cannot use."

166. Rudesill, "Closing the Legislative Experience Gap," 700.

167. Ibid.

168. *See Chevron U.S.A. Inc. v. Natural Res. Def. Council, Inc.*, 467 U.S. 837, 866 (1984).

CHAPTER 4 Petty Textualism, Canons, and Cognitive Bias

1. Orrin Hatch, "Legislative History: Tool of Construction or Destruction," *Harvard J. Law and Public Policy* 11 (1988), 43.

2. Joan Biskupic, "Scalia Takes a Narrow View in Seeking Congress's Will," *Cong. Q. Wkly. Rep.* 48 (1990), 913, 917.

3. On Congress's lack of awareness of canons, *see* Victoria F. Nourse and Jane S. Schacter, "The Politics of Legislative Drafting: A Congressional Case Study," *New York Univ. Law Rev.* 77 (2002), 575; Abbe Gluck and Lisa Schultz Bressman, "Statutory Interpretation from the Inside: An Empirical Study of Congressional Drafting, Delegation, and Canons: Part I," *Stanford Law Rev.* 65 (2013), 901, 965.

4. Antonin Scalia and Bryan A. Garner, *Reading Law: The Interpretation of Legal Texts* (St. Paul, MN: Thomson / West, 2012); ibid., 8 (ignorance of lawyers about *ejusdem generis*).

5. *See*, e.g., *Yates v. United States*, 135 S. Ct. 1074 (2015). One study estimated that, in a particular set of cases, canons were used 30 to 40 percent of the time. James J. Brudney and Corey Ditslear, "Canons of Construction and the Elusive Quest for Neutral Reasoning," *Vanderbilt Law Rev.* 58 (2005), 1, 30. Anita Krisnakumar's more recent study of 295 Roberts Court cases shows that substantive canons have not had as much of an effect as is often thought. *See* Anita S. Krishnakumar, *Reconsidering Substantive Canons* (draft 2016).

6. Westlaw search 1/13/2016.

7. Richard A. Posner, "The Incoherence of Antonin Scalia," *New Republic*, Aug. 24, 2012, https://newrepublic.com/article/106441/scalia-garner-reading-the-law-textual-originalism.

8. Geoffrey P. Miller, "Pragmatics and the Maxims of Interpretation," *Wis. Law Rev.* (1990), 1179; Cass R. Sunstein, "Interpreting Statutes in the Regulatory State," *Harvard Law Rev.* 103 (1989), 405, 451–462.

9. Posner, "Richard Posner Responds to Antonin Scalia's Accusation of Lying," *New Republic*, Sept. 20, 2012, https://newrepublic.com/article/107549

/richard-posner-responds-antonin-scalias-accusation-lying. (quoting Justice Scalia's use of the term "garbage" to refer to legislative materials).

10. Geoffrey Miller has traced this history through Judaic and Christian traditions. *See* Miller, "Pragmatics," 1184–1191.

11. Scalia and Garner, *Reading Law* at 369 ("The false notion that committee reports and floor speeches are worthwhile aids in statutory construction.").

12. Antonin Scalia, "Common Law Courts in a Civil-Law System: The Role of United States Federal Courts in Interpreting the Constitution and Laws," in *A Matter of Interpretation: Federal Courts and the Law*, ed. Amy Gutmann (Princeton, NJ: Princeton Univ. Press, 1997), 29.

13. Amy Coney Barrett, "Substantive Canons and Faithful Agency," *Boston Univ. Law Rev.* 90 (2010), 121–125.

14. *See generally* Abbe Gluck, "The Federal Common Law of Statutory Interpretation: Erie for the Age of Statutes," *Williams and Mary Law Rev.* 54 (2013), 753.

15. Richard Posner, *Reflections on Judging* (Cambridge, MA: Harvard Univ. Press, 2013), 217.

16. Ibid., 209.

17. William N. Eskridge, Jr., *Interpreting the Law: A Primer on How to Read Statutes and the Constitution* iii (St. Paul MN: Thomson/West, 2016) (foreword by John Paul Stevens).

18. Jacob Scott, "Codified Canons and the Common Law of Interpretation," *Georgetown Law J.* 98 (2010), 341.

19. Gluck and Bressman, "Statutory Interpretation, Part I," 901, 940–948.

20. For a description of these canons, see Eskridge, *Interpreting the Law*, ch. 4.

21. Scott, "Codified Canons," 358–359 ("Lawmaking bodies across the United States have uniformly adopted the bad grammar rule, preserving statutes marred by straightforward grammar errors and subordinating grammar to the evident intent of the legislature." Ibid., 357 (table 1 summarizing results).

22. Scalia and Garner, transcript.

23. Special thanks to Lisa Heinzerling for this phrase.

24. Richard Ekins and Jeffrey Goldsworthy, "The Reality and Indispensability of Legislative Intention," *Sydney Law Rev.* 36 (2014), 39, 55.

25. Stephen F. Ross and Daniel Tranen, "The Modern Parol Evidence Rule and Its Implication for New Textualist Statutory Interpretation," *Georgetown Law J.* 87 (1998), 195, 197 (quoting Arthur L. Corbin, "The Interpretation of Words and the Parol Evidence Rule," *Cornell Law Q.* 50 (1965), 161, 164) (emphasis added).

26. *King v. Burwell*, 135 S. Ct. 2480 (2015).

27. Ordinarily, a statutory interpretation could be reversed by Congress, but given the high salience of the issue, and the change in the composition of Congress, most people believed that the statutory challenge would have meant the end of the health care law.

28. 26 U.S.C. 36B (b)(2)(A) ("enrolled in through an Exchange established by the State").

29. 135 S. Ct. at 2495 ("Petitioners' arguments about the plain meaning of Section 36B are strong.").

30. John M. Conley, "Can You Talk Like a Lawyer and Still Think Like a Human Being? Mertz's *The Language of the Law School*," *Law and Soc. Inquiry* 34 (2009), 983, 994.

31. Douglas Walton and Fabrizio Macagno, "Wrenching from Context: The Manipulation of Commitments," *Argumentation* 24 (2010), 297 (discussing the fallacy of wrenching from context as a fallacy of bias).

32. Paul Grice, *Studies in the Way of Words* (Cambridge, MA: Harvard Univ. Press, 1989), 31–39.

33. Brian G. Slocum, *Ordinary Meaning: A Theory of the Most Fundamental Principle of Legal Interpretation* (Chicago, IL: Univ. of Chicago Press 2015), 191–196.

34. *King v. Burwell*, 135 S. Ct. at 2495.

35. *Ibid.*, 2490.

36. *Ibid.*, 2489 ("The meaning of that phrase ["established by the State"] may not be as clear as it appears when read out of context.")

37. *Ibid.* at 2495.

38. The federal exchange statute, 42 U.S.C. 18041 (c)(1), provides that the HHS Secretary shall establish "such Exchange within the State." *Ibid.*, 2487 (quoting the statute).

39. *Ibid.*, 2487 ("if a State nonetheless chooses not to establish its own Exchange, the Act provides that the Secretary of Health and Human Services 'shall . . . establish and operate such Exchange within the State.' ") (citing 42 U.S.C. 18041 (c) (1)).

40. The federal exchange statute, 42 U.S.C. 18041, would literally contradict itself since it would read that the Secretary of HHS "shall establish and operate" an "[exchange created by a State] within the State."

41. *King v. Burwell*, 2485 ("But in petitioners' view, Congress made the viability of the entire Affordable Care Act turn on the ultimate ancillary provision: a sub-sub-sub section of the Tax Code."

42. Slocum, *Ordinary Meaning*.

43. *McBoyle v. United States*, 283 U.S. 25 (1931).

44. *Ibid.*, 26.

45. *Ibid.* ("the Government suggests, rather to enlarge than to restrict the definition," that the law applied to airplanes).

46. *Ibid.*

47. *Ibid.*, 27.

48. 143 U.S. 457 (1892). *See* Chapter 2 and 3 for a more extended analysis of *Holy Trinity*.

49. *Ibid.*, 459 (quoting the statute). *See* Antonin Scalia, "Common Law Courts in a Civil-Law System: The Role of United States Federal Courts in Interpreting the Constitution and Laws," in *A Matter of Interpretation: Federal Courts and the Law*, ed. Amy Gutmann (Princeton, NJ: Princeton Univ. Press, 1997), 19–20.

50. William Eskridge, Abbe Gluck and Victoria Nourse, *Statutes, Regulation, and Interpretation* (St. Paul, MN: West Publishing, 2014), 305 (quoting the full statute).

51. 499 U.S. 83 (1991). Compare *ibid.* at 84 (42 U.S.C. sec. 1988, which permits the award of "a reasonable attorney's fee") with *ibid.* at 103 ("a reasonable attorney's fee as part of the costs.") (Stevens, J. dissenting).

52. 501 U.S. 380, 406 (1991). The full statute refers to voting and elections and specifically provides a violation is established by a showing that protected voters "have less opportunity than other members of the electorate to participate in the political process and to elect representatives of their choice." *Ibid.*, 395 (quoting statute).

53. 515 U.S. 687 (1995). For the analysis of *Babbitt* legislative history, *see* Victoria F. Nourse, "Decision Theory and *Babbitt v. Sweet Home*: Skepticism about Norms, Discretion, and the Virtues of Purposivism," *St. Louis Univ. Law J.* 57 (2013), 909; for the analysis of the legislative evidence in *Chisom*, see Justice Steven's opinion for the majority, 501 U.S. 380, 395 (1991).

54. *See* Max Bazerman, *Blind Spots: Why We Fail to Do What's Right and What to Do About It* (Princeton, NJ: Princeton Univ. Press, 2011) (arguing that unconscious bias accompanies conflicts of interest).

55. Ward Farnsworth, Dustin F. Guzior, and Anup Malani, "Ambiguity about Ambiguity: An Empirical Inquiry into Legal Interpretation," *J. Legal Analysis* 2 (Spring 2000), 257.

56. David A. Schkade and Daniel Kahneman, "Does Living in California Make People Happy? A Focusing Illusion in Judgments of Life Satisfaction," *Psychol. Sci.* 9 (1998), 340; Daniel Kahneman, et al., "Would You Be Happier If You Were Richer? A Focusing Illusion," *Science* 312 (2006), 1908; *see generally* Amos Tversky and Daniel Kahneman, "Judgment Under Uncertainty: Heuristics and Biases," *Science* 185 (1974), 1124.

57. The work originates in the 1970s with Tversky and Kahneman, [ibid.] 19, and is supported by work from others in cognition. *See*, e.g., P. Legrenzi et al., "Focussing in Reasoning and Decisionmaking," *Cognition* 49 (1993), 37. For more in related disciplines, see Nathaniel J. S. Ashby et al., "Focusing on What You Own: Biased Information Uptake Due to Ownership," *Judgment and Decision Making* 7 (2012), 254; David A. Comerford, "Attenuating Focalism in Affective Forecasts of the Commuting Experience: Implications for Economic Decisions and Policymaking," *J. Econ. Psychol.* 32 (2011), 691; Klatan Krizan and Jerry Suls, "Losing Sight of Oneself in the Above-Average Effect: When Egocentrism, Focalism, and Group Diffuseness Collide," *J. Experimental Soc. Psych.* 44 (2008), 929; Daniel Kahneman and Robert Sugden, "Experienced Utility as a Standard of Policy Evaluation," *Envtl. and Resource Econ.* 32 (2005), 161; Peter A. Ubel et al., "Disability and Sunshine: Can Hedonic Predictions Be Improved by Drawing Attention to Focusing Illusions or Emotional Adaptation?" *J. Experimental Psychol.: Applied* 11 (2005), 111.

58. Cynthia Farina and Jeff Rachlinski, "Cognitive Psychology and Optimal Government Design," *Cornell Law Rev.* 87 (2002), 549.

59. Alexander Platt, "Debiasing Statutory Interpretation," *Ohio Northern Univ. Law Rev.* 39 (2012), 275.

60. Frederick Schauer, "Do Cases Make Bad Law?," *Univ. Chicago Law Rev.* 73 (2006), 883.

61. *See* Cass Sunstein, "Behavioral Analysis of Law," *Univ. Chicago Law Rev.* 64 (1997), 1175.

62. Dolly Chugh and Max H. Bazerman, "Bounded Awareness: What You Fail to See Can Hurt You," *Mind and Society* 6 (2007), 1; Avishalom Tor and Max

H. Bazerman, "Focusing Failures in Competitive Environments: Explaining Decision Errors in the Monty Hall Game, the Acquiring a Company Problem, and Multiparty Ultimatums," *J. Behav. Dec. Making* 16 (2003), 353.

63. Daniel Kahneman, *Thinking Fast and Thinking Slow* (New York, NY: Farrar Straus & Giroux 2011), 23–24; Bazerman, *Blind Spots*, 78–79 (similar study).

64. Douglas Hofstadter and Emmanuel Sander, *Surfaces and Essences: Analogy as the Fuel and Fire of Thinking* (New York: Basic Books, 2013), 293.

65. *See infra* notes 56 and 57.

66. Kahneman, *Thinking Fast and Thinking Slow*, 85–88.

67. Tor and Bazerman, "Focusing Failures," 355 ("focusing of study participants, and specifically the tendency to leave the decisions of others and the rules of the game out of the focus, is responsible for failure in all three tasks."); on debiasing, see Katherine L. Milkman, Dolly Chugh, and Max H. Bazerman, "How Can Decision Making Be Improved?" *Perspectives on Psychological Science* 4 (July 2009), 379.

68. Kahneman, *Thinking Fast and Thinking Slow*, 85–88.

69. Tor and Bazerman, "Focusing Failures," 355.

70. Chugh and Bazerman, "Bounded Awareness," 10–11.

71. W.F. Samuelson and M. H. Bazerman, "Negotiating under the Winner's Curse," in *Research in Experimental Economics*, ed. Vernon Smith (Greenwich, CT: JAI Press, 1985), 105–137.

72. Chugh and Bazerman, "Bounded Awareness," 8.

73. *Pepper v. Hart, House of Lords for the United Kingdom*, [1993] 1 All E. R. 42.

74. *TVA v. Hill*, 437 U.S. 153 (1978). See Chapter 3 for a fuller discussion.

75. *United Steelworkers of Am. v. Weber*, 443 U.S. 193 (1979). See Chapter 3 for a fuller discussion.

76. *Griggs v. Duke Power Co.*, 420 F.2d 1225, 1239–1240 (4th Cir. 1970), rev'd in part, 401 U.S. 424 (1971). See Chapter 3 for a fuller discussion.

77. *Amalgamated Transit Union Local 1309 v. Laidlaw Transit Servs., Inc.*, 425 F.3d 1140 (9th Cir. 2006).

78. Matthew Christiansen and William N. Eskridge, Jr., "Congressional Overrides of Supreme Court Statutory Interpretation Decisions, 1967–2011," *Tex. Law Rev.* 92 (May 2014), 1317, 1321 (reporting that plain meaning decisions were more likely to be overridden by Congress); *see* William N. Eskridge, Jr., "Overriding Supreme Court Statutory Interpretation Decisions," *Yale Law J.* 101 (1991), 331, 421 (reporting statutory overrides of 121 Supreme Court statutory interpretation decisions).

79. Karl N. Llewellyn, "Remarks on the Theory of Appellate Decision and the Rules or Canons about How Statutes Are to Be Construed," *Vanderbilt Law Rev.* 3 (1949–1950), 395, 400.

80. Posner, *Reflections*, 52.

81. Eskridge, *Interpreting the Law*, 20.

82. *Yates v. United States*, 135 S. Ct. 1074 (2015).

83. *Ibid.*, 1085–1087.

84. *Ibid.*, 1081, 1084 (Justice Ginsburg, plurality opinion). Mr. Yates was

indicted and convicted under §2232(a), a general destruction of property to prevent seizure statute, which Mr. Yates did not contest.

85. *Ibid.*, 1089–1090 (Justice Alito, concurring in result).

86. *Ibid.*, 1091–1094 (Justice Kagan, dissenting).

87. Brief for the Honorable Michael Oxley as amicus curiae supporting petitioner at 8, *Yates v. United States*, 135 S. Ct. 1074 (2015) (No. 13-7451).

88. *Ibid.*

89. 148 Cong. Rec. S6767 (July 9, 2002) (statement of Sen. Leahy).

90. The Lott amendment applied to section 1512 (not at issue in *Yates* itself), the general witness tampering statute. That law could be considered a general obstruction statute. See 148 Cong. Rec. S6545 (Lott Amendment) (July 10, 2002). As Senator Hatch indicated, that amendment "like the new documents destruction provisions contained in S. 2010" [referring to the Leahy amendment] were separate provisions. The Leahy amendment created 18 U.S.C. 1519. 148 Cong. Rec. S6550 (July 10, 2002). (statement of Sen. Hatch, emphasis added).

91. Moreover, the report had "additional views" suggesting disagreements among members on some issues, although even the additional views referred to section 1519 as an anti-shredding statute. S. Rep. No. 107-146 at 27 (additional views of Senators Hatch, Thurmond, Grassley, Kyl, DeWine, Sessions, Brownback, and McConnell). Justice Kagan, in her dissent, quotes selectively from this report, relying upon complaints about a different statute, namely the general witness tampering statute, section 1512. Yates was prosecuted under SOX's new 18 U.S.C. 1519.

92. *Yates*, 135 S. Ct. at 1091–1094 (Justice Kagan, dissenting).

93. William N. Eskridge, Jr., "Norms, Empiricism, and Canons in Statutory Interpretation," *Univ. Chicago Law Rev.* 66 (1999), 671, 674.

94. Anita S. Krishnakumar, *Reconsidering Substantive Canons* (draft 2016).

95. Eskridge, Gluck, and Nourse, *Statutes, Regulation and Interpretation*, 490–493.

96. *Public Citizen v. U.S. Dep't of Justice*, 491 U.S. 440, 454 (1989) (citing *Holy Trinity Church v. United States*, 143 U.S. 457, 459 (1892).

97. *Ibid*, 465–466 (avoiding constitutional questions); *ibid.*, 482 (Justice Kennedy, concurring) (constitutional violation).

98. Gluck and Bressman, "Statutory Interpretation," 901, 940–948.

99. *TVA v. Hill*, 437 U.S. 153, 189 (1978).

100. *Ibid.*, 189.

101. Pub. L. 95–96, tit. IV, 91 Stat. 797, 808 (1977). *See* Eskridge, Gluck, and Nourse, *Statutes, Regulation, and Interpretation*, 366. *But see TVA v. Hill*, 437 U.S. at 189 ("There is nothing in the appropriations measures, as passed, which states that the Tellico Project was to be completed irrespective of the requirements of the Endangered Species Act.") My thanks to Emily Lanza, Georgetown University class of 2013, for discovering the 1977 appropriations statute.

102. 148 Cong. Rec. 12,481, 12,504 (July 10, 2002) (statement of Senator Durbin) ("Do you know what happened? As soon as Enron got in trouble, they called some of their buddies at Arthur Andersen, and the next thing you know,

the documents are being *shredded*, evidence is disappearing. This underlying amendment, the Leahy-Daschle-Durbin amendment, addresses that specifically.") (emphasis added); ibid., 12,507 (statement of Senator Harkin) ("The people who would *shred* documents to cover up criminal behavior are not better than the "wheel man" in a robbery. They may not have pulled the robbery, but the crook cannot get away without them. This amendment would make sure the *shredders* are held accountable as well.") (emphasis added); ibid., 12,517 (statement of Sen. Hatch ("Like the new *document destruction* provision contained in S. 2010 [referring to section 1519 in reference to the Lott amendment on section 1512 of U.S.Code title 18) (emphasis added). When other persons referred to the amendment more generally, they did not speak of a general obstruction statute, but of corporate fraud and "documents or falsifying records." Ibid., S. 12,505 (statement of Sen. Sarbanes).

103. For example, Brian Slocum has given us a rather informative analysis of *ejusdem generis* by reference to the theory of scalar implicatures. The general term in a list is to be interpreted as stereotypically exemplified, not expanded. Slocum, *Ordinary Meaning*, 197–198. This supports my reading of *Yates*.

104. Jonathan T. Molot, "The Rise and Fall of Textualism," *Columbia Law Rev.* 106 (2006), 1, 43.

105. Scalia and Garner, *Reading Law*, 6.

CHAPTER 5 What Is Legislative Intent? Evidence of Context

1. James M. Landis, "A Note on 'Statutory Interpretation,'" *Harvard Law Rev.* 43 (1930), 886, 888.

2. Ibid.

3. *Conroy v. Aniskoff*, 507 U.S. 511, 519 (1993) (Justice Scalia, concurring in judgment) (emphasis added).

4. *See generally* Alan Turing, "Computing Machinery and Intelligence," *Mind* 59 (1950), 433.

5. J. L. Austin, "Performative Utterances," in *The Philosophy of Language*, ed. A. P. Martinich and David Sosa., 6th ed. (New York: Oxford Univ. Press, 2013), 291, 293.

6. *See generally* G. E. M. Anscombe, *Intention*, 2d ed. (Ithaca, NY: Cornell Univ. Press, 1963) (providing a seminal philosophical analysis of intention); Michael E. Bratman, *Faces of Intention: Selected Essays on Intention and Agency* (New York: Cambridge Univ. Press, 1999) (discussing intention generally and in the context of shared cooperative activity); Daniel C. Dennett, *The Intentional Stance* (Cambridge, MA: MIT Press, 1989) (presenting a theory of intentionality and mind); John R. Searle, *Intentionality: An Essay in the Philosophy of Mind* (New York: Cambridge Univ. Press, 1983) (explaining intentional phenomena); Kieran Setiya, "Intention," in *The Stanford Encyclopedia of Philosophy*, ed. Edward N. Zalta (2014), http://plato.stanford./archives/spr2014/entries/intention/, archived at http://perma.cc/BXS4-HPF9 (discussing theories of intention).

7. *See* Paul Grice, *Studies in the Way of Words* (Cambridge, MA: Harvard Univ. Press, 1989), 86–116; James Tully, ed., *Meaning and Context: Quentin*

Skinner and His Critics (Princeton, NJ: Princeton Univ. Press, 1989), 73–78. *See generally* Bertram F. Malle et al., eds., *Intentions and Intentionality: Foundations of Social Cognition* (Cambridge, MA: Bradford Books, 2003) (providing analyses of intention by psychologists, social psychologists and philosophers).

8. Amanda Woodward, et al., "How Infants Make Sense of Intentional Action," in *Intentions and Intentionality: Foundations of Social Cognition*, ibid., 150–151 (summarizing existing theories and contending that "infants, before they acquire the communicative tool box of the 12–24-month-old, understand some aspects of intentional action").

9. *See* Dennett, *Intentional Stance*, 51 ("Folk psychology . . . can explain the fact that we do so well predicting each other's behavior on such slender and peripheral evidence; treating each other as intentional systems works . . . because we really are well designed by evolution. . . .").

10. *See* Max Radin, "Statutory Interpretation," *Harvard Law Rev.* 43 (1930), 863, 870. For only some of the citations to Radin's intent argument by two prominent statutory interpretation scholars, see the work of purposivist William N. Eskridge, Jr., and textualist John F. Manning. *See*, e.g., William N. Eskridge, Jr., "Dynamic Statutory Interpretation," *Univ. of Penn. Law Rev.* 135 (1987), 1479, 1507 note 113; William N. Eskridge, Jr., "Gadamer/Statutory Interpretation," *Columbia Law Rev.* 90 (1990), 609, 635 note 118; William N. Eskridge, Jr., "Public Values in Statutory Interpretation," *Univ. of Penn. Law Rev.* 137 (1989), 1007, 1012 note 13; William N. Eskridge, Jr., and Philip P. Frickey, "Statutory Interpretation as Practical Reasoning," *Stanford Law Rev.* 42 (1990), 321, 332; William N. Eskridge, Jr., "The Case of the Speluncean Explorers: Twentieth-Century Statutory Interpretation in a Nutshell," *George Washington Law Rev.* 61 (1993), 1731, 1736 note 32; John F. Manning, "Textualism and Legislative Intent," *Virginia Law Rev.* 91 (2005), 419, 430 note 34; John F. Manning, "The Necessary and Proper Clause and Its Legal Antecedents," *Boston Univ. Law Rev.* 92 (2012), 1349, 1364–1365; John F. Manning, "The Role of the Philadelphia Convention in Constitutional Adjudication," *George Washington Law. Rev.* 80 (2012), 1753, 1761 note 37; Antonin Scalia and John F. Manning, "A Dialogue on Statutory and Constitutional Interpretation," *George Washington Law Rev.* 80 (2012), 1610, 1611–1613.

11. John W. Manning, "The Supreme Court 2013 Term: Foreword: The Means of Constitutional Power," *Harvard Law Rev.* 128 (2014), 1, 18 (quoting Radin).

12. *See* Eskridge, "The New Textualism," *U.C.L.A. Law Rev.* 37 (1990), 621, 651–652 ("Scalia followed the Radin critique of the concept of legislative intent.").

13. Henry M. Hart and Albert M. Sacks, *The Legal Process: Basic Problems in the Making and Application of Law* (Cambridge, MA: Harvard Univ. Press, 1958).

14. William Blackstone, *Commentaries on the Laws of England 1* (Chicago, IL: Univ. of Chicago Press, 1979), 59. "The fairest and most rational method to interpret the will of the legislator, is by exploring his intentions at the time when the law was made, by *signs* the most natural and probable."); *see also* Thomas Hobbes, *Leviathan* (Lexington, KY: Empire Books, 2011), 133 ("It is not the

Letter, but the Intendment, or Meaning; that is to say, the authentique Interpretation of the Law (which is the sense of the Legislator) in which the nature of the Law consisteth."); *see also* John Finnis, *Aquinas: Moral, Political and Legal Theory* (New York: Oxford Univ. Press, 1998), 255–258, 257 note 19.

15. Purposivists in the Dworkinian tradition would reply that they are not looking for a collective intent of persons but are finding the best normative purpose in the law. This raises its own problems, however, as it privileges judicial to legislative norms.

16. The group objection is the basis for claims both that there is no single purpose to be found in a statute's history and that purposes can be stated at varied levels of generality. *See* Radin, "Statutory Interpretation," 878 ("To interpret a law by its purposes requires the court to select one of a concatenated sequence of purposes, and this choice is to be determined by motives which are usually suppressed."); ibid., 876 (If one carries purpose as far as it will go, "the avowed and ultimate purposes of all statutes, because of all law, are justice and security.").

17. *See* Ronald Dworkin, *Law's Empire* (Cambridge, MA: Belknap Press, 1986), 314, 315. ("When a friend says something, we may ask, 'What did he mean by that?' . . . Our answer to that question describes something about his state of mind when he spoke."); ibid. (Under the "speakers' meaning" view, judges look to legislative history . . . to discover what "state of mind" the legislators tried to communicate.); ibid., 314 (Legislative materials are "evidence" of the legislators' "mental states."); *see* ibid., 314–315 ("So long as we think legislative intention is a matter of what someone has in mind and means to communicate by a vote, we must take as primary the mental states of particular people because institutions do not have minds.") Dworkin misunderstood the notion of speaker's meaning derived from the philosophy of language, which focuses on the meaning the speaker intended to convey to her audience based on the audience's recognition of the speaker's communicative intentions. *See* H. P. Grice, "Utterer's Meaning, Sentence-Meaning, and Word-Meaning," in *Foundations of Language* 4 (1968), 225, 230.

18. *See* Dworkin, *Law's Empire*, 336 ("We must worry about how to consolidate individual intentions into a collective, fictitious group intention.")

19. *See* Jeremy Waldron, *Law and Disagreement* (New York: Oxford Univ. Press, 1999), 128.

20. Kenneth Shepsle, "Congress Is a 'They,' Not an 'It': Legislative Intent as Oxymoron," *Int'l Review of Law and Econ.* 12 (1992), 239, 254.

21. Mark I. Levy, "Plurality Opinions," *National Law J.* 13 (Feb. 12, 2007).

22. *See*, e.g., *Youngstown Sheet and Tube v. Sawyer*, 343 U.S. 579, 634 (1952) (Justice Jackson, concurring).

23. Michael Eber, "When the Dissent Creates the Law: Cross-Cutting Majorities and the Prediction Model of Precedent," *Emory Law J.* 58 (2007), 207–208.

24. Dworkin, *Law's Empire*, Chapter 9; Waldron, *Law and Disagreement*, 119–146; *see* John Gardner, "Some Types of Law," in *Common Law Theory*, ed. Douglas E. Edlin (New York: Cambridge Univ. Press, 2007), 51, 56 note 14

(identifying Dworkin and Waldron as "notable doubters" of the thought that an institution may have intentions).

25. Joseph Raz, *Between Authority and Interpretation: On the Theory of Law and Practical Reason* (New York: Oxford Univ. Press, 2009), 284 (arguing that law is intentional, but the intention involved in the act of legislating is "very minimal" and "does not include any understanding of the content of the legislation"); Gardner, "Some Types of Law," 56 (arguing that "parliament often has no intention to make the particular changes in the law that it ends up making when it legislates," but has a more humble intention to act to change the law).

26. Richard Ekins, *The Nature of Legislative Intent* (Oxford, UK: Oxford Univ. Press, 2012).

27. Christian List and Philip Pettit, *Group Agency: The Possibility, Design, and Status of Corporate Agents* (New York: Oxford Univ. Press, 2011), 4.

28. Austin, "Performative Utterances," 291, 292.

29. For example, just as a corporate report, such as a 10-K filing, is viewed as a legitimate group action even though it may have been written by a part of the organization and may never be read by the board of directors, so too similar actions (committee reports) should be viewed as legitimate public acts of Congress, not mental states. This applies to acts attributable to individuals as well as collective acts. When an individual offers an amendment, the amendment is his own, but to be a legitimate group act, it must follow group-authorized procedure. On the other hand, an offhand statement made by an individual legislator or a colloquy that did not follow the rules would not be considered a group act. *See Hamdan v. Rumsfeld*, 548 U.S. 557, 665–667 (2005) (Justice Scalia, dissenting: "Whether the floor statements are spoken where no Senator hears, or written where no Senator reads, they represent at most the views of a single Senator.").

30. Richard A. Posner, "Statutory Interpretation—In the Classroom and in the Courtroom," *Univ. Chicago Law Rev.* 50 (1983), 800, 817 ("I suggest that the task for the judge called upon to interpret a statute is best described as one of imaginative reconstruction.").

31. *See* Richard A. Posner, "Legislation and Its Interpretation: A Primer," *Nebraska Law Rev.* 68 (1989), 431, 448 (positing a hypothetical involving a commander giving garbled orders).

32. Dworkin, *Law's Empire*, 315–316. Dworkin's target is the species of constitutional argument known as originalism, but his arguments are couched in more general interpretive guise and are in part focused on statutory interpretation. *See* ibid., 313–354.

33. Ibid., 315.

34. Stanley Fish, "The Play of Surfaces," in *Legal Hermeneutics: History, Theory, and Practice*, ed. Gregory Leyh (Berkeley, CA: Univ. of Calif. Press, 1992), 300–301.

35. Ibid., 301.

36. I am rejecting a theory of communication in which the speaker encodes and the listener decodes the utterance. That theory would allow for secret intentions that no listener could have grasped. Instead, the theory of communi-

cation asserted here depends upon the communicative intentions of the speaker. *See* Grice, *Studies*, 86–116.

37. *See* Elizabeth Mertz, "Teaching Lawyers the Language of Law: Legal and Anthropological Translations," *John Marshall Law Rev.* 34 (2000), 91, 102–104.

38. Bratman, *Faces of Intention*, 2 (Intentions are "elements of stable, partial plans of action concerning present and future conduct."); ibid., 4 (Intending involves "a commitment . . . over time. . . .").

39. Ibid., 2 ("Many times, in the face of new and relevant information, we recognize that it would be folly to stick rigidly with our prior intention.").

40. One potential meaning absent from this list is "intent as reason." *See* Blackstone, *Commentaries*, 58–61. In statutory interpretation, a purposivist might argue that intent reflects a reason about a statute, for example, and that this is what is meant by "intent." Like motivation or other meanings for intent, this idea is subject to all of the claims I make here about intent as mental state, assuming it is static, private, and idealized as a mental event. Moreover, to think of intent as reason is unhelpful in situations of group agents since the implicit analogy to mind causes worries about whether groups can have internal, private, mental reasons.

41. Bratman, *Faces of Intention*, 110 ("That we do sometimes have intentions that are in an important sense shared seems clear. We commonly report or express such shared intentions by speaking of what *we* intend or of what *we* are going to do or are doing."). If action reflects intent, then a group of two or more individuals acting in a coordinated manner can be recognized as sharing an intention.

42. Radin, "Statutory Interpretation," 870.

43. Ibid. This was how James Landis, in his response, understood Radin's argument: "To insist that *each individual legislator* besides his aye vote must also have expressed the meaning he attaches to the bill . . . is to disregard the realities of legislative procedure." (Landis, "A Note," 888 (emphasis added).)

44. Radin, "Statutory Interpretation," 870.

45. The "same intent" problem may not be unique to Radin. Professor Ekins argues that theories of minimal or humble intention suffer from this problem. Ekins, *The Nature*, 114 ("Raz and Gardner . . . [make] the unsound assumption that the legislature's intention must be an intention held by each legislator (or each legislator in the majority).").

46. One might argue that some of the organizations I have identified are not necessarily "democratic" but follow hierarchical norms. In fact, school boards, unions, nonprofit organizations, and the proverbial town hall purport to operate by democratic, majoritarian principles. Even the modern corporation has a form, at least in theory, of shareholder democracy. These organizations operate with respect to some form of procedure seen as legitimate for that form of organization. Most organizations include some forms of hierarchy even as they claim resolute democracy; the House of Representatives and labor unions are examples.

47. Diego Gambetta, "'Claro!': An Essay on Discursive Machismo," in *Deliberative Democracy*, ed. Jon Elster (New York: Cambridge Univ. Press, 1998), 19,

21 (which provides a contrarian example proving the oddity of the assumption that intent is instantaneous).

48. *See* U.S. Const., art. I, § 5 (providing that each House of Congress may "determine the rules of its proceedings. . . ."). The House and Senate rules can be easily found online. *See Rules of the House of Representatives*, H. R. Doc. No. 112–161 (2013), http://clerk.house.gov//house-rules.pdf, archived at http://perma.cc/98BQ-SSMZ; *Standing Rules of the Senate*, S. Doc. No. 112–1 (2011), http://www.rules.senate.gov/public/index.cfm?p=RulesOf, archived at http://perma.cc/PC3A-RC68.

49. Waldron, *Law and Disagreement*, 123.

50. Radin, "Statutory Interpretation," 870.

51. Richard L. Hall, *Participation in Congress* (New Haven, CT: Yale Univ. Press, 1996), 3–4.

52. Almost every bill requires a supermajority in the Senate to pass the cloture barrier. *See* Gregory J. Wawro and Eric Schickler, *Filibuster: Obstruction and Lawmaking in the U.S. Senate* (Princeton, NJ: Princeton Univ. Press, 2006), 10 ("The Senate's rules that protect unlimited debate . . . effectively require supermajorities for the passage of legislation. . . ."); *see also* 157 Cong. Rec. S311 (daily ed. Jan. 27, 2011) (statement of Sen. Harkin, noting that in the 110th and 111th Congresses, there were 275 filibusters in just over 4 years: "It has spun out of control. This is not just a cold statistic of 275 filibusters. It means the filibuster, instead of a rare tool to slow things down, has become an everyday weapon of obstruction, of veto.").

53. It is well known that to draft legislation is an act of anticipation of others' preferences. *See* R. Douglas Arnold, *The Logic of Congressional Action* (New Haven, CT: Yale Univ. Press, 1990), 10. One must draft to satisfy not only one's own constituents but also other members and their constituents. *See* ibid. If the sole representative wants her draft to become law, she must anticipate a tremendous variety of "vetogates"—hurdles that must be surpassed before a proposed bill becomes law. *See* William N. Eskridge, Jr., "Vetogates, *Chevron*, Preemption," *Notre Dame Law Rev.* 83 (2008): 1441, 1444–1447 (laying out a vetogates model for lawmaking in the United States and describing nine such vetogates).

54. Note that this partiality critique applies to the *text* as much as to the legislative history. Partiality is a reason to be skeptical of the entire legislative process, including legislative text: if the few write the text, then it has no priority, nor legitimacy, as the product of the group, since formal adoption by the whole rests upon a false sense of legitimacy.

55. Organizational literature takes delegation as a basic part of proper management. Andrew J. DuBrin, *Essentials of Management*, 9th ed. (Mason, OH: South-Western, 2012), 152 ("A well-planned and highly structured organization reduces the number of nonprogrammed decisions."); Harold Koontz. et al., *Essentials of Management*, 5th ed. (New York: McGraw-Hill, 1990), 184 ("Delegation is . . . an elementary act of managing."); William M. Pride, Robert J. Hughes, and Jack R. Kapoor, *Business* (Mason, Ohio: South-Western Cengage Learning 2014), 190 ("The third major step in the organizing process is to distribute power in the organization. . . . The degree of centralization or

decentralization of authority is determined by the overall pattern of delegation within the organization.

56. List and Pettit, *Group Agency*, 74.

57. Radin, "Statutory Interpretation," 870 (emphasis added).

58. Ibid. (emphasis added).

59. Ibid. (emphasis added).

60. Dworkin, *Law's Empire*, 335–336. Dworkin states:

> So long as we think legislative intention is a matter of what someone has in mind and means to communicate by a vote, we must take as primary the mental states of particular people because institutions do not have minds, and then we must worry about how to consolidate individual intentions into a collective, fictitious group intention.

61. Ibid., 335–336 (emphasis added).

62. *See generally* Charles W. Whalen and Barbara Whalen, *The Longest Debate: A Legislative History of the 1964 Civil Rights Act* (Washington, DC: Seven Locks Press, 1985).

63. *See* Austin, "Performative Utterances," 293.

64. *See* Waldron, *Law and Disagreement*, 145.

65. This explains why canons of interpretation cannot act as substitutes for an understanding of legislative context. Miller's fine article on Grice and canons elaborates the argument for canons, but does not address the assumption that members are engaged in ordinary speech. Geoffrey P. Miller, "Pragmatics and the Maxims of Interpretation," *Wis. Law Rev.* (1990), 1179, 1183. At the most crucial point of legislative compromise, the places we most want to know legislators' meaning, they are not likely to be engaged in a cooperative enterprise.

66. Scott J. Shapiro, *Legality* (Cambridge, MA: Harvard Univ. Press, 2011); Bratman, *Faces of Intention*, 2 (Intentions are "elements of stable, partial plans of action concerning present and future conduct.").

67. To borrow another disembodied metaphor, consider a computer programmed to spit out legislation, a metaphor used by Jeremy Waldron to reject the notion of group intent. *See* Waldron, *Law and Disagreement*, 129–136 (discussing the Wollheim machine). In my view, the program for that computer operates just like congressional procedure. In this sense, the computer metaphor supports—rather than undermines—claims for the functional equivalent of group intent.

68. Michael E. Bratman, "Shared Cooperative Activity," *Philosophical Rev.* 101 (1992), 327, 331–333.

69. No one should misconstrue this as the claim that Congress has only group intent with respect to its procedures. Consider an example from chess. No one says that the game cannot have taken place or that any move is not the playing of chess because individuals sat at the board. Simply because they are playing by the rules of the game, we can infer a shared intent to play the game and conclude that each game and each move conducted pursuant to the rules is a legitimate action of a group activity conducted with the group intent to "play chess." Lest this not convince, consider the actions of corporations pursuant to rules. We can say that action following the corporation's procedures to issue

10-K reports is a group action and reflects group intent to issue the 10-K. We do not dismiss this action because there were individuals involved or because the individuals had minds or because individuals talked to each other, creating the report.

70. Special thanks to my colleague Georgetown law professor David Luban for clarifying this distinction.

71. Nothing in my claim about a "we-intention" to act pursuant to the rules requires that there be a we-intent on any particular statute, whereby intent means shared mental states or statements or even votes.

72. Compare Shepsle, "Congress Is a 'They,'" 254 (arguing against the notion of legislative intent), with Kenneth A. Shepsle, *Analyzing Politics: Rationality, Behavior, and Institutions*, 2d ed. (New York: Norton, 2010), 374 (arguing that "procedures are required to cut through all this instability," given that "there is no equilibrium to majority voting").

73. List and Pettit, *Group Agency*. Their argument is aimed at addressing the problems of incoherency suggested by positive political theory and Kenneth Arrow's theorem. That part of their analysis is beyond the scope of this paper.

74. Ibid., 81.

75. Ibid., 63.

76. Ibid., 74.

77. List and Pettit (ibid., 65) explain supervenience as follows:

> Think of the relation between the shapes made by dots on a grid and the positions or coordinates of the dots. . . . Nothing causal needs to happen in order for the positions to give rise to the shapes; suitably positioned, the dots simply constitute the shapes. . . . Fix the number and positions of the dots and, as a matter of logical necessity, the shapes will be fixed as well.

78. *See* ibid., 63.

79. Franz Dietrich and Christian List, "Where Do Preferences Come From?" *Int'l. J. Game Theory* 42 (2013), 613, 614.

80. Economists have been grappling with this for some time and concede that preferences can change with new information, as in Bayesian analysis, where initial probabilities are changed on the basis of new information. Dietrich and List argue that differing alternatives can change one's preferences, even if there is no new information. Dietrich and List, "Where Do Preferences Come From?" 613. One need not accept that account to accept the relevance of sequential procedures asserted here, as these procedures are means to provide new information (about the voting preferences of other members).

81. I am not arguing against the relative stability of members' preferences. *See*, e.g., Keith T. Poole and Howard Rosenthal, "Patterns of Congressional Voting," *American Journal of Political Sci.* 35 (1991), 228. Aggregate data prove the obvious truth that members try to vote consistently on issues; no one wants to be a "flip-flopper" at election time. *See* ibid., 261. However, at the margin, on first votes, non-roll call votes, important procedural motions (i.e. cloture), or on votes for which there is no clear precedent or effect, members have considerable leeway to form their preferences. Political pressure and social change may as

well yield "evolution" of members' views on controversial issues. For example, consider recent transformations on the question of gay marriage by various politicians. *See* "Sen. Nelson Endorses Same-Sex Marriage," CNN: Political Ticker, Apr. 4, 2013, http://politicalticker.blogs.cnn.com/2013/04/04/sen-nelson-endorses-same-sex-marriage/, *archived at* http://perma.cc/DN63-4HS6 ("Florida Sen. Bill Nelson . . . joined a wave of Democratic senators announcing their support for same sex marriage, reversing his position. . . .").

82. Civil Rights Act of 1964, Pub. L. No. 88–352, 78 Stat. 241 (codified as amended in scattered sections of 28 and 42 U.S.C. (2006)).

83. *Landmark Legislation: The Civil Rights Act of 1964*, U.S. Senate, http://www.senate.gov//history/common/generic/CivilRightsAc-t1964.htm, archived at http://perma.cc/CP4Q-N27C.

84. *See* Barbara Sinclair, *Unorthodox Lawmaking: New Legislative Processes in the U.S. Congress*, 4th ed. (Washington, DC: CQ Press, 2011), 19–21. This example reveals what is implicit in the examples given in this part: perceived electoral pressure (a bill whose "time" has come) is an important and often dominant force motivating individuals to shift preferences.

85. In the House, the Rules Committee, which issues the rules for debate on any bill, can second-guess committees' judgments and offer the opportunity for amendments. *See* ibid., 36–44.

86. Ibid., 50, 53–56, 72–85.

87. William Eskridge, Abbe Gluck, and Victoria Nourse, *Statutes, Regulations, and Interpretation: Legislation and Administration in the Republic of Statutes* (St. Paul, MN: West Publishing, 2014), 49.

88. *United Steelworkers v. Weber*, 443 U.S. 193, 230–252 (1979) (Justice Rehnquist, dissenting).

89. Civil Rights Act of 1964, 42 U.S.C. § 2000e-2(j) (2006) ("Nothing contained in this subchapter shall be interpreted to require any employer, employment agency, labor organization, or joint labor-management committee . . . to grant preferential treatment to any individual or to any group."). Cloture was voted on June 10, 1964. *See* 110 Cong. Rec. 13,327 (1964). Section 703(j) is reprinted in the pre-cloture bill at 110 Cong. Rec. 13,315 (1964). *See* Eskridge, Gluck, and Nourse, *Statutes*, 106–108 (discussing the relevant history of the bill).

90. *Public Citizen v. American Bar Association*, 491 U.S. 440 (1989).

91. *Green v. Bock Laundry Machine Co.*, 490 U.S. 504, 528 (1989).

92. *Griggs v. Duke Power Co.*, 420 F.2d 1225, 1239–1240 (4th Cir. 1970), rev'd in part, 401 U.S. 424 (1971).

93. James M. Landis, "A Note on 'Statutory Interpretation,'" *Harvard Law Rev.* 43 (1930), 886, 888 ("Intent is unfortunately a confusing word."); *Hamdan v. Rumsfeld*, 548 U.S. 557 (U.S. 2005).

94. Peter Brooks "Law and Humanities: Two Attempts," *Boston Univ. Law Rev.* 93 (2013), 1437, 1458 (quoting Gérard Genette, "Likelihood and Motivation," in Gérard Genette, "'Vraisemblance' and Motivation," trans. David Gorman, Narrative 9, no. 3 (2001), 239, 252), *Figures II* (1969), 94 (the work of a literary theorist)).

95. Ibid.

96. *See generally* Manning, "The Supreme Court 2013 Term," 1, 18.

CHAPTER 6 The Constitutional Argument for Legislative Evidence

1. Jeremy Waldron, *Law and Disagreement* (New York: Oxford Univ. Press, 1999), 70.

2. John F. Manning, "Second-Generation Textualism," *Calif. Law Rev.* 98 (2010), 1287, 1304–1305 (emphasizing that "second-generation textualists" have shifted away from positive political theory and toward "formal constitutional arguments"); ibid., 1304 ("Leading textualists—Justice Scalia, in particular—placed greater stress on formal constitutional arguments."); *see* John F. Manning, "Textualism as Nondelegation Doctrine," *Columbia Law Rev.* 97 (1997), 695 ("Textualists argue that crediting unenacted expressions of legislative intent contravenes the constitutional requirement of bicameralism and presentment.").

3. The Supreme Court's affirmance of the practice of citing legislative history, over a dissenting opinion, is *Wisconsin Public Intervenor v. Mortier*, 501 U.S. 597, 610 note 4 (1991). Recent cases in which the Supreme Court has debated or discussed legislative history include *Lockhart v. United States*, 136 S. Ct. 958 (2016); *T-Mobile v. City of Roswell*, 135 S. Ct. 808 (2015); *Yates v. United States*, 135 S. Ct. 1074 (2015); *Burwell v. Hobby Lobby Stores, Inc.*, 134 S. Ct. 2751 (2014); *Lawson v. FMR LLC*, 134 S. Ct. 1158 (2014); *Bilski v. Kappos*, 561 U.S. 593 (2015); *Brusewitz v. Wyeth*, 562 U.S. 223 (2011); *Graham County Soil and Water Conservation Dist. v. United States*, 559 U.S. 280 (2010); *L.A. County v. Humphries*, 562 U.S. 29 (2010); *Jerman v. Carlisle*, 559 U.S. 573 (2010); Corley v. U.S., 556 U.S. 303 (2009); *Boumediene v. Bush*, 553 U.S. 723 (2008); *Doe v. Chao*, 540 U.S. 614 (2004); *Small v. United States*, 544 U.S. 385 (2004); *Hamdan v. Rumsfeld*, 548 U.S. 557 (2006). Estimates vary about the usage of legislative evidence over time—from 17 percent of cases (2004) to 75 percent of cases (in 1988)—according to Justice Antonin Scalia and professor Bryan A. Garner, *Reading Law: The Interpretation of Legal Texts* (St. Paul, MN: Thomson/West 2012), 374.

4. Scalia and Garner, *Reading Law*, 388.

5. *Watkins v. Holman's Lessee*, 41 U.S. 25, 56 (1842).

6. "Each House may determine the Rules of its Proceedings . . ." U.S. Const., art. I, § 5, cl. 2. See also the Journal Clause: "Each House shall keep a Journal of its Proceedings, and from time to time publish the same . . ." U.S. Const., art. I, § 5, cl. 3.

7. My hat is off to Professor Jim Brudney, who first discussed this argument. *See* James J. Brudney, "Canon Shortfalls and the Virtues of Political Branch Interpretive Assets," *Calif. Law Rev.* 98 (2010), 1199, 1218–1224. Professor Brudney tends to emphasize the Journal Clause, but my focus here is on the Rules of Proceedings Clause, which is central to my argument for legislative history, both to make its use more disciplined and also to support its constitutionality. Its full treatment is developed more fully in Victoria Nourse, "The Constitution and Legislative History," *Univ. Pennsylvania Con. Rev.* 17 (2014), 313.

8. Barbara Sinclair, *Unorthodox Lawmaking: New Legislative Processes in the U.S. Congress*, 4th ed. (Washington, DC: CQ Press, 2012), 5 ("Filibuster threats are an everyday fact of life, affecting all aspects of the legislative process"); ibid., 50 ("The Senate is not a majority-rule chamber like the House. In the

House the majority can always prevail; in the Senate minorities can often block majorities.").

9. "Each House shall keep a Journal of its Proceedings, and from time to time publish the same . . ." U.S. Const., art. I, § 5, cl. 3.

10. U.S. Const., art. III, § 2 ("The judicial Power shall extend to all Cases, in Law and Equity . . . and Controversies. . . .").

11. Illustrative cases are discussed below, including cases not cited or discussed in Nourse, "The Constitution and Legislative History." That article, however, includes more citations on particular matters.

12. *Conroy v. Aniskoff*, 507 U.S. 511, 519 (1993) (Justice Scalia, concurring in the judgment: "The greatest defect of legislative history is its illegitimacy."); *see also ACLU v. FCC*, 823 F.2d 1554, 1583 (D.C. Cir. 1987) (Judge Starr, dissenting in part: "We in the judiciary have become shamelessly profligate and unthinking in our use of legislative history. . . .").

13. Senator Chuck Grassley (R–Iowa), "Transcript: Day Three of the Roberts Confirmation Hearings," *Washington Post*, Sept. 14, 2005 ("Justice Scalia is of the opinion that most expressions of legislative history . . . are not entitled to great weight. . . . Now, obviously, I have great regard for Justice Scalia, his intellect and legal reasoning. But, of course, . . . I don't really agree with his position.").

14. *See*, e.g., Transcript of Oral Argument, *Richlin Security Service v. Chertoff*, 553 U.S. 571 (2008) (No. 06-1717), 34–38; Transcript of Oral Argument, *Arlington Central School v. Murphy*, 548 U.S. 291 (2006) (No. 05-18) (debating the meaning of a conference report). My thanks to Professor Peter Strauss for pointing to the latter case, to Barbara Monroe and Juyoun Han, at the Georgetown library for finding the former case, among many others.

15. For support for this claim, *see* Victoria Nourse, "A Decision Theory of Statutory Interpretation: Legislative History by the Rules," *Yale Law J.* 122 (2012), 70.

16. *Lockhart v. United States*, 136 S. Ct. 958, 973 (2016).

17. *Warger v. Shauers*, 135 S. Ct. 521, 527 (2014) ("For those who consider legislative history relevant, here it confirms that this choice of language was no accident.")

18. *See* James J. Brudney, "Canon Shortfalls" at 1218–1224.

19. "Every Bill which shall have passed the House of Representatives and the Senate, shall, before it becomes a Law, be presented to the President of the United States; If he approve he shall sign it, but if not he shall return it . . ." U.S. Const., art. I, § 7, cl. 2.

20. Manning, "Textualism as Nondelegation Doctrine," 695.

21. John F. Manning, "The New Purposivism," *Supreme Court Rev.* 2011 (2011), 113, 167–168.

22. *See*, e.g., U.S. Const., art. I, § 7, cl. 2 ("Every Bill which shall have passed the House of Representatives and the Senate, shall, before it becomes a Law . . ."); Antonin Scalia, "Common Law Courts in a Civil-Law System: The Role of United States Federal Courts in Interpreting the Constitution and Laws," in *A Matter of Interpretation: Federal Courts and the Law*, ed. Amy Gutmann (Princeton, NJ: Princeton Univ. Press, 1997), 3, 31 ("I object to the use of

legislative history on principle, since I reject intent of the legislature as the proper criterion of law.").

23. *See* 157 Cong. Rec. S313 (daily ed. Jan. 27, 2011) (statement of Sen. Harkin: "I often hear opponents of reform claim that what I am proposing [reform of the filibuster] would turn the Senate into the House of Representatives because . . . 51 votes could move something."); ibid., S300–S302 (statement of Sen. Alexander, arguing that changing the filibuster rule would in fact change the character of the Senate).

24. Justice Scalia suggested that the enrolled bill doctrine could bar judicial review of some legislative rules. *United States v. Munoz-Flores*, 495 U.S. 385, 409–410 (1990) (Justice Scalia, concurring in judgment).

25. *See* Ittai Bar-Siman-Tov, "Legislative Supremacy in the United States? Rethinking the 'Enrolled Bill' Doctrine," *Georgetown Law Journal* 97 (2009), 323. In fact, the enrolled bill doctrine has not forced the court to ignore Congress's rules; *see United States v. Munoz-Flores*, 495 U.S. 385, 396–397 (1990) (adjudicating an Origination Clause case, despite Justice Scalia's argument, in a concurrence, that the enrolled bill doctrine applied). Although the doctrine's basis is obscure, its principal doctrinal foundation is not Article I, section 5. Ibid., 378 ("the *Field* Court itself did not base [the Enrolled Bill Doctrine] on . . . the Rulemaking Clause . . .").

26. *Annals of Congress* (Gales and Seaton, 1834); ibid., 20–21 (Senate); ibid., 102–106, 127–128 (House). *See also* ibid., 19 (conference procedure for resolving disagreements between the two Houses). *See generally* "The Constitution in Congress: The First Congress and the Structure of Government, 1789–1791," *Univ. Chicago L. Roundtable* 2 (1995), 61, 165 note 27.

27. A legislative journal sets forth votes, amendments, and dates of consideration, not a verbatim report of the debate. The early Congress's journals were more elaborate, however, than mere vote counts. *See* Brudney, "Canon Shortfalls," 1218.

28. Brudney, "Canon Shortfalls," 1221–1223.

29. Thomas Jefferson, *A Manual of Parliamentary Practice* (Old Saybrook, CT: Applewood Press, 1801); ibid., sec. XXVII (discussing the "Report of Committee[s]"); ibid., XLVI ("Conferences"—referring to conference committees); ibid. (stating "it is on the occasion of amendments between the houses that conferences are usually asked: but they may be asked in all cases of difference of opinion between the two Houses on matters depending between them.").

30. Thomas Jefferson, *The Papers of Thomas Jefferson*, vol. 17, ed. Julian Boyd and Barbara Oberg (Princeton, NJ: Princeton Univ. Press, 1965), 195.

31. Francis Lieber, *Manual of Political Ethics* (London: William Smith, 1839), 381.

32. Francis Lieber, *On Civil Liberty and Self-Government*, 3d rev. ed. (Philadelphia: J. B. Lippincott, 1888), 189.

33. Scalia & Garner, *Reading Law*, 370–372.

34. *Roach v. The Commonwealth*, 2 U.S. 206, 207 (1793).

35. *United States v. Fisher*, 6 U.S. (2 Cranch) 358, 386 (1805).

36. *Fletcher v. Peck*, 10 U.S. (6 Cranch) 87, 107–108, 110 (1810).

37. 1 Wall C. C. 51, 12 F. Cas. 356, 357 (Cir. Ct. D. Pa. May 18, 1801).

38. *Commonwealth v. Cushing*, 11 Mass. 67, 69 (1814).

39. *Dorsey's Executors v. Worthington*, 4H & McH. 533, 535 (Provincial Court of Maryland 1771).

40. *Marbury v. Madison*, 5 U.S. (1 Cranch) 137, 139 (1803).

41. *The Venus, Rae, Master*, 12 U.S. (8 Cranch) 253, 264 (1814).

42. *The Antelope*, 23 U.S. (6 Cranch) 66, 91 (1825).

43. *Ex Parte in the Matter of Duncan N. Hennen*, 38 U.S. 230, 233, 237–238, 240 (1839).

44. *Bingham v. Cabot*, 3 U.S. (3 Dall.) 19, 20–21, 23 (1795).

45. *Worcester v. Georgia*, 31 U.S. (6 Pet.) 515, 549 (1832) (Marshall, C. J.).

46. *Cherokee Nation v. Georgia*, 30 U.S. (5 Pet.) 1, 32, 34–35 (Justice Baldwin).

47. *Cherokee Nation v. Georgia*, 30 U.S. (5 Pet.) 1, 63 (Justice Thompson, dissenting).

48. *Wheaton v. Peters*, 33 U.S. 591, 681, 690–691 (8 Pet.) (1834) (Justice Thompson, dissenting) (The Justice cites the Acts of Congress and then writes, "And the report of the judiciary committee, to whom the subject was referred, shows in what point of light the subject was presented to congress.")

49. *Blake v. National Banks*, 90 U.S. 307, 319 (1874) ("Under these circumstances, we are compelled to ascertain the legislative intention by a recurrence to the mode in which the embarrassing words were introduced, as shown by the journals and records, and by giving such construction to the statute as we believe will carry out the intentions of Congress.")

50. For other cases and authorities, see Victoria Nourse, "The Constitution and Legislative History," 339, notes 134, 135.

51. *Eakin v. Raub*, 12 Serg and Rawle 330, 352 (Pa. Supreme Ct. 1825) (Justice Gibson, dissenting).

52. *Commonwealth ex rel. Bache v. Binns*, 17 Serg. and Rawle 219, 229–230 (Pa. Supreme Court. 1828)

53. *Hill's Adm'rs v. Mitchell*, 5 Ark. 608, 608 (1844).

54. *Sisk v. Smith*, 6 Ill. 503, 518 (1844).

55. For examples after the Civil War, *see*, e.g., *Edger v. Bd. of Com'rs of Randolph Cnty*, 70 Ind. 331, 338 (1880) ("we know of no better means for ascertaining the will and intention of the Legislature, than that which is afforded, in this case, by the history of the statute, as found in the journals of the two legislative bodies."), *State ex rel. Coleman v. Kelly*, 71 Kan. 811, 81 P. 450, 453 (1905) ("The respective journals of the Senate and House of Representatives, containing the proceedings in reference to a bill enacted into a statute, may be looked to by the courts to ascertain the intention of the Legislature in enacting such a statute, if it be ambiguous.").

56. *Dred Scott v. Sandford*, 60 U.S. 393 (1856).

57. *Aldridge v. Williams*, 44 U.S. (3 How.) 9, 15 (1845).

58. *Lochner v. New York*, 198 U.S. 45 (1905).

59. *United States v. Trans-Missouri Freight Ass'n*, 166 U.S. 290, 318 (1897). This statement appears to be swallowed, over time, by an exception to the rule, providing that courts could look to the legislative record for the "history of the times." The full statement in *Aldridge v. Williams*, 44 U.S. (3 How.) 9, 15 (1845) provides that "we must gather [Congress's] intention from the language there

used, comparing it, when any ambiguity exists, with the laws upon the same subject, and looking, if necessary, to the public history of the times in which it was passed." *But see United States v. Union Pacific R.R. Co.*, 91 U.S. 72, (1875) ("The act itself speaks the will of Congress . . . But courts, in construing a statute, may with propriety recur to the history of the times when it was passed; and this is frequently necessary, in order to ascertain the reason as well as the meaning of particular provisions in it." *United States v. Union Pacific R.R. Co.*, 91 U.S. 72 (1875).

60. Scalia and Garner, *Reading Law*, 388.

61. William N. Eskridge Jr. & John Ferejohn, *A Republic of Statutes: The New American Constitution* (New Haven CT: 2010).

62. Nicholas R. Parrillo, "Leviathan and Interpretive Revolution: The Administrative State, the Judiciary, and the Rise of Legislative History," *Yale Law J.* 123 (2013), 266.

63. Scalia and Garner, *Reading Law*, 380 (quoting Stephen L. Wasby, "Legislative Materials as an Aid to Statutory Interpretation: A Caveat," *Journal Pub. Law.* 12 (1963), 263–264).

64. Ibid.

65. Scalia & Garner, *Reading Law*, 378.

66. Ibid. at 376.

67. Ibid.

68. Manning, "Textualism as Nondelegation Doctrine," 695.

69. Manning, "Textualism as Nondelegation Doctrine," 675 ("Textualism should be understood as a means of implementing a central and increasingly well-settled element of the separation of powers—the prohibition against legislative self-delegation."). *See Bank One Chi., N. A. v. Midwest Bank & Trust Co.*, 516 U.S. 264, 280 (1996) (Justice Scalia, concurring in judgment: "But assuming Justice Stevens is right about this desire to leave details to the committees, the very first provision of the Constitution forbids it. Article I, § 1 provides that 'all legislative Powers herein granted shall be vested in a Congress of the United States, which shall consist of a Senate and a House of Representatives.' . . . No one would think that the House of Representatives could operate in such fashion that only the broad outlines of bills would be adopted by vote of the full House, leaving minor details to be written, adopted, and voted upon only by cognizant committees.").

70. Manning, "Textualism as Nondelegation Doctrine," 706 (emphasis in original).

71. Textualists concede that the problem with legislative history is not *de jure* delegation. This is why cases like *INS v. Chadha*, 462 U.S. 919 (1983), which struck down the legislative veto, are correct but irrelevant to the legislative history critique.

72. U.S. Const., art. I, § 1. "All legislative Powers herein granted shall be vested in a Congress of the United States, which shall consist of a Senate and House of Representatives."

73. *INS v. Chadha*, 462 U.S. 919 (1983).

74. "Congress cannot leave the formation of [an] intent to a small band of its number, but must, as the Constitution says, form an intent of the Congress."

Bank One Chicago, N. A. v. Midwest Bank & Trust Co., 516 U.S. 264, 280 (1996) (Justice Scalia, concurring in judgment).

75. *Public Citizen v. U.S. Dep't of Justice*, 491 U.S. 440 (1989).

76. Senate Rule XXVIII, Standing Rules of the Senate ("Conferees shall not insert in their report matter not committed to them by either House, nor shall they strike from the bill matter agreed to by both Houses."). The standing rules can be found at http://www.rules.senate.gov, *See also Senate Manual Containing the Standing Rules, Orders, Laws, and Resolutions Affecting the Business of the United States Senate*, S. Doc. No. 113–1 (2014), http://www.gpo.gov/fdsys/pkg/SMAN-113/pdf/SMAN-113.pdf. last visited September 22, 2015.

77. Nourse, "The Constitution and Legislative History," 344 ("the departments created by our Constitution are not free of conflict of interest. For example, Congress may set its own rules; and the courts may create prudential limits on their jurisdiction."); ibid. ("In some cases, departments are the judges in their own cause. This after all, is the claim of unitary executivists who argue that the President has the right to remove his subordinates, for any and all reasons. If self-delegation is appropriate there, why not in the case of Congress?")

78. Robert A. Katzmann, *Judging Statutes* (New York: Oxford Univ. Press 2014), 95.

79. Victoria F. Nourse and Jane S. Schacter, "The Politics of Legislative Drafting: A Congressional Case Study," *New York Univ. Law Rev.* 77 (2002), 575; Abbe Gluck and Lisa Bressman, "Statutory Interpretation from the Inside: An Empirical Study of Congressional Drafting, Delegation, and the Canons: Part I," *Stanford Law Rev.* (2013), 901.

80. Joan Biskupic, "Scalia Takes a Narrow View in Seeking Congress's Will," *Cong. Q. Wkly. Rep.* 48 (1990) (quoting Specter, then R–Penn); *see also* Senator Chuck Grassley (R–Iowa), "Transcript: Day Three of the Roberts Confirmation Hearings," *Washington Post*, Sept. 14, 2005 ("Justice Scalia is of the opinion that most expressions of legislative history . . . are not entitled to great weight. . . . Now, obviously, I have great regard for Justice Scalia, his intellect and legal reasoning. But, of course, . . . I don't really agree with his position.").

81. U.S. Const., art. II, § 1 ("The executive Power shall be vested in a President of the United States of America.")

82. U.S. Const., art. II, § 7 ("Every Bill . . . shall, before it become a Law . . . be presented to the President of the United States; If he approve he shall sign it, but if not he shall return it, with his Objections . . .").

83. U.S. Const., art. III, § 1 ("The judicial power of the United States shall be vested in one supreme Court, and in such inferior Courts as the Congress may from time to time ordain and establish.").

84. U.S. Const., art. I, § 3, cl. 6 ("The Senate shall have the sole Power to try all impeachments . . .").

85. U.S. Const., art. I, § 1 ("All legislative Powers herein granted shall be vested in a Congress of the United States, which shall consist of a Senate and House of Representatives.").

86. U.S. Const., art. III, § 3, cl. 2 ("The Congress shall have Power to declare the Punishment of Treason . . .").

87. U.S. Const., art. IV, § 3, cl. 2 ("The Congress shall have Power to dispose

of and make all needful Rules and Regulations respecting the Territory or other Property belonging to the United States.").

88. William Eskridge, "All about Words: Early Understandings of the 'Judicial Power' in Statutory Interpretation 1776–1806," *Columbia Law Rev.* 101 (2001), 990.

89. John Manning, "Textualism and the Equity of the Statute," *Columbia Law Rev.* 101 (2001), 1; *see* John Manning, "What Divides Textualists from Purposivists," *Columbia Law Rev.* 106 (2006), 70.

90. William Blackstone, *Commentaries on the Laws of England* 1 (Chicago, IL: Univ. of Chicago Press, 1979), 61 ("The most universal and effectual way of discovering the true meaning of a law, when the words are dubious, is by considering the *reason* and *spirit* of it; or the cause which moved the legislator to enact it.").

91. Victoria Nourse, "Toward a New Constitutional Anatomy," *Stanford Law Rev.* 56 (2004), 835; Victoria Nourse, "The Vertical Separation of Powers," *Duke Law J.* 49 (1999), 749; Victoria Nourse, "Toward a 'Due Foundation' for the Separation of Powers: *The Federalist Papers* as Political Narrative," *Texas Law Rev.* 74 (1996), 447; *see also* Victoria Nourse and John Figura, "Toward a Representational Theory of Executive Power," *Boston Univ. Law Rev.* 91 (2011), 273.

92. U.S. Const., art. I, §§ 2 and 3, amended by U.S. Const. amend XVII (authorizing the "people" to vote for the House and Senate); ibid., art. II, § 1, cls. 2–3, amended by U.S. Const. amend. XII (authorizing the people to vote for a president and vice president through an electoral college).

93. Thomas Jefferson, *The Papers of Thomas Jefferson* 17 (Julian P. Boyd ed. 1965), 195 (emphasis in original)

94. *Hamdan v. Rumsfeld*, 548 U.S. 557, 579–580 & note 10 (2006).

95. *King v. Burwell*, 135 S. Ct. 2480, 2492 (2015).

Epilogue

1. William Eskridge, "Textualism, the Unknown Ideal?" *Michigan Law Rev.* 96 (1998), 1509, 1549 (ashtray example); William Eskridge, "Spinning Legislative Supremacy," *Georgetown Law J.* 78 (1989), 319, 323.

2. John Manning, "Foreword: The Means of Constitutional Power," *Harvard Law Rev.* 128 (2013), 1, 15; John Manning, "Continuity and the Legislative Design," *Notre Dame Law Rev.* 79 (2004), 1863, 1878 note 61.

3. *Marbury v. Madison*, 5 U.S. (1 Cranch) 137 (1803).

4. I am indebted to the work of Paul Kahn and Kiel Brennan Marquez for this insight. Paul W. Kahn and Kiel Brennan-Marquez, "Statutes and Democratic Self-Authorship," *William and Mary Law Rev.* 56 (2014), 115.

5. I do not reject the idea that Congress, too, has a conflict of interest and that there are cases when members can act in ways that seek to exploit that conflict of interest which should be rejected by courts—particularly when they seek to claim the authority of the group for individualistic or contrarian interpretations. *See infra* Chapter 4.

Acknowledgments

I WANT TO thank many on the faculties of Georgetown, Yale, Columbia, and Northwestern law schools for listening to these ideas over the past few years. I am particularly indebted to Yale's Bill Eskridge and Columbia's Tom Merrill and Peter Strauss for their support and interest in my work on legislation over the years. Comments by many have helped to shape the manuscript, but particular thanks go to Peter Byrne, Chai Feldblum, Lisa Heinzerling, Tonja Jacobi, Paul Kahn, Greg Klass, Dean Daniel Rodriguez, Dakota Rudesill, Michael Seidman, Larry Solum, David Super, Emerson Tiller, Dean Bill Treanor, Robin West, Tim Westmoreland, and Kathy Zeiler. My thanks as well to the Yale, Georgetown, Brooklyn, Boston College, and Pennsylvania constitutional law reviews for allowing me to reprise, in different forms, arguments made there.

More importantly, thanks are owed to the judges who have encouraged work on legislative procedure, particularly Judge Katzmann and Judge Posner, and the judges I have debated on such topics, who have treated the ideas with respectful criticism, such as Judge Easterbrook. I was delighted to receive invitations from the Judicial Center, the Seventh Circuit, and the bankruptcy judges to test some of these ideas at conferences over the past few years. This book has been longer in arriving than expected because of a year spent at the

White House, as Chief Counsel to Vice President Biden. Of course, without the opportunity to serve my country some years ago in the Senate for then-Senator Biden, I could never have written this book. Thanks to the white house legislative affairs staff for adding to my store of arcane knowledge of the legislative process, and to the former Senate Parliamentarian, Alan Frumin, for correcting my errors and urging me to try to correct others. After my return to Georgetown, my research assistants, Meghan Breen and Alexandra Langton, worked diligently to check and update the manuscript. Morgan Stoddard, my super-librarian at Georgetown, along with her colleagues, provided essential help in mastering databases and finding materials. Finally, to Dr. Richard Cupitt, my favorite diplomat and political scientist, there are no words to describe the delight of sharing ideas on a daily basis. For my children, Mia and Jack Cudahy, I hope that, when they are older, they will forgive me the time I have spent writing. Yes, Mia, someday I will "step away" from the big fat law books.

Index

Absurdity, 8, 86, 87–88, 174, 185
Action, inference from, 142–44
  group action, 148–51
Acts recognized as group action, 141
Act to Prevent Costly Litigation, 188
Adjectives, 176–77
Advisory committee, 130, 174
Affirmative action (section 703[j]), 74, 82–83, 123, 154, 158
Affordable Care Act (ACA), 71–72, 108–11
Aldridge v. Williams, 171
Alien Contract Labor Act of 1885, 34, 76, 89
Alito, S., 126
Allison, G., 17
Amalgamated Transit Union Local 1309 v. Laidlaw Transit Servs., Inc., 68, 90, 123
Ambiguity
  in conference committees, 87–88
  keep-all-the-voters-happy problem, 30, 31
  legislative process and, 29
  ships-passing-in-the-night problem, 30–31
  structure-induced, 28–30, 44
  textualists' view of, 44–45
  theorizing, 30–32
  unprovided-for-case problem, 30, 32
American Bar Association (ABA), 23, 68, 84, 85, 155, 188
  Public Citizen v. American Bar Association, 85–88, 91–92, 94–95, 130, 155, 174
American Law Institute, 84, 188
Andersen, A., 129
Anti-delegation argument, 139, 162, 173–74
Anti-obstruction statute, 128–30
Anti-racketeering law (RICO), 75–76
Anti-shredding statute (section 1519), 125–26, 128–30, 132
Anti-tampering statute (section 1512), 128–29
Appropriations bills, 93–94
Appropriations laws, 131
Arena legislature, 21
Arguments in legislative decision theory, 95–101
  democracy deficit argument, 100–101
  "it's too complex" argument, 95–97
  legislative history "costs too much" argument, 97–98
  "let's discipline congress" argument, 99–100
Arnold, D., 19, 20
Arrow's cycling theorem, 33, 38, 151

Article I
Section 5, 6, 12, 37, 162–72, 173, 175 (*See also* Proceedings Clause)
Section 7, 12, 162, 165–66, 175 (*See also* Bicameralism Clause)
Article II, 177, 178
Article III, 164, 177
Article IV, 177
Attention bias, 118
Audience
costs, 59–60
importance of, 20–21
multiple-audience problem, 26, 44
Austin, J., 136

Babbitt v. Sweet Home, 115
Baldwin, H., 170
Bargaining, 15, 29, 54, 59
Barrett, A., 105, 125, 130
Bazerman, M., 120, 121
Behavioral economists, 117
"Behind closed doors," 71, 73
Bicameralism, 28, 39, 166–67, 172–75, 177
Bicameralism Clause, 12, 162, 165–66, 175
Biden, J. R., 1, 22
Bingham v. Cabot, 170
Black, C., 19
Blackstone, W., 35, 39, 41, 43, 138, 178
Blair, H., 77–78
Blake v. National Banks, 170–71
Bona fide merit systems, 58–60, 75
Boreman, J., 75
Bratman, M., 148
Brennan, W. J., Jr., 131, 154
Bressman, L., 4, 79, 131
Brewer, D. J., 36, 46–47, 89
Breyer, S., 3, 15, 104
British Parliament, 21, 177
Brudney, J., 4, 165
Bruhl, A., 4
Buckley, J. L., 23
Budget Act, 34
Burger, W. E., 93, 131

Canons, 103–34
of construction, 103, 106, 110, 117, 124
focalism and, 124–33
Judaic and Christian traditions in, 104
overview of, 103–6
petty textualism and, 106–33
semantic, 130–31
substantive, 130–31
Yates v. United States and, 125–29, 132
Cheap intent skepticism, 11, 16, 135, 151
Cheap talk, 54–55, 56, 75
Cherokee Nation v. Georgia, 170
Chinese Exclusion Act, 77
Chisom v. Roemer, 115
Chomsky, C., 47, 76–78
Chugh, D., 120, 121
Citizens United v. FEC, 23
Civil Procedure 101, 5, 65
Civil Rights Act of 1964, 31, 38, 56, 74
congressional context and, 147
disparate impact and, 31, 60, 76, 158
Mansfield-Dirksen substitute, 57–60, 81, 153, 158
Title VII of, 74
Class Action Fairness Act, 90–91
Cloture
compromise in, 153–55
motion, 27
post-cloture amendments, 57–59, 80, 93 (*See also* Tower amendment)
rules, 4, 65–66, 92–93
substitute text needed to obtain, 58, 80, 81, 157 (*See also* Mansfield-Dirksen substitute)
Cloture rule (Rule 22), 4, 65–66, 92–93
Code of Federal Regulations, 95–96
Cognitive bias, 116–18, 123
Cognitive scientists, 5, 10, 117
Collective intent, 137–38, 141, 146
Collectivity objection, 141
Committee reports, 88–91
conference reports distinguished from, 90
typological analysis of, 89–90
Commonwealth ex rel. Bache v. Binns, 171
Commonwealth v. Cushing, 169–70
Communicative intent, 141, 142, 146
Compromise
after narrative, 156–57, 158
in cloture, 153–55
in contract theories, 56–61
in group authority principle, 156
no compromise compromise, 49–50
theorizing ambiguity and, 30, 31
Compromise amendment, 31
Concurring opinions, 126, 140, 150

Conference committees, 3, 12, 27
ambiguity created in, 87–88
proceedings, 175
reports, 79, 80–81, 86
rules, 84, 86–88, 96, 131, 133, 163, 168, 174
self-delegations in, 175
Conference reports, 90, 91–92
committee reports distinguished from, 90
Congress
audience and, 20–21, 26, 44
constituent-talk and, 22–25, 59–60
as democratic fiduciaries, 186–88
electoral connection, 18–20
overview of, 14–33
supermajoritarian difficulty, 27–32
Congress 101 principles, 64–95
Congress's rules can help interpret statutes, 69, 85–88
overview of, 64–69
statutes are elections, 68–69, 70–79
statutes follow a sequence, 69, 79–85
typologies of legislative history may mislead, 69, 88–91
what is unthinkable to a judge may be quite thinkable to a member of congress, 69, 91–95
Congress.gov, 5, 97, 186–87
Congressional Record, 9, 13, 20, 39, 46, 53, 66, 72, 73, 100, 123, 168, 187
Constituent-talk, 22–25, 59–60
Constitutional critique of legislative history, 161–81
bicameralism paradox, 172–75
overview of, 161–64
Rules of Proceedings Clause, 165–72
separation of powers, 176–79
Constitutional originalism, 3
Constitution of the United States. *See* United States Constitution
Contract theories, 7, 34, 53–62
Contract theorists, 56, 63
Cooly labor, 47
Cooly practices, 77
Cornyn, J., 73
Costly concessions, 54, 61, 79
Costly signaling, 54–55
Costs, use of term, 114–15
Countermajoritarian difficulty, 1–2, 45, 63, 95
Courts' duties as democratic fiduciaries, 182–86
Criminal, use of term, 84
Criminal defendants, 32, 83–85, 92, 155
Cross, F., 44
Cross-cutting majority, 140
C-SPAN, 20, 39, 139, 180
Cycling theory. *See* Arrow's cycling theorem

Dahl, R., 27
Dan-Cohen, M., 26
Databases, 5, 39, 66, 70, 97, 187
D.C. Code, 84
Decision making
de-biasing technique, 120
delegating, 145, 153
majoritarian, 155–56
Monty Hall game, 120–21
reverse engineering in, 80–81
transactions costs of, 145
Decision process approach, 120
Decision theorists, 117
Decision theory. *See* Legislative decision theory
Decontextualization
cognitive bias and, 116–22
petty textualism and, 107, 110, 111–12, 113, 115
Defendants, use of term, 83–85
Delegation objection, 144–45
Democracy deficit argument, 100–101
Democratic fiduciaries, 104, 182–88
Congress's duties as, 186–88
courts' duties as, 182–86
Devil/angel view of Congress, 37–40
Dirksen, E., 56, 57, 59–60. *See also* Mansfield-Dirksen substitute
Discrimination, 9
defining, 154
in employee testing, 31, 57–58
Griggs v. Duke Power Co., 75–76, 80, 81, 92, 94, 123, 155, 158
tests used to discriminate, 59, 60, 76
United Steelworkers of America v. Weber, 68, 73–74, 81, 82–83, 123, 154, 158
Disparate impact, 31, 60, 76, 158
Dissenting opinions, 82, 91, 126, 140
Dorsey's Executors v. Worthington, 170
Douglas, M., 48
Drafting errors, 123

Dred Scott case, 171
Dworkin, R., 138, 141, 142, 146–47, 183

Eakin v. Raub, 171
Easterbrook, F. H., 44, 90
E-discovery, 66, 186
EEOC (Equal Employment Opportunity Commission), 75
Ekins, R., 108, 141, 147
Electoral connection, 18–20
Elhauge, E., 3, 99
Employee testing, 31, 57–58
Endangered Species Act (ESA), 93–94, 131–32
Enrolled bill doctrine, 167
Entextualization, 109
Equal Employment Opportunity Commission (EEOC), 75
Eskridge, W., 3–4, 35, 48–49, 52, 53, 123–24, 130, 172, 177, 183
"Established by the State," 108–9, 111–12
Establish/established, use of term, 86, 92
Ex ante, 147, 152–53, 173
Ex Parte in the Matter of Duncan N. Hennen, 170
Extensivist meaning, 18, 114, 115

Farina, C., 117
Farnsworth, W., 44
Fearon, J., 59
Federal Advisory Committee Act (FACA), 85, 86, 155
Federal exchange statute, 112–13
Federalist Papers, 21, 39
Federal Rules of Civil Procedure, 95–96, 188
Federal Rules of Evidence, 83–84, 95–96, 188
  Rule 609, 32, 83–85
Feedback, legislative intent and, 152–53
Fenno, R., 19
Ferejohn, J., 19, 53, 61
Fiduciaries, 104, 182–88
  congress's duties as, 186–88
  courts' duties as, 182–86
Fifth, use of term, 107–8
Filibuster, 4
  Affordable Care Act, 71–73
  Civil Rights Act of 1964, 74, 136, 153
  Griggs v. Duke Power Co., 75, 81
  rules, 62, 66, 163, 167
  of senators' views, 155–56
  supermajoritarian difficulty and, 27–32, 73, 98, 163
  Tower, 31, 57–60, 75–76, 81, 92, 158
  United Steelworkers of America v. Weber, 74, 82
  vote requirements, 57, 71
Financial record preservation act (section 1520), 129
Fiorina, M., 19
Fish, S., 142
Fish coverup case. *See Yates v. United States*
The floor, 147
Floor debates, 56–57. *See also* Filibuster
Focalism, 117
Focusing illusion, 5, 10, 117–19
  focal bias and, 120, 127, 130
  focusing failures and, 122
  Monty Hall game and, 120–21
  statutory interpretation and, 122–24
Frankfurter, F., 37
Fundamental rights, 31

Game theorists/theory, 7, 10, 29, 54, 55, 59, 61
Gardner, J., 141
Garner, B., 3, 103–4, 105, 133
General Agreement on Trade and Tariffs, 95–96
Generality
  in legislative evidence, 67, 124–25, 127, 157, 158, 159
  in legislative intent, 138
Gerry, E., 168
Gibson, J. B., 171
Ginsburg, R. B., 104, 120, 127
Gluck, A., 4, 79, 105, 131
Goldsworthy, J., 108
Grammar errors in statutes, 124
Grassley, C., 13, 165
Green v. Bock Laundry Machine Co., 68, 81, 83–85, 92, 155
Grice, P., 111, 148
Griggs v. Duke Power Co., 75–76, 80, 81, 92, 94, 123, 155, 158
Group action, 141–44, 147–51
  acts recognized as, 141
  group agency and, 141
  inferring group intent from, 148–51
  reconciling with group intent, 141–44, 147

Group agency, 151–53
feedback and, 152–53
group action and, 141
sequential procedure and, 150, 152
Group attribution, process-tracing and, 154–55
Group evidence, legislative evidence as, 155–56
Group intent, 138, 141, 146–51
group action reconciling with, 141–44, 147
inferring group intent from group action, 148–51
legislative context and, 147–48
objection, 138, 141, 146, 150, 151, 160
reconstructed, 146–51
skepticism, 151
Guzior, D., 44

Hall, R., 19
Hamdan v. Rumsfeld, 156, 180
Harlan, J. M., 107
Hart, H., 3, 15, 16, 42, 47, 51–52, 137
Harvard Law Review, 71, 137
Hatch, O., 8, 103, 129, 176
Hawley, J. R., 78
Health Care and Education Reconciliation Act of 2010, 72
Hill's Adm'rs v. Mitchell, 171
Hollingsworth v. Duane, 169
Holmes, O. W., 107, 113–14
Holy Trinity. See Rector, Church of the Holy Trinity v. United States
House rules, 27, 86–87, 95–96
House Rules Committee, 27
Humphrey, H., 31, 56, 60

Impeachment of witnesses by prior felonies (Rule 609), 32, 83–85
Implicatures, 110, 111
Inference
from action, 142–44
from group action, 148–51
from mind, 141–42
from speech, 142
Instantaneous legislative intent, 144
INS v. Chadha, 173
Intent. *See* Legislative intent
Intent, use of term, 68, 137, 140, 149, 160
Intentionalism, 42, 54
Interest groups, 25, 33, 38, 99
Interest group theory, 33
Interpretive, use of term, 176
Irrationality thesis, 15
Isolation of text, 10, 110, 116
"It's too complex" argument, 95–97

Jefferson, T., 168, 180, 182
Job-relatedness rule, 75
Journal Clause, 12, 163, 166, 168, 178
Judicial power, 104–5, 125, 159, 176–78, 184
Judicial review, theory of, 51

Kagan, E., 3, 126, 129
Kahneman, D., 117, 119, 120
Katzmann, R., 12, 47, 65, 99, 175, 186
Keep-all-the-voters-happy problem, 30, 31
Kennedy, A., 23, 86, 131
Kingdon, J., 19
King v. Burwell, 2, 68, 95, 115–16, 127, 180
inartful drafting and, 71–72
petty textualism and, 108–9, 115–16, 127
spurious interpretation and, 110–12
Krehbiel, K., 27, 33, 57
Krishnakumar, A., 4, 130

Labor, use of term, 77, 114
"Labor or service of any kind," 36, 40, 76, 114
Ladd, D., 84
Landis, D., 42
Law, D., 4, 130
Law of the majority, 168, 180
Leahy, P., 129, 130
Lecturers on religious topics, 79
Legalist meaning, 27, 32, 40–45, 51, 62
Legal Process, The (Hart and Sacks), 3, 15, 16, 47, 51–52, 137
Legislative absurdity, 8, 86, 87–88, 174, 185
Legislative behavior, 17, 21, 99
Legislative canons, 66, 106
Legislative compromise. *See* Compromise
Legislative context
evidence of, 68, 125, 135–60 (*See also* Legislative intent)
group intent and, 147–48

Legislative debate
  beginning, 20
  purposivism and, 50
  reading, 79–80
  strategic use of, 30
Legislative decision theory
  arguments, 95–101
  Congress 101 principles, 64–65, 68–95
  defined, 9, 17
  legislative intent and, 135
  petty textualism and, 132
  process tracing and, 154
Legislative evidence, 18
  change in, over time, 139
  constitutional argument for, 161–81 (*See also* Constitutional critique of legislative history)
  generality in, 67, 124–25, 127, 157, 158, 159
  legislative history as, 153–59
  legislative history distinguished from, 156–59
  as legitimate group evidence, 155–56
  process-tracing and group attribution and, 154–55
Legislative game, rules of, 33, 62
Legislative history. *See also* Constitutional critique of legislative history
  "costs too much" argument, 97–98
  as legislative evidence, 153–59
  legislative evidence distinguished from, 156–59
  narratives, 156–59
  process tracing and, 154–55
Legislative intent, 135–60
  collectivity objection to, 141
  communicative, 141, 142, 146
  feedback and, 152–53
  generality in, 138
  group agency and, 151–53
  group intent and, 146–51
  instantaneous, 144
  legislative history as legislative evidence and, 153–59
  mental, 141–42
  metaphysical objection, 136–40
  overview of, 135–36
  pragmatic, 142–44
  sequential procedure and, 152
  state of mind as, 143, 144–46
  subjectivity objection, 139–40
  use of term, 6, 68, 160
Legislative journals, 163, 167–72
Legislative materials, 67, 104, 165, 169, 172, 175
Legislative process, 4
  ambiguity and, 29
  contract theories and, 53–56
  Manning's adjectives for describing, 37–38
  rules governing (*See* Legislative decision theory)
  Schoolhouse Rock views of, 81
  traditional, 71
Legislative self-delegation, 172–75, 180
Legislative speech, 148
Legitimate group action, 150
Lenity rule, 114
Less, use of term, 123
"Let's discipline congress" argument, 99–100
Levinson, S., 27, 111
Lexis, 187
Lieber, F., 168–69, 183
List, C., 141, 145, 147, 151–52, 153
Llewellyn, K., 124
Lochner v. New York, 171
Locke, J., 24, 41
Loser's history, 56
Lott, T., 129
Luck doctrine, 84

Machiavelli, N., 24
Madison, J., 21, 26, 170, 184
Majority
  cross-cutting, 140
  law of, 168, 180
  leaders, 14, 187
  opinions, *vs.* dissenting, 65, 66, 68
  supermajority, 2, 28, 56, 58, 98, 101, 145, 152, 154
  votes, 150, 152
Managerial judging, 66
Manning, J. F., 3, 35, 37, 38, 42, 44, 137, 159, 172, 175, 177, 183
Mansfield-Dirksen substitute, 57–60, 81, 153, 158
Manual labor, 40, 43, 46–47, 49, 51, 55, 77, 78, 114
Marbury v. Madison, 170, 184
Marshall, J., 107, 169, 170, 184

Mashaw, J., 16
Matthews, D., 19
Mayhew, D., 19, 59
McBoyle v. United States, 113–14
McCain-Feingold campaign finance bill, 22
McCarty, N., 59
McCubbins, M., 94
McNollgast, 54–56
Median voter model, 33
Melville, H., 183
Mental state error, 144
Merit systems, bona fide, 58, 60, 75
Merrill, T., 42
Metaphysical claim, 137
Metaphysical difficulty, 138
Metaphysical objection, 136–40
Mikva, A. J., 75, 76
Mill, J. S., 24
Miller, G., 125
Mind, inference from, 141–42
Minimalist theory, 15
Minority leaders, 187
Minority reports, 56, 74, 154
Mischief rule, 40, 51
Mitchell, G., 14
M'Kean, T., 169
Molot, J., 36, 133
Monty Hall game, 120–21
Morgan, J. T., 34, 77–79
Mulani, A., 44
Multi-district litigation, 66, 186
Multiple-audience problem, 26, 44
Myart v. Motorola, 75

Narratives, 156–59
Nation, use of term, 170–71
New textualism, 35–37, 44, 45–46, 53
New textualist, 37, 38, 42, 44, 45, 51, 57, 110, 114, 116, 127, 154
Nondelegation argument, 174–75

One Fish Two Fish Red Fish Blue Fish (Dr. Seuss), 126
O'Neill, J., 34
Opinions
  concurring, 126, 140, 150
  dissenting, 65, 66, 68, 82, 91, 126, 140
  majority, 65, 66, 68
  plurality, 139
  subplurality, 139
  Supreme Court, 6, 19, 23, 57, 114, 129, 139–40, 160, 167
Ordinary meaning, 40, 43–44, 86, 113, 116–17, 133
Ordinary speech, 142, 148
Originalism, 3
Oxley, M., 128–29

Paradigm cases, 51
Parillo, N., 172
Party-driven model, 33
Peckham, R. W., 171
Pepper v. Hart, 123
Peripheral meaning, 41–42, 44
Pettit, P., 141, 145, 147, 151–52, 153
Petty textualism, 106–24
  cognitive bias and, 116–17
  decontextualization and, 116–22
  overview of, 106–8
  spurious interpretation and, 108–16
  statutory interpretation and, 122–24
Plain meaning, 5, 7, 15, 17–18
  in devil/angel view of Congress, 38
  kinds of, 40–45
  spurious, 111–12
Platt, A., 117
Platt, O., 78
Plurality opinions, 139
Political scientists, theories of. *See* Positive political theory (PPT)
Polsby, N., 21
Positive political theorists, 54, 73, 94, 96
Positive political theory (PPT), 7, 15, 53–54, 57, 67, 138
Posner, R., 3, 64, 65, 104, 105, 124, 186
Post-cloture amendments, 31, 57–59, 80, 93
Post hoc speeches, 155
PPT. *See* Positive political theory (PPT)
Pragmatic intent, 142–44
Precedence of motions (Rule XXII), 92–93
Pre-cloture, 57–58, 83, 187
Preferences, 17, 151–53
Proceedings, use of term, 175
Proceedings Clause, 6, 12, 37, 162–72, 173, 175
  history of, 167–72
  rules of, 165–67
  self-delegation in, 173, 175
ProQuest, 97, 187

Prototypical meaning, 7, 18, 27, 32, 40–45, 49, 50–51, 62, 77–78, 113, 133
Public Citizen v. American Bar Association, 85–88, 91–92, 94–95, 130, 155, 174
Public Law 111-148. *See* Affordable Care Act (ACA)
Public Law 111-152. *See* Health Care and Education Reconciliation Act of 2010
Purpose, use of term, 52, 137
Purposivism/purposivists, 45–53

Quotas, post-cloture statements against, 83

Rachlinski, J., 117
Radin, M., 11, 137–38, 144–46. *See also* State of mind, intent as
Raz, J., 141
Reading Law (Scalia and Garner), 3, 103–4, 105, 133
Realist purposivism, 50–51, 62
Reconciliation bill, 71–72
Rector, Church of the Holy Trinity v. United States, 36, 40, 46, 49, 51, 53, 55, 68, 76–79, 89, 114
Rehnquist, W., 73–74, 81–83
Reid, H., 81
Relational agent, 183
Religious topics, lecturers on, 79
Report, use of term, 90–91
Representation, 176–79
Reverse engineering, 8, 66, 80–81, 84–85, 98
RICO (anti-racketeering law), 75–76
Roach v. Commonwealth, 169
Roberts, J. G., 111, 130
Rodriguez, D., 3, 54, 56, 94
Rubenfeld, J., 51
Rule 22 (cloture rule), 4, 65, 92
Rule 609 (impeachment of witnesses by prior felonies), 32, 83–85
Rulemaking and Proceedings Clause. *See* Proceedings Clause
Rules
- cloture, 4, 65–66, 92–93
- conference committees, 84, 86–88, 96, 131, 133, 163, 168, 174
- Congress's, to help interpret statutes, 69, 85–88
- filibuster, 62, 66, 163, 167
- governing legislative process (*See* Legislative decision theory)
- House, 27, 86–87, 95–96
- legislative game, 33, 62
- lenity, 114
- mischief, 40, 51
- Proceedings Clause, 165–67
- Senate, 61, 86–87, 93, 95–96
- standing, 96

Rule XXII (precedence of motions), 92–93

Sacks, A., 3, 15, 16, 47, 51–52, 137
Sarbanes-Oxley (SOX), 125–26, 128–30, 132
Scalia, A.
- canons and, 103–34
- *Holy Trinity* and, 36, 40, 46, 49, 51, 53, 55, 68, 76–79, 89, 114
- legislative history and, 55, 161–62, 165–66, 169
- legislative intent and, 137
- *Reading Law*, 3, 103–4, 105, 133
- Scalia Tanner lectures, 35
- textualism and, 4–5, 15, 35–44, 51, 114–15, 137

Schacter, J., 3, 28, 37
Schauer, F., 47, 117
Schoolhouse Rock, 81, 90
Scriveners, 20, 37, 39–40, 52, 90, 107, 183–84, 185
Second-generation textualism, 54
Section 703(j) (affirmative action), 74, 82–83, 123, 154, 158
Section 1512 (anti-tampering statute), 128–29
Section 1519 (anti-shredding statute), 125–26, 128–30, 132
Section 1520 (financial record preservation act), 129
Self-delegation, 172–75, 180
Self-serving bias, 10
Semantic canons, 130–31
Semantic isolation, 110
Senate Judiciary Committee, 14, 28–29, 129, 165
Senate rules, 61, 86–87, 93, 95–96
Senate Rule XXII, 92–93
Separability, 61
Separation of powers, 176–79
- adjectives, 176–77
- representation, 176–79

Sequential procedure, 150, 152
Shapiro, S., 3, 148

Shepsle, K., 53, 138, 150
Ships-passing-in-the-night problem, 30–31
Siegel, J., 173
Sisk v. Smith, 171
Slave labor importation, 43, 47, 76–77, 114
Snowe, O., 22
Solan, L., 40
"Speakers' meaning" view, 138
Speeches
  as cheap talk, 56
  inference from, 142
  legislative, 148
  ordinary, 142, 148
  post hoc, 155
  statutory, 148
Spirit of the law, 41, 68, 135, 178
Spurious plain meaning, 111–12
Standing rules, 96
Stasis objection, 144
State, use of term, 109–10
State of mind, intent as, 143, 144–46
  delegation objection and, 144–45
  mental state error and, 144
  stasis objection and, 144
  unanimity problem and, 144
Statutes
  anti-obstruction statute, 128–30
  anti-shredding statute, 125–26, 128–30, 132
  anti-tampering statute, 128–29
  Congress's rules to help interpret, 69, 85–88
  as elections, 68–69, 70–79
  federal exchange statute, 112–13
  following a sequence, 69, 79–85
  grammar errors in, 124
  interpreting (*See* Statutory interpretation)
Statutory interpretation, 34–63
  contract theories, 53–62
  defined, 15
  democratic theory of, 180
  focusing illusion and, 122–24
  legislative decision theory of, 64–102
  purposivism, 45–53
  study of, 3
  textualism, 35–45
Statutory speech, 148
Statutory text, 20, 26–27, 33, 35, 47, 88, 89, 95, 100, 142, 147
Stephenson, M., 3–4
Stevens, J. P., 81, 83–84, 105
Structure-induced ambiguity, 28–30, 44
Structure-induced misunderstandings, 91–93
Subjectivity, 139–40
Subplurality opinions, 139
Substantive canons, 130–31
Substitute bill, 31, 57–58, 60, 74, 79, 81, 92, 187. *See also* Mansfield-Dirksen substitute
Substitute relationship text, 112
Sunstein, C., 49
Supermajoritarian difficulty, 27–32
  filibuster and, 27–32, 73, 98, 163
  structure-induced ambiguity and, 28–30
  theorizing ambiguity and, 30–32
Supermajority, 2, 4, 28, 56, 58, 98, 101, 145, 152, 154
Supervenience, 151–52
Supreme Court, 6, 19, 23, 57, 114, 129, 139–40, 160, 167
  Aldridge v. Williams, 171
  Amalgamated Transit Union Local 1309 v. Laidlaw Transit Servs., Inc., 68, 90, 123
  Babbitt v. Sweet Home, 115
  Bingham v. Cabot, 170
  Blake v. National Banks, 170–71
  Cherokee Nation v. Georgia, 170
  Chisom v. Roemer, 115
  Citizens United v. FEC, 23
  Commonwealth ex rel. Bache v. Binns, 171
  Commonwealth v. Cushing, 169–70
  Dorsey's Executors v. Worthington, 170
  Dred Scott case, 171
  Eakin v. Raub, 171
  Ex Parte in the Matter of Duncan N. Hennen, 170
  Green v. Bock Laundry Machine Co., 68, 81, 83–85, 92, 155
  Griggs v. Duke Power Co., 75–76, 80, 81, 92, 94, 123, 155, 158
  Hamdan v. Rumsfeld, 156, 180
  Hill's Adm'rs v. Mitchell, 171
  Hollingsworth v. Duane, 169
  INS v. Chadha, 173
  King v. Burwell, 2, 68, 71, 95, 108, 111, 115–16, 127, 180
  Lochner v. New York, 171

Supreme Court (*continued*)
- *Marbury v. Madison*, 170, 184
- *McBoyle v. United States*, 113–14
- *Myart v. Motorola*, 75
- *Pepper v. Hart*, 123
- *Public Citizen v. American Bar Association*, 85–88, 91–92, 94–95, 130, 155, 174
- *Rector, Church of the Holy Trinity v. United States*, 36, 40, 46, 49, 51, 53, 55, 68, 76–79, 89, 114
- *Roach v. Commonwealth*, 169
- *Sisk v. Smith*, 171
- *Teague v. Lane*, 31
- *Tennessee Valley Authority v. Hill*, 68, 93–94, 123, 131, 132
- *United States v. Fisher*, 169
- *United States v. Trans-Missouri Freight Ass'n*, 171
- *United Steelworkers of America v. Weber*, 68, 73–74, 81, 82–83, 123, 154, 158
- *West Virginia v. Casey*, 114
- *Wheaton v. Peters*, 170
- *Worcester v. Georgia*, 170
- *Yates v. United States*, 125–29, 132

Take, use of term, 115
Taney, R. B., 171
Tangible object, use of term, 126–29, 132
Teague v. Lane, 31
Tellico Dam, 93
Tennessee Valley Authority v. Hill, 68, 93–94, 123, 131, 132
Tests used to discriminate, 59, 60, 76
Textualism/textualists, 35–45. *See also* Petty textualism
- devil/angel view of Congress, 37–40
- plain meaning, 40–45
- Scalia and, 4–5, 15, 35–44, 51, 114–15, 137

Thompson, S., 170
Title VII of Civil Rights Act of 1964, 74
Tor, A., 120, 121
Tower, J., 31, 57–60, 75–76, 81, 92, 158
Tower amendment, 31, 57–60, 75–76, 81, 92, 158
Transformative legislature, 21
Tribe, use of term, 170–71
Turing, A., 11, 135, 146–47
Typological analysis of committee reports, 89–90

Unanimity problem, 144
United States Constitution. *See also* Constitutional critique of legislative history
- Article I, Section 5, 6, 12, 37, 162–72, 173, 175
- Article I, Section 7, 12, 162, 165–66, 175
- Article II, 177, 178
- Article III, 164, 177
- Article IV, 177
- Fifth Amendment, 8, 107–8
- First Amendment, 23
- Leahy amendment, 129–30
- post-cloture amendment, 31, 57–59, 80, 81, 92–93, 155, 157
- substitute bill, 31, 57–58, 60, 74, 76, 79, 81, 92, 153, 158, 187
- Tower amendment, 31, 59–60, 76, 81, 158

United States v. Fisher, 169
United States v. Trans-Missouri Freight Ass'n, 171
United Steelworkers of America v. Weber, 68, 73–74, 81, 82–83, 123, 154, 158
Unprovided-for-case problem, 30, 32
Utilize/utilized, use of term, 85–88, 130–31

"Vehicle in the park" case. *See McBoyle v. United States*
Venus, Rae, Master, The, 170
Vermeule, A., 4, 35, 46, 70, 76–78, 88–89, 97–98, 99
Veto, 29, 166, 173, 177, 178
Violence Against Women Act, 22, 25, 31, 38, 60
Voting
- cloture rule and, 4, 57–58
- congressional context and, 147
- contract theory and, 59, 61
- filibuster and, 56–58
- legislative intent and, 6
- legislative precedent and, 96
- majority, 150, 152
- petty textualism and, 115, 124
- preferences revealed by, 152
- scores, to define moderate member, 59
- subjectivity and, 140
- vesting clauses and, 178

Waldron, J., 4, 16, 22, 24, 138, 141, 144, 148, 161

Weingast, B., 19, 54, 56
We-intentions, 143, 149–50
Wellstone, P., 22
Westlaw, 97, 187
West Virginia v. Casey, 114
"What you see is all there is" principle, 119
Wheaton v. Peters, 170
Worcester v. Georgia, 170
Workplace prejudice against African-Americans. *See United Steelworkers of America v. Weber*

Yates, J., 125
Yates v. United States, 125–29, 132